Cycling's 50 Triumphs and Tragedies

The Rise and Fall of Bicycle Racing's Champions

Les Woodland

McGann Publishing
McMinnville, Oregon

Published by McGann Publishing
P.O. Box 864
McMinnville, OR 72525
USA

www.mcgannpublishing.com

McGann
Publishing

Table of Contents

Many sports have sacred and tragic places. There's nothing special in that. But other sports have stadiums and running tracks and boxing rings. The place is as important as the moment. Well, so it is in cycling. But only to an extent. In cycling you have to go to an anonymous road, a bend, a hill. And then you have to close your eyes and hear the sound of days long gone and sense that mix of embrocation and sweat and fear. For cycling is the people's sport, contested not in bright red cars that no man could afford, but on a bicycle. Not the sort of bicycle you'd ride to the post office, it's true, but closer to your everyday clunker than a race car is to a Volkswagen.

There are sports where the champions are visible for longer. And there are those in which they suffer more tangibly. Boxing is a case in point. But there's no sport but cycling for suffering so visibly, for so long and in so many places. And so many places in a single day.

Sometimes what happens there is heroic, sometimes triumphant. But for every winner in cycling there have to be a hundred losers, and sometimes their tale is better or sadder than the winner's.

Join me, then, on a journey round fifty sites of success and sorrow. Some of them, tragically, combined.

Les Woodland

1

Murderous Climber on a Murderous Climb

It was, said one writer, a prehistoric race never equaled in post-war racing. Triumph met tragedy that day because an angel flew and then fell to earth.

Monte Bondone, Italy, June 8, 1956: It stands a little to the west of Trento, a beautiful city in northern Italy, a fourteen-kilometer climb with thirty hairpins in the Italian Alps. The mountain itself reaches 2,180 meters, the road across it 1,300. The actual climbing from bottom to top is 1,008. It was no surprise that it was in the Giro d'Italia of 1956. Why would it not be?

It was no surprise, either, when Charly Gaul broke away. He was one of the most talented climbers of his era and a man who did best when the weather was against him. And that day it was against everyone. Snow began falling and Gaul, sensing his day, was alone with 88 kilometers still to go. And the snow carried on falling. Riders scattered across the countryside, more concerned with their future than that of the race and their rivals.

That morning, Gaul said to Raphaël Géminiani: "Go and tell your guy [Louison Bobet, whom he disliked with a passion] that if he's got good toe-straps, he's going to find them useful." Riders in those days used toe-straps to pull up the pedals as they climbed hills. Géminiani dutifully told Bobet, his team leader. "So, stick on his wheel," Bobet told him.

"But after a kilometer, Gaul had dropped me," Géminiani remembered. "Bobet asked me why I'd let him go. I said: 'Some hope! He didn't even ask my permission!'"

Géminiani said Gaul was "a murderous climber, always the same sustained rhythm, a little machine with a slightly higher gear than the rest, turning his legs at a speed that would break your heart: tick tock, tick tock, tick tock." And Gaul tick-tocked on upwards.

VeloNews recalled: "The weather turned colder and colder, and on the long, steep slopes of the Giro's final mountain, light snow soon turned to a full blizzard as the temperature dropped to freezing point. [Leader Pasquale] Fornara was overcome by the cold and took refuge in a farmhouse. Other race leaders rode to a standstill before keeling over in the ditches. Some stopped to drink hot chocolate or dip their freezing hands in bowls of hot water offered by the spectators."

Managers turned up the heating in their cars and hoped for the best, peering through clogged windshields which wipers struggled to clear. René de Latour wrote in *Sporting Cyclist*: "A search was going on for a missing man. The searcher-in-chief was former world champion Learco Guerra, now manager of the Faema team. The man he was looking for was Charly Gaul, who had not been seen for the last twenty minutes. Guerra was driving his car up the mountain pass, peering through the clogged-up windscreen when, by sheer chance, he saw a bike leaning against the wall of a shabby mountain *trattoria*. 'That's Charly's bike!' he exclaimed to his mechanic.

"They rushed into the bar and there, sitting on a chair sipping hot coffee, was Charly Gaul, exhausted, so dead to the world that he could hardly speak. Guerra knows bike riders. He talked gently to Gaul. 'Take your time, Charly,' he said. 'We're going to take care of you.' While a masseur was ripping off Gaul's wet jersey, Guerra had some water warmed and poured it over the rider's body. Then, rubbed down from head to toes, Gaul's body gradually came back to life. He lost that glassy look and in a few minutes he was a new man again."

Gaul had been riding in shorts and short sleeves, foolish, naive or impervious.

"With the encouragement of his followers he managed to reach the top, literally miles ahead of Fiorenzo Magni, who finished second at 12¼ minutes. The cheering spectators could hardly believe that men

Les Woodland

had suffered such hardships up there in the icy mountain. On the way, 44 had fallen by the wayside." Other reports say it was 46, some even 60, but with numbers like that it hardly matters. Gaul got to the top more than twelve minutes before Magni, the previous year's winner.

Magni recalled years later: "It snowed the whole day and it was very cold. I hadn't noticed how much. Along the way I saw many bikes parked next to bars and I asked what was going on. They told me that most of the peloton froze and had to quit. Then, before reaching Trento, I saw the race leader [Pasquale Fornara] quitting too! What? Am I seeing things, I wondered. If I were the Pink Jersey I would have continued even if I had to walk, but I would never abandon."

Federico Bahamontes could have led the race had he stayed with Magni. But he and Jesús Galdeano preferred to struggle through the snow to an empty farmhouse. There they found pajamas and put them on. "I had frostbite in my hands and feet," Bahamontes said. "I couldn't use them properly for a month. I'd never known such bad weather. It was really frightening. We just stopped wherever we could, two here, six there, wherever you were, you abandoned."

Another version is that a peasant found Bahamontes in a ditch and called the finish to say: "I've got a cyclist here with me and he doesn't speak Italian. What should I do with him?"

Others had no choice. Nino de Filippis rode to a standstill and, his frozen fingers clamped to the handlebars, simply keeled over sideways. Some say it was then that Bahamontes decided to pull out.

Gaul was too cold and tired after nine hours and 242 kilometers to lift a hand to acknowledge the cheers of those courageous enough to brave the weather and who had, in any case, been lucky to get up there and were now concerned with how they were going to get back down again. Soldiers pulled him from his bike and wrapped him in blankets. They carried him to a hut where they gave him coffee and more blankets. Legend says that, even an hour later, his soigneur had to cut his jersey off because Gaul's frozen skin was too tender for the jersey to be pulled off. Gaul then fainted. When he came round, Gilles Le Roc'h said, he could no longer remember what had happened.

It was a prehistoric stage, Philippe Brunel wrote in *L'Équipe,* "never equaled in the long history of post-war road racing." Few riders that day rode all the way by bike. Most had taken a truck, anything that offered a lift, some of the way. All Gaul's team pulled out and went home.

"We were picked up by a truck," Bahamontes said. "We all quit. Anybody who says the opposite is lying because then they came by the hotels next day asking who wanted to finish the Giro."

They hold a cyclosportive ride over the Bondone these days and they name it in honor of the man who made it famous. The first was in 2006 and not surprisingly there were 40 from Luxembourg, Gaul's home country, to keep the memory alive. Not bad for a story 50 years old and a country smaller than Rhode Island. And that same year the Giro ended one of its stages on the Bondone in tribute.

It was Pierre About, writing in *L'Équipe*, who first referred to Gaul as the angel of the mountains. The phrase came to him after he'd seen Gaul's expressionless, childlike face—Gaul was only 21 at the time, riding a race restricted to riders under 25—as he won the Circuit des Six Provinces in eastern central France. About wrote: "When Charly Gaul met with the terrible ascent of the Chaubouret, one forgot that he had been looking like a man who fought and suffered. An irresistible lightness suddenly took hold of this young boy with the doll's eyes, and he gave the impression of an angel for whom nothing is difficult. Light, harmonious, he rode away from the field."

Gaul had turned professional the previous summer for a French team, Terrot, and had immediately startled the old guard by coming second in the Dauphiné Libéré and winning the mountains competition. In the Six Provinces he had ridden alone over the Croix du Chaubouret into the bike-making city of St-Étienne.

Legend says Gaul sometimes received 60 letters a day from lip-smacking women. He gave some to his team-mate, Marcel Ernzer, after which Ernzer said he wasn't at all sure he'd marry if that was what women wanted.

Men with prickly personalities fall out badly over the most trivial things. For Gaul and Louison Bobet, the French star, it was the etiquette of peeing beside the road. Etiquette said stars respected each other and didn't attack when one stopped. But in a Giro stage to Trieste, Jan Heine recorded: "Bobet stopped to relieve himself, and Gaul did the same. It is a slow stage, so Gaul gave his bike to Ernzer and stepped off the road. Suddenly, he heard his teammates shout and saw Bobet and the French racing off."

Gaul had to chase for 80 kilometers and lost the lead. He never forgave Bobet's duplicity, as he saw it. He reminded Bobet he'd worked in an abattoir at Bettembourg and that, if the Frenchman carried on annoying him, he'd pick up a knife and take revenge. That same year— 1958—he taunted Bobet by telling him just where he'd attack in the mountains and defying him to follow. It was when he attacked on the Col de Luitel as he warned and had to keep going for fear that Bobet would catch him that he pioneered peeing as he rode, which earned him the nickname Monsieur Pee-Pee. It haunted him for the rest of his life.

Bahamontes, his rival in the mountains, said Gaul "had a very strong character, terrible even." He was so unpopular, says Heine, that "many of his problems appear to have been caused by a hostile peloton, which often seemed to do anything to make Gaul lose." Philippe Brunel assessed his personality as "notorious: he was a man of the cold, a man who created great impressions [but was] taciturn, a man of few words who spoke only to close acquaintances." He was, Géminiani said: "A man with two faces and a paradox in the way he behaved. He could have the most violent of tempers but he could also have the most gentle of characters."

Gaul came close to retiring in 1962, declining fast, rootless after Ernzer called it a day. He left the Gazzola team to its relief, made a mess of a comeback with Peugeot and then with Lamote-Libertas— when he was jeered by a crowd in his own country—then gave up. He rode his last race not on the road but on the Niederkom velodrome, in 1965. He opened a bar near the train station in Luxembourg City but closed the doors again six months later.

He threw up everything and went off to live in a forest hut on the Lipperscheid hill in the Ardennes. And there he disappeared, far from welcoming to the few who found him and unrecognizable to many. He grew fat and grew a beard. He dressed in hunter's green fatigues and walked the woods, watching the deer, listening to the birds. He had a phone but never answered it. He took his name out of the directory.

Local shopkeepers said he had never recovered from the end of his second marriage. But nobody knew. To anyone who asked for an interview, he said: "I don't feel like talking. Sorry. It was all so long ago. Please, leave me in peace. I'm just a grumpy old man."

Sometimes, though, he'd stand beside the road during the Tour of Luxembourg, just another spectator that few recognized. And then, in 1983 and on the twenty-fifth anniversary of winning the Tour, his debt to himself paid, he came back to life. The impassive blue eyes were still there but little else. He did, though, have a third wife, Josée, and a daughter, Fabienne. They lived at Itzigerste, a suburb to the southwest.

"I bought myself a little portable TV," he told Pilo Fonck, a journalist who said he had "the interview of my life; I was as happy as a little kid."

Gaul told him: "I connected it to the battery of my car so that I could watch stages of the Tour de France. When the battery got flat, I called the man at the garage. I didn't travel much. I said to myself: 'You're at peace here, you're happy.' There's nothing but trees and water. I spent my days planting vegetables and the deer came to eat at the end of my garden."

Why the breakdown and reclusion? Maybe because he had never been an easy man, never at ease with others. Maybe because he had had enough of a life that had turned from adulation to being whistled by his own people. And perhaps because of amphetamine psychosis.

Gaul often rode with staring if expressionless eyes and with flecks of foam on his lips. Bahamontes said tactfully that he liked hot days "because my rivals did less well." Amphetamine, then common in cycling and still not against the rules, was less effective in the heat. And Gaul always rode best in the cold. Amphetamine also played with the mind, as Erik De Vlaeminck found.

Marcel Ernzer remembered a conversation with his leader and room-mate:

"Charly is going to die," Gaul said of himself.

"Why do you say that?"

"Because Charly takes too many pills."

"But everybody takes them."

"Yes, but Charly takes a lot more than the others."

The nation decided in time that it could no longer ignore the greatest hero so small a country had produced. It suggested he work as an archivist at the sports ministry. And there he began working out his life, what he'd done, recompiling it like a puzzling jigsaw.

In 1989 the Tour started in Luxembourg City and the organizer, Jean-Marie Leblanc, gave Gaul the Tour de France's commemorative medal. In 2000 he invited him to sit on the podium as its star guest at the end of stages. Spectators who remembered his exploits as a lean and pale-faced boy stood in admiration but wondered if this was the man they had adored. Gaul sat staring back at them. It was impossible to read his thoughts. It was hard to say if he even knew what was going on.

Charly Gaul died on December 6, 2005.

Charly Gaul late in life, at the Tour de France

2
The Crazy Irishman

Little saddens the heart more than losing in front of your home crowd. Especially when you've been built up as favorite and then given all you had. Only to be beaten not by someone who could ride faster up hills but also down them.

Poggio, Italy, March 15, 1986: It's just another hill, nothing at all like the Monte Bondone. If you were out for a drive and looking for a place to picnic, you wouldn't even notice it. Not if you weren't a cyclist, you wouldn't. You could drive up it without effort and you'd be more taken by the descent, which is a snaking line of road that repeatedly doubles back on itself. Even the Italians who named it couldn't have thought much of it. They called it just Poggio. So, if you call it the Poggio hill, you're saying "hill hill" or perhaps "top of the hill." There's even a village partway up called Poggio, so presumably its address is Poggio, Poggio.

There are Poggio hills and villages everywhere, both in Italy and in the southeastern part of France that Italy once owned. The one we're talking about now, though, is just above San Remo and it's that twisted bootlace of a descent that brings the huge field of Milan–San Remo down to sea level after a long but undemanding bowl from the north.

Of all the spring classics, Milan–San Remo is unusual in having been international from the start. Look at Liège–Bastogne–Liège or the Ronde van Vlaanderen or Paris–Roubaix and you see that not only did home riders win them for years but also that nobody else was even interested in trying. By contrast, the first winner in San Remo, in 1907, was Lucien Petit-Breton, who had been born in Argentina. He won

300 lire in gold, an amount difficult to translate to modern money but worth perhaps $1,100 today. Six foreigners and five Italians won in the first eleven years. And then Italy retaliated, winning every year from 1914 to 1933.

Milan–San Remo closes the first phase of each year's season with the Italian exuberance that shows that not all stereotypes are dangerous. Riders who once were in training camps along the Mediterranean coast, and who now spend their winters in Australia and Malaysia, meet for their first serious clash of legs when they gather near the university in the center of Milan. It often seems that anyone who cares to have a go will be given a ride.

Cycling explained that "there is something of a formula. There is an early break—sometimes a lone rider, sometimes a group of three or four—which can forge a lead of as much as thirty minutes in the first 160 or so kilometers. Once the race reaches the coast, the deep blue of the Mediterranean teases the peloton all the way over the climbs to San Remo."

The Poggio is a newcomer. The final test used to be the Cipressa, which was and still is harder but which lay 22 kilometers from the finish. Since anything that happened there could be put to rights on the long descent into San Remo, year after year the race finished with a huge sprint which led many to wonder what the point had been of all that riding from Milan. It was then that the organizers caught on to the Poggio and put it right at the end. The race now goes over the Cipressa and follows the sea, and could follow the sea all the way to the end. Except that it now comes across an easily missed road to the right for which the signpost says simply "Poggio."

This, the last of those hills, isn't all that much. It averages only 3.7 per cent and it's just four kilometers long. It gets to no more than 169 meters above the sea. Any Sunday racer can take it in his stride. But that's because nothing depends on it and because they haven't also just ridden 288 kilometers to get there. It gives the race its biggest attraction and its biggest fault: fault because the race is often only half-heartedly contested until the Poggio, attraction because so often the winner is decided there.

And you know what's oddest? It's that the winner is often not who gets over the top first, although that's a natural advantage, but who can go down it fastest. "The only safe place is right at the front, where no one can crash in your path," *Cycling* considered in 2001, adding that the also-rans whose legs or nerves weren't up to the rush "were sent slipping and sliding across the road in front of the San Remo fountain." The world's best sprinters, therefore, start their battle with a helter-skelter whirl down the Poggio to rejoin the sea at Voltri.

The days have gone when the climb itself counted. It hurts many legs, of course, and a great many find they slip back through the team cars there. The steepest bit is after a kilometer and a half. And then comes the narrow, twisting descent which creates the only real climax before the finish. It was there in 1992 that the stoic Irishman, Sean Kelly, caught the local hope, Moreno Argentin. The Italian, who never did win Milan–San Remo but who had six wins already that early in the season, had dominated on the Cipressa. He was riding for a team sponsored by a flooring concern, Ariostea. He had given his riders such confidence in his chances of winning that they set an alarming pace up the hill to keep their man in front.

Now, on the Poggio, he was climbing with his hands on the drops of his bars, his yellow and red jersey stretched on his arched back. Behind him, several seconds behind, the best in the world were in a straggled line, watching each other, some suffering too much to react, others unsure what to do. Maurizio Fondriest moved tentatively to the front to see who would join him. When he eased, to see who would come past, it wasn't one of the safer workhorses that he wanted, someone who would crush his legs to get up to Argentin, but the pale, freckled form of Sean Kelly in the light blue jersey of the Festina team.

Kelly was the oldest man in the race, 36, his hair thinning. He'd once said: "If you have a 100-meter lead at the top of the Poggio, you'll win." According to that formula, Argentin was about to take Milan–San Remo. Maybe Kelly remembered his words. It's unlikely that he'd forgotten them. He went by on the right and panic ensued. "The firemen are behind, pumping on the coals," the British television commentator, David Duffield, came close to screaming. "Anyone with anything left in his legs wants to get within shouting distance of Argentin."

Eight seconds, Argentin held. Bend after bend followed, between houses, round the sides of greenhouses of spring flowers waiting for market. Kelly's reaction whipped up the others and Fondriest passed him, followed by Rolf Sørensen, the most successful rider in Danish history. More bends, Argentin out of the saddle to pull out of each of them, the followers taking their time, watching each other. The road now doubled back repeatedly, each lower section parallel to the road above it, the turns at 180 degrees.

Then three kilometers from the end and only about as many minutes, Kelly went past the other two. Argentin had 15 seconds. Kelly was in his highest gear, out of the saddle, more pressing his weight on the pedals than combing them round. Argentin remained confident: he had doubled his lead, behind him three motorbikes including the television cameraman, low above him a helicopter with a further camera strapped to its rests. The only sensations Argentin knew now were tension, tiredness, nerves and noise.

And then…worry. Something was going wrong. He looked over his shoulder for the first time to see what was happening. At the same time he reached the flat stretch along the coast and the sign for the final kilometers. Then he looked back again, over his right shoulder. Clear to him now was the sight of Sean Kelly, just five lengths behind. Two of the world's greatest sprinters were now riding not elbow to elbow but a one-kilometer pursuit.

The third time Argentin looked back, he saw Kelly on his wheel, his legs quiet for a moment, his freewheel clicking. Again and again Argentin looked back. They were riding now not like pursuiters but track sprinters. At one moment Argentin even took one hand off the bars and twisted on the saddle to look back over his shoulder like a man waiting for a gap in the traffic before making a turn.

Again Argentin looked back, his hands now on the bottom of the bars, his weight out of the saddle, his legs turning the pedals no faster than they needed to. The crowd at the finish sighed; they knew from the announcer that Kelly had caught their man but the days had not yet arrived when they could watch events on a large screen.

Now Kelly too started looking back. His brain was calculating times and distances and judging the man who could yet rob him of Milan–San Remo. And distances were important because there were 400 meters stretched before him to the finish line and an uncertain distance behind him to the regrouped mass of riders racing down towards him in the hope that he and Argentin would be so distracted by their own battle that they'd let the peloton sweep by.

Both men sensed the danger. Argentin accelerated steadily, bluffing Kelly into coming by too soon, at the same time limiting the danger from behind. Then Kelly came by on the right. Argentin moved in that direction, pushing his shoulder out to discourage him. Kelly falters. The bunch, now out of the saddle themselves, is distracted by a crash on the left. Kelly accelerates just as the fallen hit the road. He and Argentin stay side by side for a second, perhaps two, and then Argentin has given all he has. Kelly doesn't accelerate so much as Argentin decelerates.

The Irishman, now three-quarters of the way to the right of the road, throws up both hands as the Italian, deprived of his glory in front of his crowd, freewheels resignedly over the line. But there is a sad outcome for Kelly, too, although he couldn't have known it at the time. He would never again win a big race and he left the peloton two years later—to join David Duffield in his commentary box.

Milan–San Remo has never been a strong race for speakers of English. The Briton, Tom Simpson, won in 1964 and the Australians, Matthew Goss and Simon Gerrans, in 2011 and 2012. But it's not a lot to show.

There was one of those we-shall-never-know moments in 1957 when another Briton, Brian Robinson, was ordered to sacrifice his chances in a doubtful commercial deal concerning an opponent. Robinson was the first British rider to finish the Tour de France, in 1955, and had a name as a rider edging on the élite. He integrated well into continental cycling but he would have got on better had he not been from Britain. Not only was it an island where, so far as anybody knew, nobody rode bikes, but the rules in those days insisted that professional teams could have only a limited number of foreigners. Given that teams were largely French or Italian, Robinson had to fight harder for his place and was offered poorer contracts because he had less choice.

That doubt over his commercial value also forced him into at least one decision he long regretted. Robinson came to Milan–San Remo in 1957 with his first pro win behind him. It was an early-season criterium around Nice, a training race in which the stars rode as far as they felt inclined and then dropped out, but plenty of others would

have liked to win instead. They included the Tour winner, Louison Bobet, who finished second to Robinson, just under a minute. Robinson's
form lasted to Italy and he was up with the leaders as he they neared
San Remo. And then he was told to throw away his chances.

Robinson was riding for St-Raphaël, a controversial team because
it had been the first in France to ignore an international ruling that
pro teams could be sponsored only by companies from the cycle trade.
The cycle trade, however, had fallen on hard times and Robinson's
team had followed others in Spain and Britain in looking for money
elsewhere: in this case from a maker of aperitif.

Miguel Poblet rode for Ignis, an Italian maker of washing machines.
He had been a late recruit because until the start of the season he
had been with Flandria, a Belgian bicycle maker. Flandria sponsored
teams for decades, the link between them all being their haphazard
organization and shortage of money. The team in 1957 was led by the
imperious sprinter, Rik van Looy, and he or Flandria or both ruled
that Poblet wasn't to ride Milan–San Remo. That mattered so much to
Poblet that he turned in his contract and signed with Ignis.

Robinson's manager, Raymond Louviot, rated Poblet and, judging
him to be an outcast in every team he joined, hoped he could be persuaded to join St-Raphaël. The team needed a good sprinter. For that,
he needed a sweetener—a sweetener that Robinson was to pay in full.

Still believing he would be allowed to win, Robinson attacked three
times, on the Capo Berta with 22 kilometers to go, then twice more
until, said *Cycling*, the "only two men who could go with him [were]
the Belgians Alfred De Bruyne, who won in 1956, and Jozef Planckaert. Under Robinson's steamrollering, they flew."

But Robinson knew something they didn't. "My manager, Raymond
Louviot, had a tie-up in the cycle trade with Miguel Poblet. He told me
that if Poblet was anywhere near me, it was my job to get him over the
line first. Poblet was riding one of our bikes."

Robinson was upset, but managers then were all-powerful, corruption was common and there was always that ruling about the permis-
sible number of foreigners. He was in little position to object. He was
in a big team for the first time, and that mattered. He remembered: "I
buggered off up a hill, then my manager came up and said: 'Remember
what I told you!' Poblet won. I was third. That is my biggest regret. If I'd

won, I'd have been made for life. I was never a sprinter, but given the right conditions—just think what difference that victory would have made to my contract!"

Cycling, unaware until years later of what had happened, truthfully but innocently called it "by far the greatest achievement by a British roadman in a single-day race since the halcyon nineteenth century days." It had been back in the 1800s that Britons had taken all the leading places in Bordeaux–Paris, before their country settled into a self-imposed exile that excluded almost all road racing.

Poblet, incidentally, never did join Louviot. He was spoiled rotten by Ignis and its owner, Giovanni Borghi, whose enthusiasm for cycling was exceeded only by the thickness of his wallet. Poblet died in 2013, Borghi in 1975 and Louviot in 1969. Brian Robinson was still riding a bike into his eighties.

3

Death of a Champion

*Sometimes stars are snuffed out before they shine.
We can only wonder what might have happened had
tragedy not struck.*

St-Pieters-Lille, Belgium, March 15, 1971: There are big everyday beers
in Belgium, like Stella Artois and Jupiler. And there are hundreds of
small beers, some once made in monasteries, and it's for those that
thousands of tourists visit one of Europe's tiniest countries every year.
And somewhere between the extremes are perfectly serviceable beers,
of which Rodenbach is one. There were four Rodenbachs—brothers
called Pedro, Alexander, Ferdinand and Constantijn—and in 1821
they agreed that for the next fifteen years they would brew beers as
partners.

They built their brewery in Roeselare, a town that French-speakers
know as Roulers and pronounce *Roule-air* as though it were a pneu-
matic tire. It's down near the French border and it forms a lopsided triangle with Lille and Roubaix to the south and Ghent to the northeast.
A lot of good riders have come from there, starting with Odile Defraye,
in 1912 the first Tour de France winner from Belgium. Patrick Sercu,
a man who could win road races, track races and as many six-days as
any man could hope also came from Roeselare. It is a good working
town and the brewery went up to one side of it.

Breweries rarely improve the aspect of a neighborhood and the
area that this one occupied became known as Krottegem, the ending
common for place names in Flanders and *krot* meaning a slum. Slum-
town. In the square there, the Onze-Lieve Vrouwmaarkt, you can find

a two-meter statue of a cyclist with his hands raised in victory. The €50,000 that it cost was raised by selling tiny copies.

The statue is of Jean-Pierre Monseré, a boyish son of the town. The name is French but the boy, who grew up and lived in Krottegem, was Flemish. His first name was shortened to Jempi and pronounced *Yempee*.

Jempi Monseré inherited his cycling genes from his father, a man who'd raced in the 1940s and quickly realized he was never going to be a star and settled instead for life on the production line of a factory making washing machines. The son was quite the opposite. He never saw himself needing a proper job. He had his first bike at twelve as a reward for doing well at school, raced that summer against riders sometimes three years older than him and came third in his first race. He won 40 races in 1966 alone and averaged 30 a season.

By 1967 he was riding for Belgium in the world championship, at Heerlen in Holland. In those days there were still amateur and professional championships. Monseré was all but a professional in reality, supporting himself through cycling, but at 18 he was barely in the senior amateur class. His talent got him into a break which showed every sign of winning. His youth, perhaps, or maybe some order he heard but we never did, made him blunder. For a long time he shared the work with the others—René Pijnen, Uwe Ampler and Tino Conti—and then he went on strike. He just rode at the back, sheltered from the wind, his legs turning more easily.

When rivals get clear of the rest of the race, they abandon their individual hopes for a moment and share the work to keep themselves in the lead. They don't have to go any faster than the chasers but they do have to work harder to do it. A cyclist's greatest enemy on the flat is the air he is pushing aside, and the faster he goes the harder that becomes. Tradition demands, therefore, that each rider spend some time breaking through the air for a short distance while the others ride in his slipstream.

It causes great bitterness when one rider refuses to cooperate. He is selfishly profiting from the toil of others and it's quickly and loudly pointed out. When that rider stops cooperating suddenly, the leading group is destabilized. The collaboration ends because there's a thief in the camp. And so it was when Monseré stopped working. Ampler was bitter: "I don't understand him. He just stayed on our wheels. If he'd shared the work with us, the chasers would never have caught us. I know he was a good sprinter and that he wanted to save himself for the finish, but doing what he did he ended not only our chances but his own as well."

Monseré came tenth and Ampler rolled over the line anonymously. The victory went instead to a tall Briton called Graham Webb, a man so lanky that his rainbow jersey barely covered his ribs. He took the last corner faster than the rest, rode like the track pursuiter that he was and crossed the line alone but worried that there was still a lap to go.

Monseré turned professional in 1969, with the characteristically cash-strapped and chaotically organized Flandria bike company and helped by whichever sponsors it could enroll season by season. Like Freddy Maertens, who took the same route and whom he was advised not to copy, he regretted it. He had a contract with the Italian kitchen maker, Salvarani, but Flandria bought it out. Monseré was bitter for the rest of his short life.

Maertens, too, wanted to ride in Italy. There he would have had an easier start as a professional and the sort of care and equipment that Flandria never had. But Flandria had a status in the small world of Belgian cycling and Monseré was flattered, as Maertens was, by the attention of the team's manager, Briek Schotte. Schotte had godlike status in Belgium after a long, grit-stained career in which he twice won the world championship and twice the Tour of Flanders, a race which counts for almost as much in Belgium.

The sad truth, though, was that Schotte was a prisoner of his era and his background, one of many children living in poverty on a small bleak farm and, as a professional, sometimes getting little more than a jersey and a bike. He paid out Flandria's money as though it was coming from his own wallet.

It was in the red and white Flandria jersey, in his first year as a professional, that Monseré won the Tour of Lombardy at twenty-one— after crossing the line second. He, who like many riders of his era was himself no stranger to doping, profited from the cheating of the Dutchman who beat him. Gerben Karstens was the most entertaining rider of his era, not just for his sprinting but for his jokes and stunts.

He once crashed in the Tour de France and lay on the road groaning and apparently close to death. He waited until the photographers had all they wanted and got back on his bike and rejoined the race.

That day in Italy, Karstens put his fingers in a pill bottle to help himself over the hills and on to the finish. And that same day in Italy, the judges decided to send him for a drugs test. The procedure was different then. Modern riders are escorted direct to the testing caravan but back then they were told to report as soon as they could manage. That gave Karstens a moment to ask his driver to fill a small bottle, perhaps a condom, which he could smuggle into his shorts and use to fill the test flasks. A week later, the postman brought a letter from the Dutch federation: the UCI, the world authority, had told it that Karstens had failed the test and had therefore lost the Tour of Lombardy.

For Karstens it was impossible. It hadn't even been his urine. It had been his driver's. And then, after a lot of pointed questions, it emerged that the driver had helped himself to Karstens' pill stocks on the long drive south from Holland. It has to be said that this story may be apocryphal. Willy Voet, a Belgian soigneur shamed by his involvement in organized doping three decades later, tells just the same story about Sean Kelly.

In 1970, Monseré went to the glum British city of Leicester to ride the world championship. Britain hadn't organized the championships since a disastrous venture in 1922 when the road race was held in secret as a time-trial to avoid the displeasure of the police. British riders took the first three places. That same caution applied in the Britain of 1970, still new to the idea of closing roads to other traffic to hold a bike race. Sid Saltmarsh, a journalist who handled press affairs for the championships, was reluctant ever to say the roads would be shut "because otherwise we'll upset the civil liberties people."

The Belgian team stayed at a hotel in central Leicester and rode out together to try the circuit, which finished on a car-racing circuit at Mallory Park. On the way back they got lost and hired a taxi to lead them through the city's streets to their hotel. And the team had other troubles. Like every team Belgium has picked, it was riven by internal politics and commerce. Riders from a small and passionate country who spend all summer in the pay and service of one star don't take easily to helping a rider from another sponsor just for a day. And rivalry divided the team's obvious leaders, so that each demanded Belgium select riders he knew would be loyal.

Monseré was embroiled in all that and determined to ride for his own gain. So whenever there was a break, however petty, he fought to get into it for fear that another Belgian would do it instead and that he'd be reduced to an impotent role in the peloton. That was demanding because, while the circuit was easy, a cold, strong wind pulled at any rider who extracted himself from the shelter.

Monseré's effort finally paid off. He got away with Felice Gimondi, who realized he stood little chance in a big sprint finish, and with Leif Mortensen and a self-deprecating Briton called Les West. For West it was a curious moment. He'd not long turned professional for the part-time Holdsworth team in Britain and he still worked in a full-time job.

"I thought 'I'm all right here,'" he recalled, "I think I'll just sit here and hope that nobody notices." And for a while nobody cared. Only one Briton in the history of cycling had ever been good enough to win the world professional championship and there was little reason to think that this dark-haired man who always rode a bike as though he'd just borrowed it from a friend was going to turn into another Tom Simpson. "And then Gimondi dropped back and said 'Come on, Leslie!' They'd been looking me up, back in the team car."

In 1966 West had come second in the amateur championship. That's what the Italians had found out. From now they were going to take him more seriously. But West was out of his class and he was never going to win. In fact he cramped up at the end and came fourth. Monseré won, Mortensen came second and Gimondi third. West went back to a team sponsored by an everyday bike shop close to the Thames in west London and Monseré won the Ghent Six with Patrick Sercu and set off on a year of racing in his new rainbow jersey.

It's often said that the jersey is a curse. Legend says that those who win it then have their worst season in years. For Monseré, it couldn't have been worse. On May 15, 1971, he signed on for an everyday race to the east of Antwerp. He had no interest in the race except to turn his legs fast before Milan–San Remo two days later. It was his third race in three days and he wouldn't have bothered had Roger De Vlaeminck not dropped by that morning to persuade him. If he could win at Retie, fine. If not, he'd had an outing.

After 70 kilometers he was in the leading group, one of sixteen that included De Vlaeminck, an equal who was at the same time a friend and a rival. A side wind pushed the riders into a protective line, shoulder to shoulder across the road. Riders take turn in sheltering others from the wind, just as they did in Monseré's world championship, but in a side wind they move progressively from one side of the road to the other. Monseré had just done a stint on the right and he'd moved to the left of the row to take his turn in the shelter.

Riding on the left meant he was on the side of the road normally reserved for traffic coming the other way. That day the road wasn't formally closed as it would be in bigger races but oncoming traffic should have been brought to a halt by escorts preceding the riders. Except that suddenly a car was coming the other way.

The other riders braked and avoided it. But Monseré's view had been blocked for a moment by a rider in front of him. He hit the Mercedes flat out and head on and was thrown from one side of the road to the other. There he lay motionless with blood trickling from one ear. The British magazine *Cycling* refused to print the pictures.

Monseré lay motionless, then opened his unfocussed eyes, began to sit up and then fell back again. He was dead by the time a doctor arrived. There's a monument there now and the local club organizes a race each year in his memory. His medals are in the national cycling museum at Roeselare.

It has to be said that Monseré wasn't a likable man. He had a sense of humor and he was fond of practical jokes, especially at the expense of Briek Schotte. But he was young and emotionally immature, and immediate success and popular lauding made him, says the writer Michel Crépel, "a man with an extravagant personality on the edge of being unbearable. He had no scruples and he'd break contracts that he'd agreed to and denounce those around him." He was, said Crépel (who, alarmingly, has been described as Monseré's fan...), "a spoilt child."

But that didn't mean he deserved the tragedy that befell him in an almost anonymous race in a village that nobody has heard of, in the Grand Prix Retie, at St-Pieters-Lille, near Turnhout. Nor, posthumously, the tragedy of his son. Giovanni Monseré was seven in 1976. He had a tiny world champion jersey and a little racing bike that Freddy Maertens had given him for his communion, three weeks earlier. The two families were close because Monseré had introduced Maertens to Carine Brouckaert, the girl who became his wife. Carine was the niece of Annie Monseré, Jempi's wife.

"I was barely fifteen," she said. "I went [to a cycling club dance] and Jempi introduced me to one of the riders, Freddy Maertens. I'd never heard of him. 'He's going to go a long way,' Monseré said, and I had a little dance with this Maertens boy. And that's how it started."

Maertens said: "The news [of Monseré's death] finished me for days. What a loss! Jempi knew his way through life, he was intelligent and he knew what to do. If only I could have grown up in his shadow as a rider." And that led to his gift to young Giovanni. A gift the boy was riding when he too was hit by a car and died.

De Vlaeminck told the magazine *Primo*: "I still think of Jempi's accident. Nightmares about it, in fact. The start of every season, in the first races of the year, I always think of him. We'd known each other since we were about sixteen and we were good friends. My daughter now is forty and she was only three months old when Jempi died."

Annie Monseré said: "What can that mean, when you lose both your husband and son, taken away so early? I've never found an answer to that. But sometimes I think everything was just too perfect. Giovanni was a treasure of a child and maybe Jean-Pierre was too good to stay alive. Very special boys, both of them."

Les Woodland

4

The Toast of France and the End of the Tour

Soccer fans, baseball fans…they love to go back to places of legend, to live past glories. But nobody these days goes to the very heart of the Tour de France. Because it was cruelly pulled down without a sou in compensation.

Paris, France, May 16, 1901: I have to tell you: there's not much there now. You get a glimpse if you follow the Paris ring road that spelled its end, and you get a better view if you take the Métro out to the Parc de Saint-Cloud. Then you just follow the signs or the crowds, because what was once the heart of the Tour de France is now a concrete soccer and rugby stadium, the home of the variable successes of Paris St-Germain. Unfriendly fences and red-and-white barriers and men in uniform with pocket radios make it clear you're not welcome without money in your hand.

They've kept the name, though. It's still called the Parc des Princes, which means what you'd guess it means. It was where the first Tour de France ended and every Tour ended until the track that once stood there was demolished. The Olympic Games were held there in 1900 and the greatest riders from around the world competed on its broad pink bankings. And then the people who thought they owned it, the people who organized the Tour de France every summer, got a letter from the lawyers of the city of Paris saying they didn't own it after all and that it was going to be demolished without a franc of compensation.

The Parc des Princes was once far from Paris, out in the country. It was a park where the aristocracy of the eighteenth-century galloped after deer. It was between the Bois de Boulogne and one of the old gates to the city, at St-Cloud. Then times and standards dropped and uncertain toffs began wobbling on velocipedes in the Champs-Elysées and someone had the idea in 1897 of building a race track. A laboratory in one corner of the park was demolished and the velodrome opened in its place. Such had been the enthusiasm to cash in on the new paying passion for watching races that it was so badly built that inspectors from the city council denied spectators its stands for the first meeting on July 18. The supports looked like giving way under them.

There was no point of reference for tracks back then. You built it to fill the space you had. And so a young and self-confident cyclist called Henri Desgrange sketched out a track shaped like an egg and almost devoid of bankings. Despite all that, and thanks largely to Desgrange's skill as a track manager, race promoter and self-publicist, the place was a success. So much so that a bunch of businessmen looking around for men to publish a new daily sports paper settled on Desgrange and his finance director, a man called Victor Goddet. They owned the track between them and so, when their new paper hit on running a Tour de France as a stunt to push up a faltering circulation, it was an obvious step to have the race finish there.

The problem was that life was different in 1903 and the people who ran Paris had no desire to have bike races pass through their city. So the first Tour started at an outlying village, Montgeron, where cyclists had long gathered at the bar and told tall tales, and it finished as close to Paris as it was allowed, at Ville d'Avray. From there, having ridden right round France, the survivors had to pedal to the Parc des Princes and then race again for the crowd that had gathered there.

The track's status was secured. The Olympic Games were held there in 1924, the track shortened to 454 meters and with space for 20,000 and a markedly lower risk of their plunging to their death. Wonderful meetings were held there. Roadmen inspired but they were distant heroes, supermen riding super-distances. It was track riders who were the stars, from the élite of sprinting to the drama and sometimes death of motor-pacing. Cyclists were the fastest men on earth and their speed brought the crowds to buy tickets and pay for the world's best to be brought before their eyes.

It's too late now to say "the race that people still talk about" but talk about it they did and for a long time. On one side was Edmond Jacquelin, the French sprint champion in 1896, 1900 and 1902 and—significantly for our story—champion of the world in 1901. He had grown so rich from cycling talent that he had a box at the Comédie Française and a habit of buying champagne for everyone in a restaurant. The President came to watch him in the Grand Prix de Paris, in which the first prize was 15,000 gold francs. Jacquelin was stocky with an almost modern haircut and strong eyebrows and a chin that cut off square at the end like a screwdriver. The crowd, with a sense of mischief, called him Pioupiou, a long-vanished word that had suggested a street urchin.

On the other side was a man also richly paid on the track but whose story, often romanticized even then, was of poverty and racial rejection and passionate religion and a sympathy that had the crowd on his side as the underdog even though he was one of the best sprinters in the world. The fact that Major Taylor was black counted for less in France than back at home in the USA. In France, which had plenty of prejudices but rarely against black people, he was simply exotic.

And so on May 16, 1901—Ascension and therefore a national holiday—the two came face to face on the cement of the Parc des Princes, Taylor the fascinating and Jacquelin the flamboyant. The Frenchman was champion of the world, a title he'd won in front of this same Parisian crowd. The American, far from a nobody with the 1899 world championship in his legs, was on his first tour of Europe. He brought a reputation which the crowd both hoped and dreaded would bring an end to their colorful hero. All 20,000 places were taken.

There were three rounds, of which one man had to win two. The pair rode elbow to elbow in the first, Jacquelin winning. Taylor knew now that the Frenchman could accelerate better. So next time he waited. And he waited too long and Jacquelin did it again. Taylor resisted, then gave up. The two rolled to a halt and Jacquelin turned to the American to sneer. He'd been reading for days about how he'd been greeted by a crowd as he stepped off his liner at Le Havre, how he'd been training at the Parc, how the world had admired his silky style and gentle manners. And he thumbed his nose at him in contempt.

The crowd, now on the side of the winner, climbed over the barriers and carried Jacquelin shoulder-high back to his dressing room. The king of Paris reigned secure.

They loved it at the ticket office, of course. Taylor wasn't going to take the first boat back to America. He could be brought back to the Parc for a revenge match. And neither he nor Jacquelin was likely to object because clicking turnstiles put money in their pockets. Separately, both noted May 27 in their diaries and began wondering how it would go.

How it went was that Taylor was determined and Jacquelin was over-confident. And Taylor wreaked revenge. The crowd cheered and booed at the same time, uncertain how to react. The order had changed and Taylor, the foreign visitor, knew that may not have been a good thing. Yes, he was pleased to have won and won so well. But "I shouldn't have, I know. I'm sorry," he conceded.

What they didn't know is that they were the beginning of the end. They met many times again but, slowly, to less and less adulation. The gold of track sprinting had turned to bronze. There'd be revivals, men like Reg Harris and Arie van Vliet and Oscar Daemers in the 1950s, but from then on it was the road that captured imagination and adulation. And more and more it was the Tour de France that captured it most.

The Tour always finished at the Parc because the organizers owned it and because they could put on a meeting before it arrived and trouser the income. It was enough of a paying venture that Desgrange and his successor, Jacques Goddet, again renovated their stadium with room for 40,000, although avariciously they crammed in 46,000 for the opening and were told never to do it again.

The Parc saw the Tour finish in its most glorious days, before soccer rose to challenge cycling and when the Tour was *disputé* by teams representing their country. It was a time when French riders were at their peak and the system suited everyone except the smaller nations that couldn't raise a full team and had to be pitched in along with Luxembourg. And then came the death knell. Suddenly and without warning. Paris was to get a bypass. Jacques Goddet was confident. It had only to pass a few hundred meters to one side and his track was safe. And, if it wasn't, well Paris would pay for its demolition and he could build again elsewhere. It was about time it was improved, anyway.

But Paris had other ideas. The track was to fall as rubble.

Goddet fought bitterly. "That the administration of the city, with an especially motivated sports adviser, should want to interrupt the activities of the company running the Parc—my company—demands explanations," he protested in his autobiography. "We had been model partners going right back to the previous century, having the most courteous, the most straightforward dealings with the administration of the city of Paris, which owned our land from its beginnings. We were its tenants and therefore we had a lease. It had all the clauses that any lease would have, right down to rights to raise the rent, terms for extension of the period of lease…

"As tenants, paying rent, we were therefore entitled to our rights, which were that when the time came to eject us, there was a duty, without discussion, to pay us the costs of the ending of the lease. Those would have been considerable sums, because our little Parc, its buildings and installations, just 32 years old, and its pretty pink track were in excellent state and produced a good income."

What happened next, he said, was "iniquitous".

"We found out that what the city of Paris had told us was a lease—something that nobody denied—wasn't one! What had been called a lease, treated as a lease, was just an error of description on the part of the city of Paris. Since 1898! And we who thought we were tenants, with all the rights of tenants, rights that until then had always been respected, suddenly found that under the law we were common concessionaires, people who could be shown the door without any legal discussion and without any damages."

Somewhere in a file-lined office in the center of town, a lawyer had discovered that the hiring agreement back in the nineteenth century dictated that a local school had free use of the stadium on Thursday afternoons. And, Paris argued in court, such a clause could never be in a tenancy agreement. A tenant would have full and exclusive use. So, if he didn't have full and exclusive use, it followed that the Tour de France had just a concession to use the land. Goddet and his company took the argument to appeal. But the judges saw the legal argument. The track's shareholders got not a centime.

The last man to win a race on it was Raymond Poulidor, whose victory in the last stage of the 1967 Tour confirmed a death warrant that had already been delivered. Roger Pingeon, the overall winner, accepted his yellow jersey in a depleted stadium in which the demolishers had already started work. The remains stayed up another two years as an ugly gravestone, and then neglect and mistreatment meant they too had to come down. The Parc des Princes became rubble for that soccer and rugby stadium.

I stood outside one day. I had to. The Parc now is all concrete and fencing and barbed wire. You're not welcome without a ticket. You're not welcome unless you have the money to buy a ticket. I suppose the bike track was no less a commercial venture but it seemed less blatant, less cold-hearted.

A man stood in a sentry box, behind a gray metal gate at the entrance. He wore the mock police uniform that private guards wear all over the world, as though they were any different from old-fashioned night-watchmen who sat beneath the stars and warmed their hands on a brazier of glowing coke. He walked to meet me as I peered through the railings, his gut hanging over his black leather belt.

"*Oui, monsieur…,*" he asked neutrally, as though he knew already that the answer, whatever the question, would be *Non.*

"Can I come in?"

"Why?"

"So I can see if anything remains of the bike track that used to stand here."

The look on his face showed he was of too late a generation to be familiar with the site's history, with the stars and the also-rans who rode there and who once were chastised in print if they left without a shower.

"There's nothing here," he said after a while.

"Where is it, then?"

I knew the answer, of course, but he confirmed it by pointing at the ground and scraping his foot on the gravel to make the point. It had been demolished and then buried. I hadn't expected anything else but it made me sad nevertheless.

Les Woodland

5
Shattered Dreams

It's bad enough to be beaten within grasp of the greatest prize. But to be consider yourself beaten not by the opposition but by your own side, that's the hardest of all.

Goodwood, England, September 5, 1982: Nobody Remembers Jonathon Boyer much now, but at the time he was big news in America, and in France, the man who held the Tour's purse-strings rather saw him as a source of American riches. For American cycling, so long the subject of sidelong glances and a long wait in the cold before all the team got home—the French daily, *L'Équipe,* once sniffed at an American amateur team "dressed in cowboy clothes, with broad-brimmed hats and rodeo trousers"—he was the end to decades of embarrassment. Not only was he riding with a small but respectable team in France but he was finishing races that those far away had actually heard of, and he was riding (pause for breath) *The Tour de France.*

And one day near the southern English horse-racing town of Goodwood, he thought he was going to be the world professional road champion. And who did him out of it a few seconds later? Another American.

He was an odd man, Boyer. His team-manager, Cyrille Guimard, called him a *marginal,* which is French word for someone who's not exactly downright bizarre but nevertheless doesn't live life the way that's expected. He was encouraged in his description not simply by Boyer's vegetarianism, which is close to illegal in France, but by the way he came to the Tour with suitcases of fruit and nuts. One day the British journalist, Dennis Donovan, took pity on him in the years when there was little English spoken in the Tour and offered some girlie magazines to pass the lonely nights in hotels.

"Thank you," Boyer said coldly. "I have my Bible."

There is unspoken Catholicism in European cycling and it's not unusual for riders to cross themselves before races. But Boyer's devotion, his nightly reading of the Scriptures, and above all his rejection of naked women, were novel. Alarming, even. Before long the Dutch got wind of it and, the biggest gossips on the race, the story was everywhere.

Boyer was the first American to ride the Tour. He was a quiet, long-faced man of 25 who, after Ed Pavelka asked him for *VeloNews* whether cyclists had groupies in the style of pop stars, dismissed him as a pervert. There is an irony in that that came back to haunt him. And put him in jail.

Boyer was no stranger to Europe. He had been racing there since he was 18, abandoning plans to become an animal doctor to ride for the club in the northern Parisian industrial suburb of Boulogne-Billancourt. The club, run by a man called Micky Weigant, had a reputation for passing its best amateurs to Peugeot, France's longest established pro team. Boyer, though, went to a smaller team, also based in Paris: Lejeune-BP. It was backed by two brothers making race bikes and by a global oil company which curiously also supported Peugeot.

He moved teams as the seasons passed and then, fifth and one of the few finishers in a cold and wet world championship in the shadow of Mont Blanc, joined the Renault team. It was there that he came into contact with Guimard, a former road-sprinter with a talent for producing champions and for predicting the day's race. "Everything he told you at the morning briefing would come true by the end of the day," said the Tour winner, Lucien van Impe, with a mixture of admiration and frustration.

"Now here he was in France's crack team," Geoffrey Nicholson wrote of Boyer. "He was an approachable person who answered questions with candor and possessed a great deal of charm, but the French couldn't work him out. While he rode, he did so with all his effort and concentration, but not simply to make money; he could earn more back home. He raced because he enjoyed it."

The Tour liked Boyer because he was American. Specifically, Félix Lévitan liked him. Lévitan was the rodent-faced despot who looked after the race's money and, when he chose, overruled judges and referees to produce a verdict he found more favorable. He was in the habit of signing race sponsors for however little they were prepared to pay and the presentations at the end of each stage, one for each backer, went on even after most of the crowd had gone home. If he could land one big American sponsor, he reasoned, he could do away with all the shoestring accounts. And just maybe he could start organizing a race in America, a dream which eventually cost him his job.

Lévitan therefore told Boyer to wear not the yellow, white and black of Renault, at the time a state-owned car company (it had been seized after the war in resentment at the way it had made tanks for the Germans), but a vivid American champion's jersey to which he wasn't entitled. Boyer obliged by going further and wearing a stetson hat after each stage and having a bucking bronco on his car license plate.

For a while all went well. Boyer finished the Tour in as good a position as any rider hired not to win but to support his betters. Everyone was as happy as anyone can be in an essentially miserable world like professional cycling. But Boyer's status as "a lone American eagle ahead of the curve," as Pavelka put it, couldn't last. Because Guimard, reasoning that where there was one there may be more, came across a younger, fresher-faced, even spotty American called Greg LeMond.

LeMond coped with an unhappy childhood by writing a list of ambitions which he kept in his school desk. He had been a skier but had turned to cycling when his father inadvertently found himself mixed up with a bike race while driving and, to the young LeMond's delight, couldn't keep up with the riders as they whizzed down hills. Somewhere around his eighteenth birthday he went to race in Belgium, still a junior and still unknown in Europe. But not for long.

A British rider of the same age, Neil Dykes, remembered the effect that LeMond caused. "We'd all be trying to get into races, because officially junior events in Belgium weren't open to foreigners, and if we got a ride we thought we'd done well if we finished in the first 20 and won a prize. We were happy if we just finished. And then this guy we'd never heard of turned up, won a race every day for a week and then went home again. For weeks afterward, people were still asking 'Who the hell was that?'"

I've no idea if Boyer saw the threat or if he resented Guimard's interest. I suspect he did, both, because it was to at least some advantage that he was the curiosity, the novelty, the one American in top-level cycling. There could be no room for two without one or the other losing. Certainly LeMond, ambitious despite his almost absent-minded manner, was aware of Boyer and he was determined not to yield right of passage. Which brings us to that day at Goodwood in fall 1982.

The circuit chosen by the British was flatter than it could have been. It could have gone in bad-tempered style up and down the South Downs, the range of low but taxing hills beyond which lay the English Channel. But it didn't. Instead it rose rather than struggled to a ridge road, followed it, dropped to a normal height and then rose on the only real hill, which took it to the finish line. It wasn't a hard ride but after eighteen laps and 275 kilometers it was plenty challenging enough.

The world championship is unusual in being disputed, as the French say, by national teams and not by the sponsored teams of many nationalities that ride all the other races. National cycling associations pick their riders and the smallest can't always afford to pay their expenses, still less fees or a bonus. The American federation was one of those and had already had the embarrassment of not paying for a women's team in 1969—only to have one of its members, Audrey McElmury, pay her own way and then win the championship.

Perhaps the Americans paid for amateurs to ride the 1982 world championships. But, according to LeMond, it hadn't paid the professionals, or at any rate it hadn't paid him. Nor was there a manager or a masseur. There was no team beyond individuals wearing jerseys they'd received through the post. In fact the American selectors had named nine riders, pretty much every professional they had, but only six had turned up. As a result, LeMond reckoned there was no contract between him and the USA, nor between him and the other members of this nominal team. Including Boyer, whom he had now come to dislike.

To his alarm, Boyer attacked on that last hill and was heading alone for the finish line, with the passion that comes to a man when he's only seconds from being champion of the world. Look at a photo taken in the last 150 meters of that race and you see the story. There is a small group maybe 25 meters behind Boyer and nobody is sure what to do. Then, just as the camera clicked, Beppe Saronni looked across at LeMond and smiled. He is smiling because LeMond had started to chase his own teammate. Saronni's only interest was in winning, but he couldn't start the pursuit himself without taking with him a dour man in green, Sean Kelly of Ireland, who was the only rider in the group capable of outsprinting him. Especially if Saronni had given him the shelter of his back wheel until just before the line.

Now, with LeMond starting the chase, unbelievably to Saronni's eyes, Kelly was obliged to chase as well. Now the fight was not between the Italian and the Irishman but between them and the two Americans.

To have won the world championship would have changed Boyer's life, his earnings and his place in history. The first American to ride the Tour, the first American man to win a world title since dandy but musty guys way back in history. The result would also have changed LeMond's life. If he won, he would have the glory and fortune, of course. But if Boyer won, LeMond would be overshadowed and, as he saw it, belittled. And so he chased Boyer. Because he had nothing to lose.

In the end, neither American won. Saronni played the role of third thief perfectly. He won, LeMond came second and Kelly third. There was just the chance that LeMond might have won had Saronni not been so pampered throughout the race by his team-mates. But the more pressing question was whether Boyer would have won had he been left alone by his own team.

I was there that day with a tape recorder and I was the only reporter for a moment to approach him as he sat dejected and alone on a low white wall soon after the finish.

"How do you feel about that?", I asked, hoping such an open question gave more scope for a reply, perhaps even an "I tried my best but it wasn't enough." Instead Boyer turned and glared and shouted so loudly that he distorted the tape.

"HOW D'YOU *THINK* I FEEL?", he snapped.

I took it the interview was over. Boyer had come tenth, forgotten by everyone, celebrated by none, and he got back on his bike and rode to the empty pits that the Americans had been allocated. Nobody else troubled to ask how he felt. Nobody cared. He was just another side player who'd tried a solo and flopped.

To his mind, he wasn't denied and he wasn't beaten: he was betrayed. And he was still bitter decades later when he spoke to the author, Richard Moore. He had watched the tape of the finish, he said, and only then realized just how disloyal LeMond had been. "I asked Greg why. He said that he didn't care who won, as long as it wasn't me; that I didn't deserve to win, didn't deserve the publicity, that I'd done nothing all year. It was a deliberate move on his part. Greg didn't like the fact that I got any publicity. He wanted his own publicity; he wanted to do it for himself."

LeMond agrees that they didn't get on, that for other than a short period they had never gotten on. He says he can understand Boyer's resentment, but then it's always easier for the victor to be gracious towards the vanquished than the other way round. And there's no doubting that LeMond was as abrasive as any other twenty-one-year-old who'd discovered a dominating talent from the moment he took up a sport. Not only did he find it easy, he had a conceited self-regard. He became more of a diplomat later, "doing anything rather than brush people up the wrong way", according to Laurent Fignon, while at the same time "his estimate of his own worth has changed very little", according to Geoffrey Nicholson.

Tactically, LeMond insisted, he was right to chase and pass and beat Boyer. His fellow American had yet to win a professional race and there was no chance he was going to hold off Saronni, Kelly, Joop Zoetemelk, Michel Pollentier or any of the nine riders who passed him. LeMond had just been one of those nine. But more than that, he could have argued a legal right. America had nine entrants in the race, six starters and only three finishers (George Mount, exactly six minutes behind in fifty-second place, was the other). Nine was too few to hold a national championship and so the governing body had decided a year earlier that the world championship would also be the American *national* championship.

If it was a national championship, it followed that those taking part were rivals and not teammates. If anybody had decreed that LeMond should chase Boyer and beat him, it was the American national federation.

In time, of course, LeMond too would become the "other" American. Boyer had eclipsed Mount (who also retained a fervent dislike of

Les Woodland

Boyer and what he called his holier-than-thou attitude) and LeMond had overtaken both of them. Then in turn LeMond, winner of the Tour de France and the world championship, was outranked by Lance Armstrong. True to history, LeMond quickly developed a dislike of Armstrong which rose to public criticism and a nearly-said claim that Armstrong was drugged to win his seven Tours. What he actually said, as Armstrong played his role of inspirational cancer survivor, was that "If Lance is clean, it is the greatest comeback in the history of sports. If he isn't, it would be the greatest fraud", adding later that Armstrong was "ready to do anything to keep his secret."

Soon afterward all was revealed: Armstrong had indeed been central to what investigators called the most organized dope ring in sports history, that professional lives had been ruined if that suited Armstrong. He was stripped of his seven wins in the Tour de France and LeMond is back to being the only American to have won the Tour.

Boyer raced for another few years, the last three until 1987 with a team sponsored by an American shop chain. He helped in team management, then retired to run a bike shop near his home in California. Still deeply religious, he nevertheless became involved with an underage girl at his church, admitting in court that he had molested an eleven-year-old girl in 1997 and continued to do so for three years. The two had sex, the girl said, and Boyer spoke French as he was climaxing. Ed Pavelka didn't know at the time that a decade earlier Boyer had called him a pervert for asking if professional cyclists had groupies but it must have produced a smile when Boyer was jailed for a year and put on probation.

Boyer sat out his punishment peacefully and for a while appeared at trade shows to sell the tools he had sold before becoming successful in Europe. He was never accepted by American cycling, though, and he began helping cyclists in Rwanda. His qualities as a *marginal* increased. He drinks water irradiated by ultraviolet light, sleeps on a pulsating bed and never watches television, listens to the radio or reads a newspaper. He reads books but only if they are "biblical or historical or nutritional," he told Steve Friedman of *Bicycling*. He skips fiction because "I have so little time and I don't want to waste it." He prays before every meal and a lot at other times. He has found another life in Rwanda just as the girl at his church has found another life.

Greg LeMond saw his suspicions justified and his role as All-American Hero restored. Lance Armstrong has become the most hated man in cycling. A long trail of ashes spreads back from that afternoon in the English countryside on September 5, 1982.

6

Beauty in the Ugliness

It's tough when a god falls to earth. You can't believe it. But now and then it happens...rarely without a good tale.

Mourenx, France, July 15, 1969: It's hard now to grasp the phenomenon of Eddy Merckx. It's not just that he won the Tour de France five times; others have done that. It's that he won everything. He won classics, he won six-day races, he won everyday races in places we have never heard of. He won so often that other teams' sponsors became hard to find because nobody wanted riders who'd never come better than second. Merckx is the only rider so successful that he put his sport into recession.

Belgium, of course, loved him. He lived in Brussels and spoke French and Dutch equally well, pleasing the sometimes bitterly divided communities of the north and south. He had matinée looks and Betty Boop eyelashes. In time he even had a Métro station named after him. His success ended a long walk in the wilderness for Belgian cycling and the country's first win in the Tour de France since 1939 put his image everywhere—on balls of chewing gum, on dish-drying cloths and, until he went to law to stop it, his naked backside on posters.

The man could do no wrong. Other riders often disliked him and complained of his moaning—if he lost, said the British rider, Barry Hoban, it was somebody or something else's fault—and they mimicked his slow, slightly mournful voice. But for the public, in Belgium and elsewhere, he was an idol.

When a dope test caught him in the Giro in June 1969, therefore, many were much more inclined to believe the theory of a plot by jealous riders or officials than to accept that he had had his fingers in the pill bottle. They felt a stab of personal pain when they saw photos of him on his bed in the Excelsior hotel in Savona, dressed in his racing gear except for the leader's pink jersey he had yet to put on when he heard of his exclusion. When he wept in front of the cameras, the world wept for him.

Merckx still insists the world was against him in Italy and in particular a coterie of riders. If the test was positive it was because it had been tricked. Many still believe that, and names have been named of riders who invited him to lose the race, or part with money to keep his name clean. Others, seeing later history, recognize that no man is perfect and that this was merely the first of so many positive dope tests that under modern rules he would have been banned for life. But the era and its attitudes were different.

On that bed in Savona, Merckx is said to have promised: "At the Tour de France I will prove what Merckx can do. I'll have had my shower and changed by the time the second rider crosses the line in the big Pyrenean stage into Mourenx."

Whether he said it or not, that was pretty much what happened. He was thrown out of the Giro but allowed to ride the Tour in a strange decision in which an international panel —which included one of the Tour's organizers, Félix Lévitan, who could hardly have been disinterested in the participation of the world's greatest rider in his race—accepted that Merckx was guilty but that he shouldn't be punished because he was Merckx.

In fact, he hadn't wanted to ride the Giro in the first place. He had won Paris–Nice, Milan–San Remo and the Tour of Flanders, all in a few weeks, and he wanted to win the Tour. The problem was that he and a bunch of other Belgians had an Italian sponsor and, although Faema sold coffee machines all over Europe, the directors wanted him in Italy, to show him off and perhaps to hobnob with him.

Faema, with Merckx, was the continent's dominant team. Merckx made enemies in Belgium, riders resented him across Europe, and Italian riders fretted at an Italian sponsor giving its money to foreigners so they could thrash them on their own soil. Hence the talk of plots and revenge in the Giro.

Merckx boasted in Savona that he'd be the first into Mourenx. Frankly, most would want to be the first to leave it. It is the ugliest concentration of factories and industrial plants in France, a place so breathtakingly ugly that many who stumble on its outskirts stop to take a photo. It started with gas plants in 1956 and grew and grew, with aluminum factories and power stations and installations of silvery pipes and tubes that defy understanding. Beside it all stands a town of 15,000 people either short-sighted or commendably resilient.

Cities, towns and even large villages pay for the Tour to start or finish a stage *chez eux* because they like the publicity. Usually it's to attract tourists, sometimes to bring in investors and employment. Mourenx paid out to bring in still more industry. And, whether that succeeded or not, it got value for money in the publicity that Merckx brought that day and was so grateful that on July 15, 1999, the thirtieth anniversary, it renovated its velodrome and renamed it after him.

Maybe it was because he knew what lay in store that Merckx was more circumspect the night before the stage started. "We'll see how things work out tomorrow but I'm not going to try anything special."

By then, in his first Tour, he was already in the yellow jersey by nine minutes. Ink flowed in discussions of whether he was bluffing about being washed and changed by the time the next man came in, or if he thought having the jersey was enough and that it was for others to attack him and not for him to attack them. A *fringale* in the mountains, a weakening because he hadn't eaten enough, would cost him if he went too wild. Why not just sit tight and wait for the others to move? It wasn't the exciting way but it had won Jacques Anquetil five Tours and it would certainly win Merckx one.

The Pyrenees, which are there to stop French and Spanish bickering turning to fisticuffs, are lower and shorter than the Alps. But they climb straight up instead of in zigzags and so they are the more destructive to ride aggressively. And that day the bunch faced the Peyresourde, the Aspin and then the highest, the col du Tourmalet, followed by the Aubisque. That's four of the race's toughest climbs in one stage, a relentlessly hot stage, although after them would come a descent and a long and unchallenging ride round to Pau and, twenty kilometers away, the industrial blot of Mourenx.

The remaining riders set off unsure what to do. The little climbers, like Joaquim Galera, could dance away and nobody would or could match them. They would have their day and then spend the rest of the Tour clinging to the back of the peloton in the hope of reaching Paris. The riders who mattered, the strongmen like Felice Gimondi in second place, could wait and then, they hoped, put all their strength into one destructive burst. The problem was that, as Cyrille Guimard used to say, the trick was to attack last but before all the others. And nobody could forget that an indiscreet attack on Merckx could rebound as terrible misfortune.

Nobody hurried, therefore. They ambled over the Peyresourde, rode down it, then ambled over the Aspin and back down the other side. That brought them to the village of Ste-Marie-de-Campan, where in the Tour's earliest years Eugène Christophe had to weld his forks together at a smithy on the outskirts. There's a plaque on the building that stands where the smithy used to be but the riders didn't see it because they turned left in the village and rode towards the highest col of the day.

The road to the Tourmalet rises briefly as it leaves Ste-Marie and then tricks the soul by holding the flat valley and even briefly descending. Then, on the right, is a small sign announcing the *lieu-dit*, the hamlet, of Grippe. It means "flu" in English. And that's where the hot fever of the long and often open climb to the café at the summit begins. It's broken on the way only by the concrete mess of the ski station at La Mongie and, just before it, the sweeping right bend beneath the open-sided tunnel that protects the road from avalanches. Many a weekend amateur has had to put foot to ground on that bend and then again by the ski-hire shops.

What's rarely observed is that Merckx was in a bad mood because his teammate, Martin Vandenbossche, had that morning told him he was leaving. The two were friends and they had often shared hotel rooms, including that night in the Excelsior at Savona. Merckx appreciated that Vandenbossche had told him first but he was cross because the two had become brothers and because he and the team "had rescued him the previous winter, without which he wouldn't have had a team."

"We'd been through hard moments together and there he was, calmly telling me he was leaving. And I took it badly and I accelerated on the Tourmalet to stop him getting to the summit first. On the way down, I wasn't sure what to do next. Should I wait or should I press on? In the end I decided to carry on alone, as far as the Aubisque, thinking the others would catch me, because there was still so far to ride. But they never caught me."

The result was that he plowed on in his round-shouldered, heaving style—he always looked more elegant in photos than real life—and soaked with sweat with bands around his wrist to keep his mitts from getting soggy. Across the mitts, he had written the letters M-E-R-C-K-X. With them he heaved on his deep Cinelli bars and reached the foot of the Aubisque with a minute and got to the summit with eight minutes' advance. He arrived in Mourenx four seconds short of those same eight minutes.

Pierre Chany, writing in *L'Équipe* next morning, said: "For a journalist sent out to follow Eddy Merckx, the first thing to do is go easy on superlatives, to have some left for the exploits still to come, and which *will* come. Let's go easy, therefore. Let's go easy." After which he said Merckx had put himself on the level of Fausto Coppi, or of Hugo Koblet when he won alone at Agen, except that Coppi had never been that audacious in the Tour and that Koblet hadn't ridden in the mountains, that Merckx had been "a proud *torero* desperate for glory, risking the bull's horn for the simple pleasure of making the crowd gasp."

Merckx won the Tour that year, and six of its stages, and the mountains and points competitions. The 17 minutes 54 seconds by which he beat the rest has never been matched in the modern era.

You can't see it clearly in pictures but the bottles on his bike, all his bottles, were marked with a red stripe. The experience in Italy had persuaded him to accept only those bottles, the ones he trusted. But Mourenx was Merckx's last dominant triumph in the mountains. That fall he was following a derny in a race on the narrow and rain-dampened track at Blois, in the Loire valley, when both he and his pacer, Fernand Wambst, ran into a couple who had fallen ahead of them and both crashed heavily. Merckx displaced a bone in his pelvis; Wambst died.

From then on Merckx was never comfortable on his bike. Ugo De Rosa, who made his bikes, supplied one minutely altered frame after another. Merckx began changing his saddle height, his handlebar settings, not just before a race but during it. He once pulled out a wrench going down the col de la Faucille, slackened his saddle bolt, adjusted it a centimeter, then re-tightened it. His Italian teammate, Vittorio Adorni, used to laugh: "If you wanted something done on your bike, there was no point in calling a mechanic for a wrench. Eddy had a pocketful of them."

Merckx was rarely a settled man after that. He slept fitfully. "He'd sit there worrying about Ghent–Wevelgem or Paris–Roubaix even though he had won the Tour of Flanders only a few hours earlier," said his wife, Claudine.

By 1977 he was a shadow of the man he was, still respected but not longer the great beast of the jungle. He suffered and stepped off in the Alps. His sponsor, Fiat, told him it planned to back a youth team the following season, that Merckx could lead it if he wanted to and to decide its program. He refused. It was beneath his pride. But his talent had declined to the point that nobody would pay the price he wanted and only after long bargaining could he make a deal with the Dutch clothing chain, C & A, which made it clear it was in the game for only a year.

The new sponsor was even more disappointed than the old. Merckx dropped out of the Omloop Het Volk, exhausted. It should have been a step to the Tour of Flanders to follow a few weeks later. He should have returned to Milan–San Remo, which he'd won so often. But the day before it, April 19, 1978, he rode an everyday race, the Omloop van het Waasland, in the flat land across the river Schelde from Antwerp.

I was there that day with Jonathon Boyer. He said Merckx looked "overweight", which I rendered into "fat" when I quoted him in *VeloNews*. Boyer rebuked me, rightly, for getting it wrong. But I had got it right. Merckx looked fat. And he rode like a fat man, a talented fat man but no better than twelfth place, and that evening he drove home to Brussels with his soigneur, Pierrot De Wit, and said he wouldn't be needing his services any more.

De Wit looked surprised and hurt. They had been together for a long time. Merckx smiled sadly and said: "I rode my last race today. This time, it's finished for good."

De Wit tried to dissuade him. But he failed. Merckx, frankly, had grown tired of being Eddy Merckx. He rode his bike again after that but the will and the body had grown tired. He gathered one infection after another. There was no surprise when he called journalists to the Brussels International Press Center on the afternoon of May 18 and said it was all over.

Herman van Springel, who in 1968 had been close to being the first Belgian to win the Tour since Sylvère Maes, said: "He wasn't that bad when he stopped, but he just wasn't what he had been, all the time. He had to be better than anyone else. Only that would do."

William Fotheringham, one of Merckx's many biographers, wrote: "Every bit of ground covered regularly by the sport's monumental events has its associations: Tom Simpson and Mont Ventoux, Eugène Christophe and the Tourmalet, Louison Bobet and the Izoard, Fausto Coppi and Gino Bartali on the Galibier, Coppi at the Stelvio and Madonna del Ghisallo in Italy, Ocaña on the col de Menté, De Vlaeminck, Moser and others on the cobbles of Paris–Roubaix. But the whole of cycling's topography can be seen in reference to Merckx: his imprint is everywhere, from the côte de Stockeu, near Liège, where his statue stands, to the Ventoux, and the heel of Italy. Every race in the cycling calendar that has any history refers back to Merckx. If there is any irony, it is that as the calendar is being globalized, the European events that are being downgraded and are disappearing are the ones where Merckx built his legend.

"*La course en tête* as Merckx forged it remains the benchmark for the entire sport. The way he raced is the gold standard to which all professional cyclists and all their victories are compared."

7

Into the Wilderness

Sport is a combination of triumph and tragedy, one man happy, the other beaten. Judges are there to see fair play. But rarely are they called on to judge the absurd.

Gap, France, July 14, 2003: Judges are troubled by many things. Should they really intervene in every misdemeanor, taking the charm out of cycling and laying down a heavy-handed law? Should they let things slide and risk a precedent they will regret as the seasons roll on? Such things have often vexed them. But rarely have they had to decide if a rider in the Tour de France has drawn an unfair advantage by turning left into a field, riding across its bumps and then back out again through a hole in a hedge.

That, though, is what they had to consider on France's national day, July 14, in 2003. Because it was that day that Lance Armstrong took just such a short cut.

Gap—pronounced more like *Gupp* than the chain store—is in southeast France. It's the country's highest *préfecture* or administrative capital, 750 meters above sea level. Napoleon turned up there when he got away from Elba and printed off thousands of leaflets so impressively revolutionary that the locals turned out to join him as he left on a horse next morning.

The travelers that day in 2003 were on bicycles rather than horses. They had been riding all day from Bourg d'Oisans, on the road from Grenoble to Briançon and at the foot of Alpe d'Huez. It's 98 kilometers by the shortest route but further the way the Tour took them. Armstrong was in the yellow jersey of leader and looking for his fifth successive win. It had been a hard day, with just four kilometers left to do, and he had been pestered all day by a gnome-like Spaniard called Joseba Beloki. The Spaniard was lighter and less muscular than Armstrong and vulnerable if the American attacked where the terrain suited him most. But that lightness helped him when the road veered upwards and all day Armstrong had been trying to swat him off in the way a cotton-picker tries to squash a mosquito.

Both were trying too hard. At stake was not only the elapsed time on which the race was judged but the mental blow one could inflict on the other by opening a gap, and then the handful of seconds that would be deducted from one man's time if he could cross the line first. For the moment, that first man looked like being the blond, sporty but unsmiling Alexandre Vinokourov, a man who could tell you he was having the happiest day of his life and still make you feel sorry for him.

Beloki was leading Armstrong by a couple of lengths. And then he crashed. He ran into tar melted by the day's heat and his back wheel swung first to the left and then to the right. It tore the tire off his back wheel. He fell so heavily to his right at approaching 60 kilometers per hour that he broke his right leg, an elbow and a wrist. He never saw the finish line because he went straight to hospital and out of the Tour.

Armstrong was behind him and slightly to the left. He had time to brake but not enough to miss him had he stayed on road. Having nowhere else to go, he steered blindly and desperately into the sun-hardened dust of the road on his left, to the outside of the bend, alarming a policeman standing there but staying upright. Other riders following had time to stop or steer clear. Armstrong, though, with the momentum of going downhill, dropping down the five kilometers of the côte de la Rochette, had to keep going as he bumped across the drought-hardened soil toward an exit he could see beside a power pylon a few hundred meters further on.

A shallow drainage ditch ran beside the road at that point and Armstrong had to dismount for a couple of steps to make it back to the road, a few meters short of the blue overhead banner that announced the last four kilometers of the day. A sweep of riders passed him as he got back to momentum, one or two muttering their admiration and Tyler Hamilton, a fellow American, reaching out his right hand to slap his back.

Les Woodland

The episode saved Armstrong a hundred meters or so—he and the others never caught Vinokourov—and that's what the judges had to decide: whether he had taken a short cut and gained in the process. It wasn't a misdemeanor on the scale of extending cycle racing by catching a train, as some of the earliest riders had done, or attaching themselves to cars by string. But rules are rules and they asked riders to stick to the course.

Beloki, meanwhile, lay on the road in the pink jersey of his sponsor, a lottery for the blind, comforted by team-mates and fussed over by nurses. His manager, the fleshy Manolo Saiz, arrived shortly afterward. He stooped over his fallen rider. The two exchanged a few words, Beloki crying and pressing his head against Saiz's chest. Saiz said the following day that he had seen him as a possible winner but that he was outclassed. "For me," he said, "there are three levels of rider: Lance Armstrong above all the others, Joseba Beloki on level two and then all the others on level three." Beloki had to be audacious to close that talent gap and his daring was what cost him the race. And, as it turned out, his career. He had impressed throughout, said *Procycling*, "but then lost everything through a combination of bad luck and poor judgment."

The medical team took him to the Albert Murat hospital in Gap, sirens on and taking short cuts in the wrong direction down several one-way streets. They reached the hospital around 5pm. Beloki had been subdued by morphine and he woke only at one the following morning, feeling hungry. The team's sports manager, Pablo Anton, had spent the night at his side. Beloki was to be repatriated to Vittoria, in Spain, to have the operation on his bones there. That morning, at 8:25, an ambulance took him to Margignan airport near Marseille, where a medical air-ambulance was waiting. It landed at Vittoria at 1:10. Beloki went to the Las Esperanzas hospital there and into its operating surgery the following morning at 9. Armstrong sent him a note of condolence; more significantly, so did the king of Spain.

Armstrong went on to finish fastest of those who made it to Paris that year and acknowledged the crowd on the Champs-Elysées. But the story turned out badly for everyone. There was no rush of teams to sign Beloki the following year. The best offer came from a lesser French team, Brioches La Boulangère. The bakery chain was the latest in a succession of sponsors that its manager, Jean-René Bernardeau, found each season to keep the team afloat. And Beloki didn't last long.

Didier Rous, himself involved in systematic doping in the Festina team which came close to bringing the 1998 Tour to a halt, said he warned Bernardeau not to sign Beloki. Bernardeau, a boyish looking former rider whose teams have an unusual reputation for steering clear of dope claims, agreed that he'd been warned. Rous, he said, had been "frightened that someone could come in and light a match under the whole group."

Rous said: "People whom I trust intimately had told me certain things about Beloki. In our team there are rules and everyone has to respect them." One was that all Bernardeau's riders had to be treated only by the team's doctor. Beloki wanted his own doctor and to use an asthma treatment, Pulmicort, a corticosteroid for which he'd need permission from the sport's panel of doctors. He threatened to sue Rous when his comments appeared in *L'Équipe*, the daily sports paper.

By the middle of April, and still with the team, he was struggling with a hurting knee and hadn't started serious racing. He left the team, rode elsewhere for another three seasons, including again for Manolo Saiz, and then stopped. He never again showed much talent. He finished seventy-fifth in the 2005 Tour and thirty-ninth in the Tour of Spain. He left the sport as an unknown. In 2006 he was named in a national doping investigation in Spain but cleared. He had never failed a dope test.

He worked after leaving the sport as a writer for a Spanish cycling magazine and as a commentator on cycling on a radio station in the Basque region of Spain where he lives. He helped coach minor professionals in the area and talked for a while of running the New York marathon. But he ruled out ever racing again on a bike. "Everything has a place in life and racing's place in mine passed some time ago," he said.

Manolo Saiz was arrested in the same national investigation that had looked at Beloki. The sport's governing body, the *Union Cycliste Internationale*, had long been offended by the rumors that surrounded him and by a the way he pulled his team out of the 1998 Tour de France and persuaded the other Spanish teams to join him, after which he spoke of "sticking a finger up the Tour's ass." The Tour made him *persona non grata* the following summer but was obliged to accept him when the UCI, perhaps reluctantly, said it had no right to tell him to keep away. Now things had gone too far and it took away his team's license and the sponsor, an insurance company, withdrew from the sport. That was the end of Beloki's time in the peloton, unable to find anyone to take him in.

Saiz was charged but cleared of damaging public health and he left cycling to run a restaurant and a catering business. "I don't think I'm a problem for the sport or the problem [itself]," he told reporters when he contemplated a return to team management. "A lot of other people who were in the sport when I was are still involved and so why am I different from them? I don't understand why people keep digging things up from the past."

Alexandre Vinokourov, who won the stage in which Beloki fell, was caught blood-doping in the Tour of 2007 and was suspended for two years. He began racing again, then crashed on the way down the Pas de Peyrol towards Aurillac in the 2011 Tour de France and said that was to be his last race. The point at which he fell, and an arrow to show the direction, have been painted on the road with the words, in English, "Vino out."

He sold the bike on which he'd won an Olympic gold medal for $243,000 and gave the money to treat five children in Kazakhstan with serious illnesses. His closeness to the Kazakh government and his status as national hero have helped his life after retirement.

Tyler Hamilton, who slapped Armstrong on the back in congratulation, was found positive for drugs in the Olympic time-trial in 2004. There was no confirmation or sentence because his second urine sample had been frozen and couldn't be tested. He then failed further tests in the Tour of Spain in 2004, finally failing another test in 2009, a year after becoming national champion. Many other allegations followed, including in the national Spanish investigation.

Hamilton lives now in Missoula, in the mountains of the northwestern American state of Montana. The air there is purer than any he breathed in his years as a racer. He now coaches other riders and works as an after-dinner speaker. His tell-all autobiography, *The Secret Race*, did much to undermine Lance Armstrong. And Armstrong's fall was greatest of them all. The US anti-doping agency said in 2012 that he had masterminded "the most sophisticated, professionalized and successful doping program the sport has ever seen." He was banned from sport for life and stripped of all seven of his Tour victories and of other races in the same period.

That fall on the côte de la Rochette was merely the first of more and worse.

8

Frozen in the Mountains

They don't make them like they used to. It's the sigh of aging sports fans everywhere, old man's disease. But sometimes it's undeniably true.

Passo del Turchino, Italy, April 3, 1910: You may not have heard of Dave Lloyd—and that's almost the point—but he has spent all his life in cycling, a short-haired man, not tall, with a convinced view of his record. And he has reason, because only two years after taking up cycling he rode four events for Britain in the world championships of 1971 and then went on to join the TI-Raleigh professional team established in Britain and then installed in Holland when Peter Post took over a few years later. That didn't work out and one by one he and the other Brits came home, persuaded perhaps rightly that Post had taken them only through a legal obligation to his British sponsors.

But while he was there, he became one of the few riders in the world—certainly among the lower ranks which he occupied—to have led Milan–San Remo for four and a half hours. With false modesty he described it as "a chance for some bronzing", meaning he was out in the Italian sun with just another British rider in the team, Phil Bayton, rather than hidden in the literal shadow of the huge main field.

The year was 1973, a period in which riders still didn't attack right from the start, least of all in Italy, because there were no crowds to flatter and no television coverage to please the sponsors. That was why Lloyd, an unknown outside his team, was allowed to bowl off by himself and stay out there until 40 kilometers from the end.

"I didn't plan to do it," he says. "I didn't say to anyone 'I'm going to attack in Milan–San Remo.' It came into my head and I went." A man more used to riding up and down seafronts in criteriums that were the backbone of an impoverished professional calendar in Britain was now elevated to leading the most glamorous race on earth.

"I remember thinking 'Bloody hell!'" Lloyd says. He was still thinking that when he was joined by the enthusiastic but ungainly Bayton, a lugubrious-looking man they called The Engine. "It was the crowds I remember," Lloyd says. "They were ten deep all through every village we went to. Not just standing on the roadside but ten deep, shouting *Allez Raleigh!* and things like that. In the end Luis Ocaña came up with another bloke, and then we were caught and the bunch came by. I was shattered. I could have gone on to the Poggio and tottered on to the finish but I packed it in. I'd done my job and I got some publicity and that was enough. I've never really regretted it."

Milan–San Remo has the reputation in Italy that the Tour of Flanders enjoys in Belgium. Almost, anyway. Many Italians would rather win once on the broad finish on the Riviera at San Remo than in a stage of the Tour de France. It is, to an Italian, the world championship.

It's an odd race. It's 294 kilometers long, for a start. It also starts in one season, in the cold spring of Milan, and ends in another: the seaside warmth of the coast. It's Paris–Nice that's called the Race to the Sun but it ought to be Milan–San Remo. Every year the riders roll away from the front of the cathedral in the main square in Milan and roll unhindered across the flat and dull plain towards the south-west. Often they don't go fast. The Dutch professional, Jac van Meer, who rode it and other races in Italy, remembers: "When you were in the Giro, particularly in the south, in the first two or three hours you were not to ride very hard, because all the people who were standing by the side of the road wanted to see Moser. They wanted to see Visentini. They wanted to see Saronni. They threw flowers into the peloton. They didn't want to see them at 60 miles an hour. No, no…*tranquillo, tranquillo.*"

It's that Italian attitude that helped Lloyd and Bayton slide away for their long break, that and the cynical attitude of riders that they weren't going to make a big effort until the television cameras were there to show it.

Les Woodland

Milan–San Remo is made not by the first hours but by the finale. It's then that the field tackles first the Turchino pass and, after it, a succession of hard but shallow hills of which the best known are the Cipressa and the Poggio. It's not hard for many professionals in mid-season now, but before the early stage races that exist today, it was tough in March when riders had only a few weeks' racing behind them.

For some, for many, it was a race to suffer and perhaps to win. For others, it was a fast but genial day out. Dominique Muret summed that up in *Humanité*: "The azure of the sea, the silver green of the olive trees, the emerald of the palm trees, the yellows and the tender pinks of the houses, the red of geraniums. And above all the warm welcome of the public, a never-ending hedge of them all along the coast. That's Milan–San Remo. With the journalists who picnic along the route, enjoying the blue of the horizon, waiting for the riders."

It is the last of the classics that echoes the classic years of cycling, the decades when riders not only went as fast as they could but had to survive as well. Men such as Eugène Christophe. If his name is familiar—and I mentioned him some pages back—it's because he was the man the rules insisted had to weld his forks back together in the Tour de France, and because he was the first *maillot jaune*. But the misery in the forge at Ste-Marie-de-Campan at the foot of the Tourmalet was a historical novelty, something that could never happen again. But we have all been horribly, bitterly cold on a bike and it's far easier to imagine Christophe's terrible, horrible day back in March four years before the world went to war.

It was 1910. Christophe was twenty-five, a perpetually sad-looking man with a heavy forehead lined by thick eyebrows and a wide mouth above a strong chin. In the days when he wore a mustache above that mouth, he looked enough like one of the old Gauls of France that that's what other riders called him: the Old Gaul. That day he was one of 71 on the line at Milan. Or, according to some reports, 65. Of whom, only three reached San Remo. Or perhaps four. Even five: it's all so very hazy. But let him tell the story in his own words…

"It was the second time I'd been to Milan and I only knew a few words of the language. With Gustave Garrigou, I went to look at the course as far as Pavia, which was 30 kilometers. That was all I knew of the 290 kilometers of the race. I took Garrigou's advice, because he'd ridden before, in deciding which gears to use on the bikes I'd use before and after the Turchino climb."

The Turchino is on a road that runs—well, I was going to say straight south but it wiggles as any mountain climb ought to wiggle. To the south is Voltri, where the road comes out on to the Mediterranean and Milan–San Remo turns right with the sea on its left. To the north is Ovada and further north, and slightly east, is Novi Ligure, where the era's leading Italian Costante Girardengo lived, and where decades later, Fausto Coppi worked in a butcher's shop. The climb itself is between Masone and Mêle, climbing only to 532 meters but no less difficult for that.

They've built a fast highway now where once only the old road snaked over the Passo del Turchino. The old road is better surfaced now than it used to be in Christophe's time, but to ride it still gives a hint of what it must have been then.

"The weather had been good at the start of the week but it turned really bad and Alphonse Baugé [the manager] told us that we'd be going over the Turchino even though the road was bad and covered with snow. Everybody was talking about it and we began wondering if the race would be postponed. François Faber and Louis Trousselier cheered us up by saying 'What does it matter if we've got Lapize and Christophe the two cyclo-cross champions with us?'

"On Sunday morning April 3, 71 riders of the 94 who'd entered were set off in a biting cold. The roads were muddy and frozen and we had to bounce along in the ruts, riding on the verges between the posts that were spaced every 20 meters as far as Pavia. We rode the first 32 kilometers in 56 minutes, the 53 kilometers from Milan to Voghera in 1 hour 50 minutes. There were attacks after attacks and it was more like a *course des primes* than a long-distance race…

"We got to the notorious col de Turchino. The clouds were low, the countryside was unattractive and we started to feel the cold more and more. We started to shiver and every turn of the pedals was heavier. The half-melted snow made the race very hard and we were struggling too with a glacial wind. I dropped my friend Ernest Paul to get up to Ganna, whom I could see on the hairpins. I got up and past him without too much trouble because he didn't seem to be standing the cold any better than I was.

"Not far from the summit I had to get off my bike because I started feeling bad. My fingers were rigid, my feet numb, my legs stiff and I was shaking continuously. I began walking and running to get my circulation back, looking at the countryside. It was bleak and the wind made a low moaning noise. I'd have felt scared if I hadn't been used to bad weather in cyclo-crosses.

"Well, I got back on my bike and I got to the top of the col. There's a tunnel at the top and I asked a soigneur how far down I was on the leader. He told me six minutes. I found van Hauwaert at the exit of the tunnel with his bike in his hand and a cloak on his back. He told me he was packing it in. I was beyond feeling happy about it and I just got on with going down through the snow that lay on the road on that side of the mountain.

"The view was totally different now. The snow made the countryside beautiful. The sky was really clear. But now it was my turn to have trouble. It was hard to keep going. In places there were 20 centimeters of snow and sometimes more. Each time I was obliged to get off and push. It was cyclo-cross—off, on, riding, walking. I could keep going but it was slowing me right down. Then I had to stop with stomach cramps. Doubled up, one hand on my bike and the other on my stomach, I collapsed on to a rock on the left side of the road. I was bitter with cold. All I could do was move my head a little from left to right and right to left.

"I saw a little house not far away but I couldn't get there. I didn't realize just what danger I was in. I just had one thought: to get to San Remo first and I attached no importance to the pain I felt…. I thought too of my contract with the bike factory. I'd get double my wages if won as well as primes and there'd be my 300 francs for first place. Happily in my misfortune a man chanced to pass by.

"'Signor, signor…'

"He stopped and spoke to me in Italian, naturally. I nodded towards the house and said *casa* [house] and he understood. He took me by the right arm while I leaned my left on my bike. The house was a tiny inn. The boss undressed me completely and wrapped me in a blanket. I murmured *aqua caldo* [hot water] and pointed at the bottles of rum.

"I did some physical exercises and my life started to come back. I wanted to go on but the boss wouldn't hear of it and pointed at the snow still falling outside. And then first van Hauwaert and then Ernest Paul came in. They were so frozen that they put their hands into the flames. Ernest Paul had lost a shoe without noticing.

"I was there for about 25 minutes. I saw four riders go by, or at least four piles of mud. I decided to press on. Ernest Paul said "You're crazy." And the innkeeper didn't want to let me go. I had to trick him by saying I could meet someone who would get me to San Remo by train. I set off and caught Cocchi and Pavesi and I got to the control just behind Ganna, who was setting off as I stopped. I set off again after Baugé told me I could win and I passed Ganna at the edge of the town. And I caught Albini a few kilometers later.

"At the control at Savona [90 kilometers] everybody was astonished to see me alone. The crowd didn't recognize me. I didn't stop long and took Trousellier's spare bike, because I knew he and Garrigou had abandoned before Ovada. I was sure of my victory and with only 100 kilometers to go I felt a new strength. The idea of crossing the line alone brought back all my energy. I got to San Remo well behind the scheduled time. It was 6pm when I stopped underneath the blowing banner that showed the end of my Calvary."

He sank into the arms of helpers. It had taken him almost twelve and a half hours—more than half the day. He won by an hour, greater than any winner since. Behind him, 60 others were scattered along the course, taking shelter where they could. Many hadn't attempted the mountain. Some, reasonably, had turned back. But help was hard to come by. Cars were rare and in their infancy. They had trouble not just plowing through snow but in driving up long climbs. They had to start with full tanks; if they didn't, the slope made the fuel well into one end of the tank and nothing reached the engine. Sometimes drivers had to go up mountains backwards, to solve the fuel problem but also because reverse gear was the only one low enough for the gradient.

In any case, there were few cars. These days bike races look like long traffic hold-ups behind a short bunch of cyclists. Then, in Milan–San Remo and every other race, riders were alone and unhelped on the road for hours, especially those who had little chance of winning. And even, as we've just seen, those who had every chance of winning.

Christophe had to spend a month in hospital to recover from frost bite to his hands and the damage the cold had done to his body. Not for another two years did he return to his original health. The records show that only three riders finished but the result never has been formalized because some reports say there'd been a fourth—van Hauwaert—and others say there hadn't been and that he had been disqualified for hanging on to a car. Other reports say it was Luigi Ganna who was disqualified, for getting into a car. Perhaps both were thrown out.

Cyclists do still hang on to cars and they still cheat in other ways. But they're not what they used to be. There was alarm in the 2001 race when mudslides and torrential rain closed the Turchino just as it had Christophe's day. Who knows whether the organizers thought back to 1910? Perhaps they did. Probably they didn't. They could have sent the riders over the mountain but they didn't. Because men like Christophe aren't born any more.

4ª · 3 APRILE 1910

IN QUATTRO AL TRAGUARDO

Un paio di caldi pantaloni di fustagno decise la quarta edizione della «Sanremo»: una corsa divenuta leggendaria negli annali del ciclismo per le condizioni atmosferiche in cui si svolse: pioggia nel tratto iniziale, neve sul Turchino, bufera in Riviera e dovunque freddo intenso. Nella discesa del Turchino i corridori trovarono 20 cm. di neve: e Van Hauwaert, che in vetta era transitato per primo, fu superato dal francese Christophe che era anche un abile «crossista» e quindi si trovava a suo agio su un fondo simile. Ma ben presto anche Christophe fu vinto dal freddo: intirizzito si rifugiò in un casolare. Poco dopo passarono di lì Van Hauwaert e Paul che, vista una bicicletta appoggiata alla soglia, si fermarono ed entrarono. E non ne vollero più sapere di riprendere la corsa. Christophe invece, rifocillatosi, si fece dare' della biancheria asciutta e un vecchio paio di pantaloni di fustagno che adattò con qualche sapiente colpo di forbice. Ripresa la corsa, egli non tardò a raggiungere Ganna e Albini. Solo quattro corridori arrivarono alla meta: anche le strade del percorso erano deserte e Christophe più di una volta temette di aver sbagliato strada.

1. EUGENIO CHRISTOPHE, km. 289,3 in 12.24', media km. 23,330; 2. Cocchi a 1.01'; 3. Marchese a 1.17'; 4. Sala E. a 2.06'. - Partiti 63, arrivati 4.

A contemporary Italian news report of the Milan–San Remo race of 1910

9

Sensation on the Boards

There are many records in cycling but the most prestigious is The Hour. It merits the capital letters. It's been held by stars and by those who've been forgotten. But some will be forever remembered.

Milan, Italy, 1942: Fausto Coppi was a perpetually depressed-looking man who led a sad and troubled life lifted from its gloom by a cycling stardom of a passion that's never been seen since. To give you an example: when Coppi moved in with his girlfriend and not his wife, the Pope refused to bless the Tour of Italy while he remained within it. The man charged with a global congregation larger than any nation on earth, who at the very least stayed silent on the slaughter of millions of God's creatures in concentration camps, concerned himself with a man who rode a bike for money…and then ex-communicated him *ad vitam aeternam* (for the rest of time) for abandoning his wife. A court had set the tone by giving him a suspended three-year prison sentence for the same thing.

When he died on the second day of 1960, of malaria caught on a hunting trip to Burkina Faso, his obituary filled two pages in *L'Équipe* and went on seemingly without end in *La Gazetta dello Sport*. The wreaths left outside the church where his funeral was conducted—the Catholic church had presumably come to terms with its fallen angel—stretched for 300 meters. Cycling's aristocracy was there—Louison Bobet, Jacques Anquetil, Gino Bartali and Roger Rivière—and a director of *La Gazetta* wrote: "I pray that the good God will one day soon send us another Coppi."

The God, that is, from whom Coppi had been ex-communicated for life.

Such was the man's brilliance, his standing in society…and his sadness. By the end he was a parody of himself, a man who had gone on too long, for whom races were shortened so he wouldn't have the indignity of being left behind. Jacques Goddet wrote in *L'Équipe*: "We would like to have cried out to him: 'Stop!' And as nobody dared to, destiny took care of it.'"

This was a different man, so very different, from what the world had known. Coppi once won the Tour by almost half an hour: 28 minutes 22 seconds, to be precise, in 1952. Pierre Chany, who died just before following his fiftieth Tour de France, said that never, between 1946 and 1954, was Coppi caught once he had broken clear of the field. And Raphaël Géminiani, who raced with Coppi, said: "When Fausto won and you wanted to check the time gap to the man in second place, you didn't need a Swiss stopwatch. The bell of the church clock tower would do the job just as well We're talking ten minutes to a quarter of an hour."

The problem was that he so often broke a bone when he fell. In those days, riders rode everything. In 1942 Coppi was national road champion and also riding, eight days later, the national pursuit. He was warming up for the final when he touched a wheel, fell to his right and broke a collar bone. The judges proposed that the other finalist, Cino Cinelli, should become the champion. But Cinelli, who later made a career of making components such as handlebars, sportingly asked for the match to be deferred until Coppi had recovered—a decision he may have seen with wry amusement because two months later Coppi not only beat but caught him with 340 meters still to ride. He had averaged 48.3 kilometers per hour.

Coppi the all-rounder then looked at the world hour record. There was a big difference in distance, of course, but the chubby but gifted French all-rounder, Maurice Archambaud, had ridden at 45.8 kilometers per hour, considerably slower than Coppi's pursuit. And that had been in November 1937. What's more, the idea had been put in his mind by a rider he saw lapping the Vigorelli when he called in one afternoon.

The man's name was Rino Benedetti, more a road than a track rider. He won stages in the Tours of France, Italy and Spain. He and Coppi knew each other well and Coppi waited for him to finish, strolled across to ask how he was and asked what he was doing. Benedetti said he had been riding 100 kilometers on the track to avoid being on the road when there was a risk of air raids. And he joked that, with all that track riding, he could have a go at the hour record.

When Coppi first looked quizzical and then laughed, Benedetti said: "Well, I could never do it—but you could." Coppi said neither yes nor no. He thought about it, though, and then spoke about it to his team manager, Eberardo Pavesi, and to his blind masseur, Bruno Cavanna, who ran a school for racing cyclists in the suburbs of Genoa.

The attraction to Coppi wasn't simply the record; it would establish him as undeniably better than his older rival, Gino Bartali, with whom he'd had to contest the leadership of the Italian team in the Tour de France. Both Pavesi and Cavanna could see the point. There'd be embarrassment if he failed, certainly, but everyone knew the hour record had a toughness that others didn't have.

Coppi trained on a fixed-wheel bike with a single brake on the flat, straight roads near his home in Novi Ligure. And, when he was ready, he drove to Milan, to just northwest of the city center, to the Vigorelli track. It had been built in 1935 and named after the bike company that paid for it. Its smooth wooden boards and perfect banking gave it the nickname of Magic Vigorelli. It had been home to the world hour record from the year it was built, when a Frenchman with the hairdresser's name of Maurice Richard rode 45.32 kilometers. Nine world hour records have been broken there.

Coppi slept badly in his hotel that night and went to the track in a gloomy mood. He hadn't prepared as he would normally have because he was in the army, in an infantry regiment at Tortona that would soon send him to Tunisia and, with little resistance on Coppi's part, his capture by the British.

While the British never knew whom they'd they put in a prison camp, the Italian army was well aware of Soldier Coppi and spared him a lot of soldiering duties to let him go out on his bike. Nevertheless, Coppi knew no more about the hour record than anyone else and nothing about how to train for it. Training knowledge then was limited to riding long distances repeatedly. He'd booked the track for two weeks of training but he still wasn't convinced. Little had gone well, but his plans had brought such publicity that he was in a weak position for pulling out.

The omens weren't good. The city had been bombed the previous night and the roof of the velodrome had holes. Cavanna tried to talk him out of his despondency, giving him a pep talk, reminding him of the prize he'd get for beating the record, the bonus he'd receive from his sponsor, telling him he could feel magic in his legs.

The story, especially the magic bit, is typical of the era. Cavanna's blindness was said to gave him an unusual understanding of what he felt through his hands. Sports reporting in those days idolized the sport and its heroes, rarely queried their shortcomings and even less frequently reported on them. Television didn't exist and fans relied on what they read in the papers. And reporters, knowing that what they wrote governed how long they kept their job, gave readers the glamor and mystery they craved.

The likely truth is that Cavanna, like most soigneurs and witch-doctors who have passed through the sport, was a glib and persuasive man, well meaning, with a lot of experience, a little knowledge and a convincing patter in a sport still short of medical science.

Coppi had a bike lighter than Archambaud's. He rode a gear, 52 x 15, which gave him six centimeters more than Archambaud with each turn of the pedals. But he was still unconvinced when he pulled on a dark green jersey and set off for his first lap at two minutes after noon.

He started too fast, paid for his effort and rode 22.946 kilometers in the first 30 minutes against the 23.007 of the record. He got back to even with Archambaud but suffered in the process. The last 30 laps were chaotic. He went fast, he slowed down, he looked smooth, he looked ragged. On one lap he could gain several meters and then on the next lose them. "After 115 laps of the track he was getting round as best he could," Jean-Paul Ollivier wrote in his biography, "no longer concerned about style, rhythm or elegance—he was suffering too much."

Finally he finished the hour 31 meters better than the Frenchman—45.871 kilometers—and the record had fallen for the first time since the world went to war. Such was his ride, and the aura that surrounded Coppi, that the record stood for fourteen years until Jacques Anquetil bettered it.

Nobody after the war held the record longer than Coppi. Only the Swiss, Oscar Egg, ever held it longer—from 1914 to 1933—but that included world war one and the destruction and disillusion with which Europe had to deal for a decade afterward.

But his ride was surrounded by doubts. Maurice Archambaud, with his "air of an old British lord", as the Tour de France archivist Jacques Augendre called him because of his quiet, introverted personality, wasn't impressed. To him, Coppi hadn't ridden the distance. He brandished photos that showed sand bags hadn't been placed on the track to make sure Coppi stayed above the blue line that marked the track's measured distance and therefore ensured Coppi hadn't ridden a shorter lap. Suddenly Archambaud was anything but a quiet British lord.

In Paris, Pierre Chany and many others had their doubts. "I can tell you," he said, "that even three years later there were still doubts about the authenticity of his hour record. Was it a political lie? A propaganda coup by the fascists? We just didn't know. All we had was a photo of the record ride, the one that you still see in all the books about cycling. And add to that that Fausto had ridden so erratically. He rode some laps at the speed of a sprinter and on others he came close to dawdling. So when the Liberation came, there were major doubts."

Archambaud complained to the UVF, the French federation, an act he must have soon regretted. Because its director, the former Legionnaire, Colonel Beaupuis, who had been head referee of the Tour de France before the war, set about the problem and decided that not only must Coppi have ridden *further* than the distance credited but that Archambaud had ridden *less*. And he illustrated his theory on a blackboard as he spoke to delegates at the international cycling body's conference in Palestine in 1947 to scrap all hour records as unreliable and start anew.

Coppi, who was riding on the track in Brussels when reporters told him the news, replied drily: "You can see that Monsieur Beaupuis has never ridden a bike." In fact, what Beaupuis was proposing was more conformity and more accuracy in records. Failing which, the UCI should scrap the lot and start again. It declined to do that but it did raise Coppi's record to what the record books show now: 45.798. And it insisted on sand bags or other obstacles along the blue marker line of the track to make sure riders from then on completed the full distance.

But still the doubt didn't go. Chany added his own: "Objectively, there *is* a doubt. I believe I was one of the journalists who looked into the affair. Astolfi and Carapezzi, the few eye-witnesses I could meet, confirmed, both of them, that the last seconds were called out by a man on the loudspeakers who was in no hurry to get to zero. So, he went like this: 'Five [Chany hesitated more than a second]...four [same hesitation]...three [same thing]...two [another delay]...one [more delay]...stop!'

"When they did the calculations afterward, the judges said Fausto had beaten the record by 31 meters. In reality, he may have beaten it by only three or four meters. And maybe he hadn't beaten it at all. But, it doesn't matter. It doesn't matter if he beat the record that day or not because he beat it [figuratively] a hundred times afterward. He was an athlete who had the record in his legs. He was higher than everyone. With good preparation, he could have taken the record even higher. That's what counts."

It's hard to see that Chany's comments about counting down the time would have fooled even the crowd, unless there was no large clock ticking for them to see. Coppi himself was misled by the clanging of a local church bell to announce the hour, but that was psychological and, anyway, the clock always chimed early. The actual timing, of course, was in the hands of a specialist: the tubby but dapper Ferruccio Massara. He used a silver Ulysse Nardin stopwatch, made in 1915, and until his death kept it carefully in its original box.

The watch was one of several auctioned by Sotheby's in Switzerland in May 2011. The auctioneers had expected between 15,000 and 28,000 euros. But either it wasn't in itself remarkable or the world had forgotten its significance. It didn't sell.

Many have beaten that record since but no one has done it as remarkably as Coppi. Eddy Merckx was better publicized, because the world by then was a media village in the way it wasn't in Coppi's day. But he won his record in the thin air of Mexico, after long preparation and with excellent support. And, as one sports scientist observed: "In spite of much better bikes, better tracks and the use of altitude training, the record set in 1972 by Eddy Merckx was only 3.5 kilometers better than that of Fausto Coppi 30 years before."

10
Kidnap

Cyclists who rouse crowds on the road can often walk unnoticed on streets. But sometimes their prominence, their fame, can lead to dangerous consequences.

Fusagasagá, Colombia, January 2000: Not all cyclists have happy lives. The Tour's first star climber, René Pottier, hanged himself in 1907. Ottavio Bottechia, the Tour winner in 1924 and 1925, was murdered in a vineyard, a crime that was never solved. Henri Pélissier, who dominated French cycling and won the Tour in 1923, was murdered by his lover. Hugo Koblet, an elegant Swiss, died in 1964 in a car crash widely considered to be suicide. Jose Diaz, a retired Spanish professional, was murdered in 1995. Shay Elliott, Ireland's first *maillot jaune*, shot himself in 1971. Thierry Claveyrolat, winner of the Tour's mountains competition in 1990, shot himself nine years later after a car crash that left a family of four badly injured.

Few, though, have been kidnapped by Marxist-Leninist guerillas.

Luis "Lucho" Herrera was an accidental consequence of a war between one of the Tour's organizers, Félix Lévitan, and the riders and officials who took part in his race. Lévitan was a dictatorial man who felt teams and their sponsors were getting too demanding, undermining his authority and not treating his race with sufficient respect. The Tour had run into ever more troubled times in the late 1970s, to the point that teams had to be begged to ride. Lévitan lacked a broad commercial vision and scraped about for small sponsors whose advertising along the route reached such an ugliness that serious commentators called for the race to be nationalized to protect it from itself.

~

Lévitan looked everywhere for money or the potential of money, which was why he insisted Jonathon Boyer wear a stars-and-stripes jersey rather than his sponsor's. And then at the start of the 1980s he realized that amateurs would be a lot less trouble and would doubtless complain less—especially those from communist countries who, he thought, would jump at a chance to ride with professionals—and even perhaps bring in lots of money. And there'd be no sponsors to irritate him.

He asked all around eastern Europe and elsewhere for teams to join his race. Most said no straight away and some hesitated and then said no. After all that, only one amateur nation wanted to come. But Lévitan wasn't disappointed because he knew that Colombians saw cycling as second only to soccer and that it was richly financed. Fausto Coppi and Hugo Koblet had raced in the mountains there and were humbled by the locals, who realized for the first time how good they were. There was money and there was talent and that suited him fine and so Colombian amateurs rode the Tour in 1983.

Colombia was still a long way from Europe in the 1980s and a country which many Europeans confused with a record label spelled only slightly differently. The idea that the passion for cycling there could be so great that 35 journalists would come to France to report on a bunch of amateurs was astounding. Many of them worked for television and radio stations. "The racket they made was deafening," the British broadcaster David Duffield said. "In those days, broadcasting cubicles were flimsy wood and canvas and all you could hear was these frantic Spanish voices. And they all chain-smoked and the area was deep in cigarette ends."

The Colombians found plenty to enthuse them. Some of their team were ordinary but some had real talent, especially when the road reared upwards. The best of them was the sad-looking and occasionally impenetrable Herrera. Another British writer, Chris Sidwells, said of Herrera: "His wiry legs simply stroked the pedals round with a rhythm all of his own." Raphaël Géminiani's assessment: "Lucho Herrera was one of the greatest climbers of his generation, a pure, light, true flier. We never saw the best of him in Europe. A Tour of Spain, two Dauphiné Libérés, that's nothing for a man with such talents as a climber."

Herrera rode the Tour every year from 1984 to 1991, never won it but won the mountains competition in 1985 and 1991. And that

Les Woodland

despite a conspiracy by the professionals, who resented having their market undercut and who would simply sit up and freewheel if an amateur ever got into a break with them.

Herrera was an exception they could admire even if they wished he wasn't there. But his heart was never in Europe. Cycling there was just a job for him and he was disillusioned when, with the onset of EPO doping, he was challenged in the mountains by riders he'd never seen alongside him before.

"When I started seeing riders with fat asses climbing like airplanes, I understood," he said colorfully but accurately.

The man who worked in the fields as a boy and was said once to have had a pet rat on a string, went back to Colombia with, it's said, $5 million profit at 1990 values. There he rejoined his wife, Judith, a former model, and made himself still richer by going into the cattle business with his brother, Rafael. His country was, by contrast, going through difficult times and he was a tempting target, not just for his money but because of his prominence as director of 25 national cycling schools.

Colombia had then and still has now a communist peasant guerilla army referred to as FARC, after the Spanish for Revolutionary Armed Forces of Colombia. It was tied up with the noticeably non-communist world of drug dealing, which founded its activities. The Colombian government estimated its strength at 13,800, of whom half were active.

Herrera knew the risk of kidnap because guerillas had already taken another cyclist, Oliverio Rincon. That was why in late January 2000 Herrera made the 90-minute journey to Bogotá, the capital: to join a protest against kidnapping. With him was the Frenchman, José Beyaert, a bespectacled hairdresser who won the Olympic road race in London in 1948. His fame and a longing for travel took him to Colombia in 1951, to open a velodrome. Instead of staying a month as planned, he stayed for the rest of his life. And a colorful life, too, because the words businessman, emerald trader, logger, smuggler, father of a child with a secret lover and "perhaps even hired killer" turn up in his biography.

Their presence didn't go unremarked. And soon seven masked men kidnapped him on his mother's doorstep. They drove away in two cars, Herrera jammed between two heavies on a back seat. Other kidnappings of prominent Colombians followed.

The cars stopped in the hills, far from anywhere, and Herrera was marched through dense vegetation up the side of a mountain. They walked, some reports say, for two hours, sometimes struggling to keep their footing. Nobody spoke beyond orders and muttered conversations. Legend says that only when they locked Herrera in a windowless room did they realize who he was: their boss, Bernardo Mosquera, had given them only an address and a description.

Herrera was always taciturn and rarely talked cycling even in his racing days. He didn't object but he soon deflected the conversation. There in his cell, though, he found his kidnappers knew all about what he'd done, that they'd followed his career thanks to those 35 noisy reporters. But instead of feeling flattered, Herrera was sure he was being softened up for worse to come. He was wrong.

What actually happened was that the public outcry convinced the FARC leadership it had blundered. Even terrorists need public support. And they need recruits. And FARC's strength was among peasants, the very people most captivated by sporting heroes. Word reached the mountain prison that Herrera was to be freed. And he was, except that the kidnappers wanted to turn him out at night, to make his own way back the way he'd come. Apart from the obvious risk, he had no wish to be mistaken on the way down by Colombian soldiers on the way up, who could well take him in the darkness for one of the terrorists. He stayed another night, trying but failing to sleep.

Next morning he stumbled back down the trail and walked into Tocaima, where he found a phone box and called Rafael, his brother, and asked for a ride home.

The kidnapping régime continued, however. Snatching television personalities brought less troublesome attention and probably greater gains. FARC freed Oliviero Rincon, too, although he had the indignity of being snatched all over again and once more allowed to go. But few prominent cyclists felt at ease. Among them was the shady Beyaert. He told Matt Rendell, his biographer, that cars began stopping outside his family house. "My neighbors alerted me," he said. "There was a car here and a car over there. It might not have been guerillas. It could have been common criminals. But someone was looking for me."

To be honest, Beyaert was hardly a big enough name in cycling for that alone to be a motive for kidnapping. He had won the Tour of

Colombia but that had been long ago and, a foreigner, he wouldn't have been remembered for long. And he reported bike races on television, but that scarcely made him a star attraction. If half the descriptions in Rendell's account are true then there's every reason the cars, if cars there were, were driven by fellow crooks anxious for revenge.

Whoever it was, Beyaert told his son to do nothing. If he was kidnapped, he said, the boy was just to let his father stay where he was. Intervening would only make things worse.

I wrote "if cars there were" because at that point Beyaert had only his neighbors' observations to go on. But Beyaert began seeing for himself what was happening. With the bravado of the brave or the foolish, he strolled out of the house and smoked a cigarette "to show them that I was still there." And then he walked back through the house, out into the back garden with clothing in a plastic bag—"a suitcase would have been too obvious"—and climbed over a fence and called Air France for a flight out of the country, using a false name.

Four months had passed since Herrera was kidnapped and freed. Beyaert, under his assumed name, made it back to Paris, where he had once lived. He died in La Rochelle, on the Atlantic coast, in June 2005.

Herrera is still well, as taciturn as ever, keeping himself to himself. He owns land, his ranch and cattle, and has two hotels, one called The Alps. He still has few friends and would rather sit alone and watch films than have a conversation.

The Tour de France will never forget him, though. A volcano killed 25,000 people in the Colombian town of Armero one night in November 1985. France sent humanitarian aid. Herrera didn't forget. The following year he arrived at the Tour de France with two lumps of the volcano's brown lava in his suitcase. If you climb the Alpe d'Huez one day, the climb he turned into "a thing of beauty" in Chris Sidwell's words, halt at by the bridge on the last but one hairpin, close to a chapel. There, beneath the bridge, is where the two brown lumps now lie in gratitude for France's help, along with a commemorative plaque.

11

Badger in a Blizzard

Nobody remembers rides in the sunshine when birds sang and lambs gamboled. Legend, personal and international, are made when nature turns against you.

Liège, Belgium, 1980: Legend says that Bernard Hinault was nicknamed Badger because he had that same stubborn, insistent character. Or because he had gray flecks in his hair. The truth, however, is simpler: "I used to ride in a group where one of the lads called everyone 'Badger'. 'How are you then, Badger?', that sort of thing. And for some reason, for me, it stuck."

Hinault needed every ounce of that badger quality on the roads of eastern Belgium in 1980. He needed the claws, the teeth and the fighting quality of a badger cornered. And he showed them, winning Liège–Bastogne–Liège by ten minutes. But there's far more to the story than that, because the Liège–Bastogne–Liège of 1980 was the Liège of Misery. Hinault rode alone, soaked and frozen, listening to rivals and teammates cheering from the warmth of their hotels. Cyclists enjoy misery, especially other people's and perhaps Hinault's more than most. A cyclist rarely understands what's shouted at him and so you can shout what you like from a distance. And they did.

Liège–Bastogne–Liège is the oldest of the classics. It started as a club race in 1894, when it ran from and returned to Spa. And why did it turn round at Bastogne and not somewhere better known? Because there was a train there from Liège and officials could get to Bastogne ahead of the riders and take their numbers before taking another train back to Liège for the finish.

For years it was all that Belgium had. The sport had all but vanished. There were only 125 licensed riders in the whole country. Tracks had shut and their bankings had cracked. This country we see now as the heartland of northern European cycling had no national road championships in 1902, 1903 and 1904 and none on the track in 1901, 1902, 1903, 1905 or 1906.

The Doyenne—so called because it's the oldest classic—restored Belgium's pride. Merely by existing and, incidentally, by being in the French-speaking south. There is a great and sometimes bitter rivalry between the south and the Dutch-speaking north. The newspaper editor, Karel van Wijnendaele, believed poor and oppressed Flanders deserved a race of the same status. Which led to the birth of the Tour of Flanders—the Ronde van Vlaanderen in Dutch—and the renaissance of Belgian cycling. By that cold day in 1980, Flanders and Liège–Bastogne–Liège were the cornerstones of the sport, Flanders more important to northerners than the world championship and Liège more important to the south for being more accessible to riders from elsewhere on the continent.

"In purely physical terms, this is probably the toughest classic," is *Cycling*'s assessment. "The climbs are long, most of them are pretty steep as well, and they come up with depressing frequency in the final kilometers." Just the sort of race in that first year of the 1980s to satisfy Bernard Hinault, already twice winner of the Tour de France and already first back to Liège in 1977.

A polar wind whipped the riders from the start. Snow began the moment the race climbed out of Liège's valley. "It was a hell of a day," Lucien van Impe remembers. "I rode ten kilometers and just got off." The first flakes turned into a storm and riders struggled on, holding their hands to their face just to keep a view of the road. The bunch was a mass of anonymous plastic jackets and windcheaters. Spectators wore goggles as they stood by the roadside like animated snowmen, red-faced in the cold. There weren't many of them. Nor after a while were there many riders. After an hour, some teams had barely a man left on the road. Riders pulled out more than a dozen at a time, shivering by the road and waiting miserably for a car to collect them. Men like Gibi Baronchelli and Beppe Saronni and Jean-René Bernardeau. And Lucien van Impe.

Les Woodland

A young Frank Vandenbroucke was among thousands excited but chilled by what they saw. He wrote: "From the pinched faces and the knocking knees you could see that it was inhumanly cold. It was cycling from the epic days. Some riders sat in a wood round a log fire, or went swearing and screaming to look for their team cars, or barged into ordinary houses or gas stations to get the cold out of their bodies. They passed round a bottle of cognac and shook their heads as they realized there were still riders on the road to Bastogne and back."

Hinault fell back to his team car. He passed Maurice Le Guilloux, a long-faced, dark-haired rider who was his only team-mate left riding, and told him he was quitting. Le Guilloux squinted through the blizzard and shouted: "Carry on to Bastogne. There's a feeding station there. Pack it in then if you want to but don't do it now." Hinault nodded and both men dropped back through the dwindling bunch to find their manager, Cyrille Guimard, and some dry gloves. Another dozen riders called it a day, dropping out at a man a minute for the first hour. Worried messages passed between the organizers.

"At this rate we won't have a race at all," someone said on the radio. There was a pause and the muffled sound of a discussion with a commissaire. And then: "Attention team managers: the commissaires have agreed that warm drinks can be passed to riders at any stage of the race." And Hinault attacked. To win the race, of course, but also to keep warm, to survive. "I was so cold," he said, "that I needed to ride hard. I did 100 kilometers on my own."

Those with long memories recalled the same race in 1957. At every bar the race passed, yet another rider disappeared to press himself into the crowd of drinkers for warmth. This was the Liège–Bastogne–Liège when the giant Frenchman, Gérard Saint, stopped in the snow to pee on his hands to bring them back to life.

Germain Derycke reached the finish alone that year, skin raw in the coldness. And then, as if there hadn't been misery enough for a man known as a sunshine *coureur*, the judges disqualified him for having jumped over a closed railway crossing. They gave the victory instead to the runner-up, Frans Schoubben, although the Belgian federation felt sorry for both and made them joint winners. The world champion, Louison Bobet, finished way down the field. When he got to his hotel and found his team washed, warm and dry, his team manager ordered: "Gentlemen, rise! A great champion is entering the room."

The snow had turned to rain by the time Hinault reached Bastogne in 1980. Only 21 began the journey back to Liège. The last, Jostein Wilmann, was 27 minutes down.

"Cyrille Guimard told me to remove my racing cape because the real race was about to start," Hinault said later. "My cape was made of waxed fabric and I was very warm inside it, but I took it off as instructed. Until then I hadn't really paid any attention to the race, but now my teeth were chattering and I had no protection. I decided the only thing to do was ride as hard as I could to keep myself warm."

He looked miserable in photos, let alone real life. The road is lightly coated with snow except where car tires have pushed through. His yellow, black and white Renault jersey had long sleeves but he wore just shorts that stretched, in the style of the time, only halfway down his thighs. He has a cotton racing cap beneath his leather helmet, which in those days only Belgium demanded. And covers for his shoes and ankles. Many have worn as much in the sun of spring.

Rudy Pévenage and Ludo Peeters had broken away before the Côte de Wanna, the shallowest of the principle climbs. Hinault was on a fresh bike, having changed at the feed at Wielsam, and he went off up the slope. He gained on the leaders, reached them on the Haute-Levée, and dropped them. He never looked round. "The rhythm had returned and I was feeling good," he said. "I didn't even need to turn round to know that my pursuers had vanished."

He rode into the boulevard de la Sauvinière in Liège to the cheers of his team and a pitiful crowd. Most who'd thought of turning out had stayed home to watch on television. Hinault had no feeling in his arms and it took three weeks to move the index and middle fingers of his right hand. They ache in cold weather even now. A bath waited at the hotel but he couldn't get in until the water was almost cold; the contrast was too great.

"Did Eddy Merckx congratulate you?", someone wanted to know decades later. "I don't remember that he did," Hinault replied with a straight face. "He didn't take to being beaten like that."

Hinault eventually parted with Cyrille Guimard. Martine Hinault said of her husband—they met at a wedding when she was eighteen—

that he wasn't a man to make concessions. "We never spoke about cycling at home so I don't know all the details. But I know they didn't see eye to eye about the races he was going to ride. Bernard thought that Renault would rather keep the rider than the manager, but in the end they decided the opposite. Bernard was a bit surprised..."

Hinault retired from cycling in November 1986, his thirty-second birthday, just as he had predicted years earlier at the world championship in Colorado Springs. He always said, too, that he'd never go into team management and he didn't.

"Nobody would ever have wanted to be in a team that I ran," he said. "I'd never have accepted it if a rider said 'I'm worth such-and-such and that's what I want to be paid.' I'd have replied: 'You'll be worth that when you show me you're worth it. I'll pay you what I think you're worth and the rest you'll have to earn.'"

He worked 100 days a year for the Tour de France behind the scenes, but also appearing on the podium each afternoon as host to local celebrities. Many think he would have been a good Tour organizer. But no. "Living in Paris, that's not for me," he said. "I'm much happier living in the countryside. And you have to *want* to do something like that. And at 50 I just don't feel it."

Hinault retired from cycling to look after his cattle. He and Martine bought the farm in 1983, when his retirement loomed. It was the year he had to skip the Tour because of a painful knee that took him to hospital for an operation. They moved to the farm definitively in 1986. It had 30 cows, one farm worker and an output of 90,000 liters of milk—the most that European quotas allowed. It never made a profit but they'd promised to keep their employee in his job and so they persevered until he retired and in 2006 they sold up.

Martine was elected mayor of the granite-walled commune of Calorguen in 2008. She succeeded another Hinault, cousin Michel. There are eleven Hinaults in the local phone book. Martine stood by the roadside—without her blue, white and red sash—to see the Tour pass through the village for the third time in its history. The Tour that her husband won five times.

He was never as widely seen or as respected at home as he was elsewhere. "People here couldn't care about him," a barman told a biographer. "Just like he couldn't care less about the people in the village.

The only time we see him is when his wife has her mayoral *voeux* [in France, politicians of all levels receive electors, journalists and others to present their wishes for the new year]."

His bust is in the town hall at Yffiniac, where he was born. And he has a street named after him not in Brittany, where he still lives, but in Blaye-les-Mines, in the Tarn area. It was named not when the Tour de France passed but on the passage of the Tour de l'Avenir, a race intended to find Tour winners of the future. France has still to find one.

12

Stop! We're On Strike!

Cyclists put up with a lot, from saddle boils to insulting fans. But they don't expect to be assaulted by their own side. And sometimes things go just too far.

Valence d'Agen, France, July 12, 1978: There had never been a strike in the Tour de France. Several disputes before the war, yes, but nothing which had brought the riders to a halt. And then, in a small town about halfway between Bordeaux and Toulouse, it happened. The riders rounded the bend into the 480 meters of the avenue Victor Guilhem and there they got off. They walked as far as the finish line, which was about where the entrance to the town's central supermarket is now, and they stopped.

It had been a while since the Tour had been to Valence d'Agen. It was on the route of the very first Tour, back in 1903, but it had been largely forgotten ever since. For this town of maybe 4,000 people, therefore, having the riders finish there was a big event for which they had paid dearly. The mayor was a man named Jean-Michel Baylet, then just thirty-one and now a national politician who still lives on the edge of town beside where the 1903 Tour passed.

Baylet had been the town's mayor for only three years, succeeding his father. Bringing the Tour to Valence was not only the town's moment of glory and publicity but a mark that the son and not the father was now in charge. As the Tour approached his town, he walked the main street, wearing a tie and a light-colored suit, doing what all mayors do—shaking hands, showing himself off as the man who'd brought the people their day of pride, and secretly hoping that nothing would go wrong and that they'd vote for him again.

But it did all go wrong. Some time through the hilly *département* of the Gers which lies on the other side of the Garonne valley from Valence, the riders began riding no faster than your everyday Sunday fat-boy. Puzzled farm workers and villagers who'd stood by the road or in bars, waiting to see their heroes, got a better if later view than they'd expected. Because the riders passed so slowly, chatting as they went.

The Tour in those days was still Félix Lévitan's personal quest for other people's money. It had long been accepted that a town would pay to have the Tour finish there and another would pay for the start next morning. What was only recently established was that two stages each day would double the money the Tour could get, and to heck with inconvenience to the riders.

The Tour the previous day had finished on the Pla d'Adet, a mountain in the Pyrenees. Mario Martinez had won after five o'clock in the afternoon and the hapless foot soldiers trudging miserably off the back of the main race got in an hour later. The riders went down to the bottom by ski lift, which was both cold and time-consuming. Buses waited for them but, by the time they got there, so had many of the thousands of spectators who'd also been up on the mountain.

The riders' buses had no priority in the traffic on the narrow roads and so they made no faster progress than anyone else. The outcome was that exhausted riders reached their accommodation so late that, after a shower, a meal and, for the lucky ones, a massage, they got to bed at midnight. Only to have to get up again at 5 for a new stage at 7:30. That was how the Tour squeezed in two races a day: by calling riders out of their beds before dawn.

And life on the Tour wasn't as it is now. Maurice Le Guilloux, who rode beside Bernard Hinault for as long as he could in that snowy Liège–Bastogne–Liège, said: "In those days we used to sleep in sports halls. Or we used to be three to a room in a hotel. If we were in a hall, there could be 50 of us in the same dormitory with one shower and toilet.

"That day we'd ridden five cols in the Pyrenees, in the sun, and there were two toilets for 50 of us, masseurs trying to prepare food and massaging riders in the corridors. When we got there, the water was cold."

The riders, predictably, slept badly. And they weren't any happier next morning. Lucien van Impe remembered: "We all started off just by talking, complaining among ourselves. At first it was just grumbling, others joining in but doing nothing." Bernard Hinault, wearing the blue, white and red of French champion and fresh from winning the Vuelta, held his tongue. Jean-Pierre Danguillaume said: "It was us, the older riders. He didn't say much at the start but, as the pressure rose, he took his stance. He got into the front line and he never conceded.

"We rode at 25 kilometers per hour. We felt exploited. We had to ride from Tarbes to Toulouse in two stages, 275 kilometers. We weren't fools. We could see it was a way for the organizers to pay their bills. And it was barely dawn when we got to the start in the square at Tarbes."

"They're riding like simple cycle-tourists looking for a coffee somewhere," said Jean-Paul Ollivier, *le sage Pollo*, commentator for France 2 that day.

"Everyone was tired and it was easy to get the whole peloton on strike," Danguillaume remembered. "We rode at walking speed. Some of the riders were riding through the fields and others were stopping to buy drinks."

The strike was on. The riders agreed. Or most. A Spaniard spotted what was happening and thought he'd profit from it. He could have escaped and ruined everything, because only Guy Sibille saw what was about to happen.

"The Spaniard was off quickly because he wanted to escape," Hinault recalled years afterward. "Only Sibille saw it coming. And bang! Next thing he was lying in the road. But it had to stop—the organizers had us riding three stages in a day. We'd been through all that for just a half stage of 80 kilometers."

Hinault's manager, Cyrille Guimard, was another who wasn't happy. Whatever the justification for the strike, he didn't want Hinault taking a prominent part. And Lévitan and his colleague, Jacques Goddet, didn't agree; they were being ridiculed, humbled and perhaps they worried Valence d'Agen would demand its money back. And at the very least the race was going to be late into Toulouse—assuming the riders would even agree to ride in the afternoon.

Goddet drove up and down the race, talking to team leaders, offering deals. "I just don't understand," he insisted. "You knew the route and the timetable of the Tour last November. That was the time to state your feelings, not now." He said he would hang on to the prizes if there was no racing, then realized his mistake. If there were to be no prizes, why get going again? "OK," he told André Chalmel, who'd become the riders' spokesman, "start racing again and there'll be prizes as usual." But prizes no longer mattered.

Ordinary folk who'd taken time off work to see their heroes pass, and often not knowing what had happened, shouted insults and even spat as the race trundled by. "They went through Fleurance at a *train de sénateur*," Ollivier said on television to pictures of perplexed, gray-haired villagers in blue overalls. Like a majestic procession. "Baffled spectators who'd come to see the excitement of the Tour wondered where the sport was in all that."

The race crossed the Garonne River and reached the middle of Valence, took the corner into the finishing straight, and then got off. Baylet, the mayor, had already been waiting for an hour more than he'd expected. With wind of what was about to happen, he was there when the brakes went on and steel-plated cycling shoes began clacking on the road. He begged riders, implored them, to save his town's day by riding at least the last few hundred meters. But Hinault insisted and the field walked on.

Jean-René Bernardeau, now a team manager, said: "We all panicked a bit, but he said 'Don't budge—I'll walk at the front.'" And that's what happened, Hinault in front with his chin defiantly high, Freddy Maertens beside him in his green jersey, Michel Pollentier in the climbers' polkadot, Gerben Karstens and Hennie Kuiper in the red, yellow and black of Raleigh. And the mayor shrieking at their side. Someone threw a tomato and Hinault went towards him, his fist raised.

Goddet defended his stance and he stuck up for giving the riders a tough time. "The Tour needs excess," he said. "A little suffering is normal." Lévitan strutted like a cockerel and said he wouldn't go back on having more than one stage in a day. But, curiously, it never happened again.

The Tour did set off again that afternoon. Hinault was still angry, now not just with the Tour but with his manager's efforts to boss him about. "So he went off flat out for 30 kilometers," Danguillaume said. "We old guys, we were really happy. We were going to get to Toulouse earlier than we thought! I think that was Hinault's way of getting rid of his anger, rather than thumping the mayor."

Years later, Hinault he said: "There was no other solution. You know what Monsieur Lévitan was like. Authoritarian, let's say. But I'm not saying that I didn't make a mistake. It would have been better to have negotiated in private." The riders had nothing against Baylet's little town, he said. It was a victim of circumstance. Could they make amends by coming back, he asked, as many stars as he could gather, to ride a criterium there for nothing? He was as good as his promise and Valence d'Agen got four hours of racing with Raphaël Géminiani as race director, talking non-stop throughout according to a local enthusiast recruited to drive him.

"The only time I think he stopped was when he got out of the car for a pee. And even then I couldn't be sure he wasn't still rattling on to himself. With Gem you don't talk; you listen."

The Tour has passed through Valence d'Agen since then. But never again has it started or finished there.

13

And Therefore, This Country Is At War

Breaking the rules just to get your own way is something your mother told you never to do. And she was right, because it would lead to anarchy. But sometimes it's needed and sometimes, however long it takes, it turns out to be right.

Wolverhampton, England, June 7, 1942: The words, however expected, chilled everyone. Neville Chamberlain has been vilified as a weak prime minister keener to placate Hitler than fight him. But that is to see history the wrong way round. Millions of British men had died in a war that ended only 25 years earlier, and hobbling men and men with hideously mutilated faces were still struggling with life.

Britain was in no position to fight Hitler even had it wanted. And it didn't want to. It had been through too much too recently. Which explains the cheering crowds and the enthusiasm of newspapers when Chamberlain waved his now notorious piece of paper and announced, although not in those precise words, that there would be peace in our time.

We now know he was wrong. On September 3, 1939, he spoke to the nation on the BBC. Germany had not replied to an ultimatum "and, therefore, this country is at war."

The little island of British cycling been at war far longer, at war with itself. The short story is that racers on one of the roads leading out of London had upset a woman in a horse-and-carriage. Little hurt was done even to the riders who fell off but the woman complained to the police, who said they'd do all they could to prevent anyone racing there again.

The position of cyclists on the road at the end of the nineteenth century was far from sure and the national body, the National Cyclists Union, played safe by confining races to the track. Not everybody lived near a track, though, and a separate organization formed to hold races at dawn and in secret. They didn't call them races and they avoided the police ban by starting riders at minute intervals, the racer with the shortest time to win. Before long, secret time-trials became the dominant sport in Britain and road racing in bunches was something that foreigners got up to but nobody heard about.

Except, that is, for a few enthusiasts who'd been and seen and couldn't fathom why they shouldn't have the same at home. Among them was a short, round-faced cycle dealer from the English Midlands called Percy Stallard.

Stallard wrote to the NCU to say that: "It is amazing to think that this is the only country in Europe where this form of sport is not permitted.... There seems to be the mistaken idea that it would be necessary to close the roads [*on which impossibility the NCU had insisted*]. This, of course, is entirely wrong.... There would be no better time than now to introduce this form of racing to the roads, what with decreased amount of motor traffic and the important part that the cycle is playing in wartime transport."

The last words played to a false patriotism but the empty roads were a fact, because fuel was rationed to the point of unavailability and the British, now in their second year of war, had been told to travel only if their journey was really necessary, as a ubiquitous poster put it.

A.P. Chamberlin—notice the difference in spelling and the enthusiasm of the era for referring to people by their initials—was the head man of the NCU and open-minded for the era. But the forces of tradition behind him were conservative in the extreme. There was no chance the NCU would agree. The NCU had long allowed massed racing where there was no traffic, which in the absence of closed roads meant the perimeter tracks of airfields. But the RAF had taken back those airfields after Neville Chamberlain's declaration of war. Stallard—"the most abrasive man I have ever met," in the words of the editor of *The Bicycle*, Peter Bryan—decided to act alone. He would organize a race from Llangollen in western Wales to his home town of Wolverhampton, near Birmingham. He'd allow 40 riders, if he could find that many willing to risk suspension, and he'd give any profit to a fund for forces' well-being.

Stallard sat at his bike shop and wrote letters to the police through whose area the route would pass. "I just explained to the police what I was doing and told them that things like that were common on the Continent, and they said they were happy and that they'd try to help."

The cycling establishment was horrified. Its time-trials were held in secret, its lists of riders were headed PRIVATE AND CONFIDENTIAL, and courses and dates were referred to in code. Both *The Bicycle* and its larger rival, *Cycling*, went along with never saying where a race had been held, even afterward, and never giving more than coded publicity beforehand. The secrecy was false, of course, because no police force in the world would have missed what was happening. There was tacit agreement and an acceptance that, this not being a race, it needed no permission.

It was the idea of putting cycling under police control that upset the grumpiest of all the old guard, the veteran George Stancer. "The rebels," he wrote, "want to go on holding races by police permit and under police protection; and when this is withdrawn they are apparently content to put up the shutters and go out of business as promoters. If we voluntarily place [racing on the road] under police control, we sign its death warrant.... If we are to race on the road, for heaven's sake let us do it as free citizens, and not by permission of the police."

Stallard was too stubborn to back down. The NCU suspended him even before the race had started and that made him more stubborn than ever. And because all the cycling bodies recognized each other's bans, Stallard had been ex-communicated from the sport. The authorities thought that would do it. But it was their biggest mistake: throw someone out of your club and he has no alternative but to start his own.

The race went ahead with ragtag riders on whatever bikes they could find. One or two were foreign servicemen in Britain. Others, accustomed to riding time-trials on fixed gears and having nothing else, rode on them. Few had any notion of tactics or, in extreme cases, of staying upright. It had never been done before.

Fifteen riders got to the finish in front of a crowd of a thousand. Far from disapproving, Wolverhampton sent its chief constable and fifteen men in uniform to secure safe passage through the town. Two riders—Albert Price and a lean, bespectacled man called Cec Anslow—arrived together and the rest a minute or so later.

The NCU, not yet realizing its error, compounded it by suspending not just Stallard but all the riders and all the officials. Within a week, they were meeting to organize still more races, no longer answerable to officialdom and by the end of the year they had created their own governing body, the British League of Racing Cyclists.

It was full of rebels, discontents, visionaries, international socialists and a heavy number of those who warmed to the sound of breaking glass. Peter Bryan, who'd reported on the race, remembered: "There were a lot more misfits than there were fitters." The BLRC was so cantankerous that in 1943 it temporarily expelled its founder for suggesting that some of its race organizers weren't as good as they might be. Given that none of them had organized races before, that was quite probably true. But the BLRC was so edgy and Stallard so prickly that a collision was inevitable.

Jimmy Kain, a leading light, wrote in retirement of "the two years of nervous and physical breakdown that followed six years of BLRC office."

The NCU old guard went the way of all old guards: they simply faded away. But a civil war of breathtaking bitterness broke out among those in everyday cycling who saw the BLRC as the savior of the sport and those who saw it as the devil that would ruin all they loved. New clubs formed just to run and to ride road races and others refused, not always because they were against but because they didn't want to take fundamental decisions in the absence of so many members abroad and at war.

The battle went on and on, each side sabotaging the other, dropping acid words in the ear of authorities, slandering each other whenever they could. It led to a trench mentality, both sides dug in because they were dug in. For many, the prize was no longer winning the battle but that the war should never end. In the end, Chas Fearnley wrote in the

BLRC's magazine in 1954 that "there is a malignant cancer prevalent in the cycling world and common to all three racing bodies in this country. It is the taint of vanity and culminates in the clash of personality."

Many took the words to refer to Stallard. And they were right. To him, the existence of the BLRC had become the cause, not the means. "In the end," he said, "even the NCU were running road races and we were running road races *and there wasn't any need for amalgamation at all.*"

But amalgamation there was. By 1958 the NCU was as exhausted and as penniless as the BLRC. Ordinary cyclists had tired of it all and so had the UCI, the world body, which more than once tried to crack heads together. The BLRC agreed that "all assets, liabilities, obligations and commitments of the British League of Racing Cyclists should be transferred or handed over to the British Cycling Federation." The NCU passed a similar ruling and on February 1, 1959, the smoke of battle cleared and Britain had one body for road and track racing.

Peter Bryan's assessment was that: "You can never say that if that didn't happen then this wouldn't have happened, but I can't see what else [other than the BLRC] would have brought it about."

There are still a few stooped and pale-eyed men who become misty at their memories of those days. They suffer from over-colored nostalgia, of course, and they miss the noisy, rebellious days of their youth. Many still have the red, white and blue lapel badges they wore to show their BLRC allegiance. And many clubs still have fancy foreign words such as *coureurs* in their title to show their role in the swashbuckling days when ordinary Englishmen yearned to be French.

By the time the BLRC and the NCU limped exhausted into each other's arms, Britain had an international stage race, albeit primitive and shaky in its organization, and it had sent a team to the Tour de France. The first riders were camping out on the Continent and struggling for a living. Among them, Brian Robinson, the first Englishman to finish the Tour.

There were ups and downs to follow and at times the sport misted into an obscurity difficult to wave away. Time-trialling remained a secretive pleasure until into the 1960s, long after any pretense that the police knew nothing of what was happening. Far from that, time-trial organizers were now legally committed to telling the police what they intended to do, even though the police were powerless to stop them.

Road racing became legally permitted—until then it had been neither allowed nor not allowed—on March 1, 1960. It, too, required notifying the police, but there they did indeed have the power of veto. For decades there was no problem. The fears that George Stancer eloquently expressed came to nothing. Or, not immediately they didn't. And then towards the end of the century police bodies across the land seem to have agreed to make life difficult. At best they wanted to be paid for giving unasked help on the day; at worst, and increasingly often, they just said No.

The irony is that just as Britain began winning Olympic medals by the cart, when Chris Hoy was knighted for success on the track and Bradley Wiggins for winning the Tour de France, it is harder than ever to organize a road race.

There's no plaque where that first race finished, close to the Wolverhampton Wanderers soccer ground. In fact there's little now but old men's memories. The BCF was reluctant to remember, that's for sure. Percy Stallard became a member of the BCF, of which he never approved, but the ban was never lifted, although he probably preferred it that way. In 1988 the BCF offered him its gold badge of honor, which at first he said he'd accept and then said he wouldn't. He had never forgiven the BCF for not making him a team manager, or anything else.

"Whatever the award is intended for, whether it is my activities of 46 years ago or my present struggle for age-related [veteran] racing, the significance of the award is nil as it does not open the locked doors of the BCF to me or to anyone else with progressive ideas," he moaned, now camped out in his self-pity. The BCF, he said, had both the ideas of the old NCU and many of its officials.

Stallard died on August 11, 2001. Many still see him as a grumpy saint who saved their sport. His shop, where the revolution began to turn, was run for years afterward by his son, Mick. Albert Price died in 1968. The British Cycling Federation is now called simply British Cycling.

14
A Troubled Winter Star

Few riders have had as much glory and few such shame.
This is the story of a man who had the world at his feet
yet threw it all away.

London, England, February 25, 1973: Everyone thought Renato Longo
would win. He was a "master of the winter", a kind of riding across
fields in the mist, according to the Belgian writer, Pascal Sergent. Longo had traveled from Italy, his home, to Beasain, in the Spanish Basque
country southwest of San Sebastian. It was February 27, 1966, and he
intended to defend the Cyclocross world champion's jersey he had
won not only the previous year but also in 1959, 1962, and 1964. The
result looked obvious, unless he had unusual competition from Rolf
Wolfshohl.

And that's much the way the race went, Longo setting the pace, the
German interfering when he could. Longo punctured and Wolfshohl
pushed on. Only to be caught from a hundred meters back by an unknown from a country which had never won a world cyclo-cross title.
And who won it by 12 seconds.

Erik de Vlaeminck won that world cyclo-cross championship in
1966 and then every year from 1968 to 1973. It's an unsurpassed
achievement that would have been even greater had his bike not broken and forced him out of the race in 1967. He also won the Belgian
championship four times, a race harder than the world championship because Belgians dominate the sport and only a limited number
are allowed in the world race whereas as many as can be accepted can
ride the national event. De Vlaeminck, brother of Roger, also won

the Tour of Belgium in 1969 and a stage of the Tour de France and the Tour of Spain.

Len Thorpe, a photographer who was in Beasain that day, wrote in *Sporting Cyclist*: "De Vlaeminck is certainly a rider of class, and I was very impressed as he just rode away from the tiring Wolfshohl on a one-in-four hill on the sixth lap. By the seventh and last lap he was well away, dashing down the hills as effectively as he climbed, sitting well back in the saddle."

De Vlaeminck, a lean, dark-haired boy barely out of his teens, with a face that was at the same time alert and vacant, could master his bike to the despair of the rest. The 1973 world championship, and his last, was in south London, the first time it had been outside the Continent. A small group of devotees in a sport seen in Britain as the province of the slightly daft found the circuit they wanted in the grounds of the former Crystal Palace, a short distance from Herne Hill track. The palace had been a glass exhibition hall built for the Exhibition of the Industry of All Nations in 1851. It was put up in Hyde Park, across from Buckingham Palace, and then moved south of London by rich financiers who couldn't bear to see it pulled down. It was the crystal palace because of the glittering glass that was its striking feature.

The place burned down in November 1936 in a fire that could be seen all over London. The grounds remained, their statues and full-sized models of pre-historic monsters untended and grubby. The road that ran round the gardens below the palace were a venue for bike races from 1869 and later became a venue for motorbike racing. And in 1973 the same grounds proved ideal for the world cyclo-cross championship.

The designer of the course was a former semi-professional whose mouth turned up at the ends like a crocodile when he smiled. Once he'd devised his circuit, he walked it and picked up more than a thousand shards of glass from that fire four decades and a world war earlier.

Johnny Morris, a Londoner, was enough of a fan of cyclo-cross that he and friends organized porn film shows to finance the teams they took to race in Belgium. He still prides himself on the circuit he devised.

"It was fast," he says. "It wasn't a muddy pit, as courses tended to be in those days, but I did put in a steep climb where I expected the riders to get off and run. And they did. Except that, on the last lap, De Vlaeminck rode it and left the others standing. He was just an exceptional rider. It was a fantastic day, tremendously fast. There was a three-man break just like in a road race."

That, he said, was the future of cyclo-cross, far from the mud-plugging sometimes still common in Britain.

John Wilcockson, the former editor of *Velo-News*, said of him: "Eric [*sic*] was a compact rider who was a virtuoso at cyclo-cross. He could punch out attacks on his bike at the top of short hills when his rivals were gasping, and his steady jogging gait up steps or steep run-ups was unmatchable. Over the 1971 New Year's holiday period, I saw him win a series of five events in Switzerland, which gave him 21 victories that cross season and he placed second in the other two races behind brother Roger."

A word now about the spelling of De Vlaeminck's name. His first name is Erik and it's the version he prefers and the way it's spelled on the certificates at home on his wall. Eric is the French variation and has become more common because there are more newspapers in French than in De Vlaeminck's native Dutch. He says, though, that he has never been upset to be called Eric.

Morris says: "He just had fantastic flair and bike-handling. I mean, regardless of what was fueling him, he was just that much better."

"Fueling him" because, while De Vlaeminck never failed a dope test, tales of his behavior after races—a period he refuses to discuss—are legion. The most common have him driving wildly round towns, shooting at lampposts, terrifying passers-by. But, especially given his refusal to talk, they can't be confirmed. Nevertheless when he decided to start riding again at the end of the 1970s, when he was working as a dumper driver in the parks of Eeklo, his home town, the Belgian federation would give him a license for only one day at a time.

An Alice-in-Wonderland situation had arisen. De Vlaeminck's doctor was Roland Marlier. He in turn was a leader of anti-doping measures in Belgium and a member of the anti-doping branch of the UCI, the world body. And why Alice in Wonderland? Because in 1976 Marlier was given a six-month suspended jail sentence and fined 30,000 Belgian francs for supplying drugs to…Erik De Vlaeminck.

By then, De Vlaeminck was notorious in Belgium and among enthusiasts elsewhere. "Nutty Erik," we used to call him, Morris says. He slowly faded away, a national embarrassment. He took a detoxification course and slowly became a normal person. His return to racing never worked and he became the national cyclo-cross coach instead. He replaced Bert Vermeire, whom journalists and federation complained achieved too little, who was too mild-mannered to bang the table and bring professional riders to order, and whom De Vlaeminck accused of wanting, unlike him and Johnny Morris, old-fashioned courses wallowing in mud.

"Young riders just don't want to struggle through mud as they did in Vermeire's time," he said. "And they should be given the chance to ride abroad more, for the experience, and given a chance to learn without the pressure to succeed all the time."

The formula got him the job and the results came: Belgium has won almost every world championship since and has even evicted every other nationality from the podium. The outcome hasn't always been happy for him, though. His son Geert died in 1993 after crashing, as national amateur champion, in a race at Heist-op-den-Berg. And relations weren't always happy with the national federation. Belgium's successes all came from cyclo-cross, he said, while all the money went to road racing. At one time he said he would welcome an offer to be the national coach in Britain.

But, says Johnny Morris, his brother Roger was still classier. "He was a far classier bike-handler," he remembers. "I went to Italy with John Atkins [a prominent British rider who came fifth in the world championship in 1968]. Roger was at the back of the riders at the start, laughing and chatting and signing autographs. Then when the race started, he rode up the left side of the field, riding on the grass, and entered the circuit in second place."

It's worth pointing out that the start of a cyclo-cross is a sprint to get to the first corner first, after which it's harder to advance through the field. Passing everyone on the grass is far from being the easiest way to do it.

"He got to the second place in the front and rode several laps with the Italian champion, for television, and then passed him."

Roger won the amateur cyclo-cross world championship in 1968, when brother Erik was the professional champion, and the professional race in 1975. He was one of few cyclo-cross riders to do well in the one race you'd think would suit them: Paris–Roubaix. But the race generally defeats them because the cobbles ask more power and more weight than cyclo-cross riders have and Roger De Vlaeminck's success there came more from his wider ability on the road. Nevertheless, the skill of winter riding showed in the way he appeared to glide over the holes and cobbles where other riders made heavy weather. He won Paris–Roubaix four times and each of the five classics: Milan–San Remo (1973, 1978, 1979), Ronde van Vlaanderen (1977), Liège–Bastogne–Liège (1970), Paris–Roubaix (1972, 1974, 1975, 1977), Tour of Lombardy (1974, 1976).

The two brothers not only look unrelated but act it. There is no affection between them.

Oh, and as a footnote, the London championships made a loss.

"Organizing a world championship ought to set the national federation up for years," Morris says. "But it made them zilch. People got in for free because there were so many milling about in the road outside that the police wanted the doors to be opened to avoid a problem. They weren't controlling them properly. I mean, there weren't so many of them by the standards of other events—maybe 15,000—but they were becoming a nuisance in the area. So it was a great day for everyone but the British Cycling Federation."

15

Birth of a Record, Rise of a Giant

Whatever he did, it would be a record. Few of us have been in that position. He could have been forgotten as a result—but he went on to become the first giant of cycling.

Paris, May 11, 1893: He was a giant who became a colossus. His name: Henri Desgrange. For decades his initials, embroidered just as he wrote them, were on the yellow jersey of the Tour de France: both of them his creation. He was a giant for his era, enormous now let alone at the end of the nineteenth century. And for decades he used that dominance, physical and administrative, to rule not just the Tour but all cycling. He could and did disqualify riders as he chose; he used his newspaper to shame those who left race meetings without a shower; his obsessive sense of competition made him hobble across the room from his death bed to see if he could do it faster than the day before.

This man who created the world's largest race—although to be truthful it wasn't his idea and he was dubious when one of his staff suggested it over coffee—was long before then an undistinguished runner, an uncoordinated swimmer ("he battled in an altogether anarchic fashion"), a reporter, an author and the holder of the world's first ratified hour record.

There had been other hour records, of course, a cluster of them. The first was by an American, Frank Dodds, who rode 26.508 kilometers on a penny-farthing in 1876. But not until formation of the International

Cycling Association, in London late in 1892, had there been any way of checking their accuracy or setting a common standard. Once that had been done, all it needed was someone to ride each of the distances, to establishing a record.

In May 1893, the man who rode 35.325 kilometers in an hour was Henri Desgrange. It wasn't fast, although it exhausted him, and it was quickly bettered by no less than three kilometers. Later that year he also set records for 50 and 100 kilometers, the second lasting for four years.

Henri Desgrange in 1893 was 28 years old. He had been racing for three years, at weekends and in the evenings after working as a legal clerk for Depeux-Dumesnil near the place de Clichy in central Paris. He cycled to work and legend says he was fired when a client complained she had seen him with bare calves, or perhaps in tight socks that outlined the lower part of his leg. It's a good tale but it's not necessarily true. What is certain is that Desgrange raced on the road and went to watch other races—including at Montgeron, a popular hangout for cyclists south of Paris, which explains why it became the start point of the first Tour de France—and that he rode well on the Vélodrome de l'Est in the avenue de Charenton. It stood close to the Gare de Lyon train station.

Desgrange, presumably by now out of a job because of his offending calves, then fell into a happy coincidence. An aristocratic British cyclist called Herbert Duncan thought that Paris, where he lived, should have a proper, decent track. He didn't have the money for it and so he went to the man who ran the Folies Bergère girlie show: Clovis Clerc. He, a showman, saw the commercial possibilities of a bike track straight away. Cycling was the sensation of the age and cyclists were the fastest creatures on earth. He chose a site near the Porte Maillot on the edge of the city and called his track the Buffalo, showing his publicist's flair because it had been there that Buffalo Bill had wowed the capital with his Wild West show. If people went to one, perhaps they'd go to the other. And, anyway, he had to call it something.

The problem was that Clovis had the money but he knew nothing about tracks, and Duncan's knowledge was limited to riding round them. Which led to Desgrange, who sounded literate and knowledgeable from his newspaper articles and who had time on his hands. And

Desgrange designed him the track of the century. It was so good that of the next ten successful attempts on the hour record, nine were set at the Buffalo.

Maybe it was Clovis who prompted Desgrange to set the first of those records. It would have fitted his wish for publicity and it would have appealed to Desgrange's undeniable sense of his own worth. And he took it seriously. He trained alone and, in his own words, "led an asthetic [sic] existence, [following] a diet based on very pure milk."

Desgrange that day dressed in a black jersey with white contrasts but no sleeves. He settled for a gear of 44 x 20, which gave him 4.7 meters with every turn of the pedals. Attached to the handlebars: a bottle of milk. Ever the perfectionist obsessed by details, he inspected his two Raleighs several times, decided a tire on his spare bike was too soft, insisted on having it pumped. The crowd grew restless because the program was running behind time.

Eugène Paz, the track's administrator, asked him to hurry and explained why.

"I don't care a thing about the crowd," Desgrange snapped.

When he was ready, he gave his mustache a final wipe, checked any last recommendations from his friend, Adolphe de Palissaux, who was in charge of the attempt, and only then climbed on his bike, a horrendous thing by today's standards but a machine that created envy at the time. It weighed 15 kilograms.

"When I climbed down from my bike," he recalled in 1939, "I was dirty, oily, snotty and covered in dust. You wouldn't have touched me with pincers. But, my god, I was happy!"

The crowd had been excited if impatient before the start but soon they didn't know what to make of it. As Serge Lacet wrote: "He pedaled 'determinedly, mathematically, with perseverance', dedicating himself body and soul in the silence of a cathedral because, surprised by the monotony and lack of drama of the spectacle, the public were cold."

All that broke the dreariness of a man circling a track for an hour were "his hands replacing his handkerchief and the movement of the scoreboard every five kilometers."

In the end, Henri Desgrange set no fewer than thirteen world records, some still on the books, others not. They included records set with pacers and one over 100 miles, categories that have long since vanished. He never stopped riding a bike—he was an exercise fanatic and his staff hid during the Tour de France's rest days for fear that he'd demand they join him in running up mountains—but that was the end of serious competition. His last race, according to René Chesal, former secretary of the French cycling federation, was to set a record for the hour, with pacers, on the Mondésir track at Bordeaux in 1895.

He could afford to call it a day. At the Vélodrome de l'Est he had met a fresh-faced man called Victor Goddet, an official there. The two men became not only friends but also business partners and in time they became the editor and financial chief of a new newspaper, L'Auto, which created the Tour de France as a publicity stunt to stem falling sales.

Desgrange ran the Tour as his personal fiefdom. It started for commercial reasons but Desgrange wanted it to inspire French youth. He had lived through the German siege of Paris in the Franco-Prussian war and he was horrified at how many young French boys were considered unfit for the army because they were underdeveloped, underfed or stricken by maladies such as rickets. He has subsequently been mocked for his wish to create a Tour so hard that only one man would finish it but he had a reason: he wanted that winner to be a superman to inspire others.

Nor was he a hypocrite, happy to criticize others' laziness from the security of an armchair. He ran for two hours a day all his life. He climbed the shingle banks beneath the ski lifts when the Tour passed into the mountains, rising in darkness to do it. It was a régime he wanted his staff to copy but not everyone was as enthusiastic. Albert Baker d'Isy, the rounded and heavy drinking founder of the Grand Prix des Nations, remembered: "His great joy was to drag along the secretary-general of the Tour, Lucien Cazalis, who didn't have the same talent and followed him sweating and panting."

Jacques Goddet, the son of Victor Goddet, who eventually succeeded Desgrange as organizer of the Tour, was one of many who made themselves scarce whenever Desgrange looked like picking up his running shoes. Goddet, too, believed in stimulating exercise for young men. He had gone to a minor private school in England and admired the way sport was, he thought, the source of Britain's "moral and social strength." It was just that he didn't share his boss's more practical enthusiasm.

Desgrange may have been exceptional but he wasn't excused the problems of life. He had a turbulent love affair with a colorful and party-loving artist called Jeanne Deley, to whom he wasn't married and who, to his discomfort, urged him repeatedly not to be so stuffy. She surrounded him with bohemian friends whom he liked but rarely understood and he even started a short-lived newspaper to cater to their theatrical interests.

Jeanne pushed him into buying a flamboyant château of arcades and courtyards at Beauvallon across the bay from an unknown fishing village called St-Tropez. He got a good deal because the previous owners wanted to get rid of it after the local council refused to let them turn it into a casino. But Desgrange was already ill with prostate problems. These days the operation is straightforward but then it had two parts. The first had gone badly and Desgrange had to wait until the pain subsided before he could have the second. The 1936 Tour de France came between the two and Desgrange insisted on being there, riding in a marshmallow of cushions with a nurse at his side. He could barely move, barely speak. And before long he gave up and handed the Tour to Jacques Goddet.

Desgrange retired to his château and defied death to take him, timing himself each day as he shuffled painfully round his room. But no man can hold off the inevitable. He died on August 16, 1940.

16

More Than a Man
Should Bear

*The Tour de France still has no Hall of Fame. Indeed,
there is no exact translation for it in French. But more
than anyone, one man would deserve his place.*

Ste-Marie-de-Campan, France, July 9, 1913: There's a hotel opposite
the road that leads up to the Tourmalet at Ste-Marie-de-Campan. The
man who runs it is used to cyclists arriving with their eyes moving
independently.

"Everyone underestimates the rise from Bagnères," he says. "It looks
like nothing but they arrive here on their knees."

Because of that, the shattered souls may not notice the life-sized
dolls which dot the roads and balconies of Campan, the main village
two-thirds of the way along the rise, and their gratitude on passing the
white sign with its red edging that announces, at last, the arrival of Ste-
Marie-de-Campan probably stops their looking to the left.

If they were to, they'd have seen where one of cycling's most famous—and heart-rending—moments took place. Because the small
house across the road is on the site of the forge where Eugène Christophe—the same Christophe who was stranded in the snow of Milan–
San Remo–was condemned to mend his own front forks in the fire.

The Tour de France didn't come from the Bagnères direction in
1913. It took the climb—the highest in the Pyrenees—from the other
side and then descended through where the hideous ski resort of La
Mongie stands now. It was the sixth stage, from Bayonne to Luchon, a

bagatelle of no less than 326 kilometers. Another two decades had to pass before the Tour could be persuaded that such distances were less races than trials of endurance.

The route to Luchon wasn't undemanding. It crossed the Aubisque and Soulor cols before going over the Tourmalet, dropping to Ste-Marie and then turning right to make an immediate start on climbing the Aspin. After that, to make misery complete, the race took the Peyresourde. It would keep modern Tour riders tossing in their sleep for days but back then it was worse: the roads were largely unsurfaced, bikes were heavy with no derailleur gears, and there was no way to help riders in physical or mental distress. They were left to themselves—until there was any hint they might break the rules, in which case race commissaires were there to watch cruelly.

That year, Christophe was riding for Peugeot. The team attacked from the start at 3am to demoralize their rivals from Alcyon, the other dominant team. The race ebbed and flowed but by the foot of the Tourmalet at Barèges, Christophe was riding with his Belgian teammate, Philippe Thys. About where La Mongie blots the landscape now, Christophe braked to a halt and waved Thys to continue.

"I felt that something was wrong with my handlebars," Christophe remembered years later. Some reports say he lost control and crashed after being hit by a car, although Christophe didn't mention it. "I pulled on my brake and stopped. I could see that the forks were broken. I can tell you now that they'd broken but I wouldn't have told you at the time because it would have been bad publicity for my *maison*.

"So there I was, left alone on the road. When I say road, I should say path. I thought one of the steep pack trails would lead me straight to Ste-Marie-de-Campan. But I was crying so badly that I couldn't see anything. With my bike on my shoulder, I walked for all those ten kilometers."

Spectators were waiting in the village to see the riders pass. They were astonished to see the man they knew as Cri-Cri walking in with his bike across his back. He was followed but not helped by race officials. Christophe approached a woman, Maria Despiau, and asked for a blacksmith's shop. She pointed him to the left, away from the way the race was going, and he walked down the slope to where the village sign stands now. A small crowd followed, including officials from rival teams anxious to see that he lost as much time as possible.

"Monsieur Lecomte was the name of the blacksmith. He was a nice man and he wanted to help me, but he wasn't allowed to. The regulations were strict. I had to do all the repair myself. I never spent a more wretched time in my life than those cruel hours in M. Lecomte's forge."

Jock Wadley, editor of *Sporting Cyclist*, wrote: "Had a spare fork stem been available, then the job would have been over much more quickly. But Christophe had to shape a piece of metal and then weld it on to the shattered stem."

The only image from that time has been so reproduced that it's hard to work out if it's a much retouched photograph—indistinct pictures had to be inked in to reproduce—or a romanticized drawing. Whichever it was, it's misleading because it shows Christophe raising a mallet high above his right shoulder, standing in his race jersey and shorts, about to bring it down not on the forks but the front of the frame. It's hard to work out why.

The forks themselves lie on the edge of the forge, the steering column seemingly heating in the glowing cinders. However accurate it is, it nevertheless gives a good idea of the absurdity and cruelty of the situation, the exhausted Christophe no more skilled in welding than any other layman, working away with a hammer as men in suits and flat caps look on.

Legend says Christophe saw the fire was growing cooler. He had the forks in one hand and the hammer in his other. He asked a seven-year-old boy called Corni to take the bellows and revive the fire, for which he was fined a further ten minutes. It's important to add "legend says" because it wasn't always that journalists of the time actually saw what they reported—it was still hard to drive across mountains and they could rarely see more than one or two riders, the field being spread over several hours—and nobody complained if they exaggerated or supplemented events for the benefit of their circulation.

Christophe remembered Lecomte as the blacksmith. In fact the blacksmith was Joseph Bayle and Henri Lecomte was the commissaire. We even know his age that day: 41. Years later, in tears, he said: "In those days riders had seals on their bikes, to make sure they started and finished on the same machine. Riders had to make all their own repairs."

The ten-minute penalty happened, though, because it was recorded and later reduced to three, as the rules insisted.

There's doubt, too, about the name of the boy. Reporters have since established that his name was Alexandrou Torné.

It was 8:44pm when Christophe reached Luchon on an uncertain bike that would have been an embarrassment to Peugeot, who took it away and made sure it was never seen again. Astonishingly, he wasn't the last to finish. He came twenty-ninth, with fifteen riders behind him.

Christophe's training diaries still exist. They're written in a neat, flowing hand, in blue ink or in pencil. One entry records: "Changing the cranks gives the impression of having a lighter bike or a lower gear (for the same size of gear) and so I had the impression of going faster without getting tired."

He rode a bike for much of the rest of his life, especially in touring rallies around Paris. "I stopped for ten minutes every two hours to eat biscuits, pears and grapes and drink a glass of Vichy water," he remembered of one ride.

Jock Wadley, who went to see him at his home in Malakoff, south of Paris, wrote: "Christophe still has a tidy mind. That is why his workshop is tidy, with every tool clean and in its place. His home is equally in order. I had merely to mention some subject and he would go to a drawer, take out an envelope or a file, marked 'Tour 1912' or 'Paris–Roubaix 1920' or 'Cyclo-Pédestre'. Every photograph had a neatly written caption on the back."

In 1951 he put on race shorts and jersey again and strung a spare tire across his shoulders and re-enacted that day in 1913. There with him in the forge—by now abandoned but made tidy for the occasion—was Lecomte, Maria Despiau and Alexandrou Torné, once the boy who'd helped him at such cost. The French cycling federation posted an engraved plaque on the wall of the house. It said: "Here, in 1913, Eugène Christophe, French racing cyclist, leader overall of the Tour de France, victim of an accident to his machine on the Tourmalet, worked in the forge to repair the fork of his bicycle. Despite having walked several kilometers on the mountain and lost several hours, Eugène Cristophe [sic] didn't just give up the race that he could have won, thereby giving an example of his sublime willpower."

The plaque, with its misspelled name, stayed there until it was replaced on the Tour's hundreth anniversary, which was equally the ninetieth anniversary of the day in the forge of Ste-Marie-de-Campan.

Astonishingly, the same thing happened in 1919. Again the stage covered an outrageous distance: 468 kilometers from Metz to Dunkirk. The Tour had survived roads torn by war and had just a further day to go. Christophe's forks snapped once more but this time there was no mountain to walk down. He was at Raismes, a mile from Valenciennes and a fully equipped forge.

Desgrange wrote in *L'Auto*: "The sky is gloomy and washed out. Huge, dirty clouds stretch to the horizon. It is as if nature itself were grieving. In the outskirts of Valenciennes, Eugène Christophe stands on the pavement. He pushes in front of him, the saddle towards the ground, his bicycle: the fork is broken. It seems to me a mighty lyre whose broken strings sing his final misery."

Desgrange's colorful phrasing survived the years but less so an explanation of why the saddle should point to the ground if the front fork had spanned.

Christophe lost two hours and that day finished tenth of the eleven riders left in the running. He had lost the Tour, finishing third. Readers of *L'Auto* sent in enough money to make up the prize that he would otherwise have won.

Still more astonishing for this man dogged by hardship, he hit a block of stone as he was descending the Galibier in 1922. He got to the next village, Valloire, and there the local parson offered him his own bike.

"Take it," the *curé* said as he stood there in his long black tunic. "It's yours."

Christophe tried it but there was no evidence the brakes would work on the flat, let alone in mountains. He smiled and handed it back. Heaven may take care of preachers but there was little sign it was taking much care of Christophe.

The famous picture of Christophe at the forge

17

Let the Best Man Win (and the Other Be Disqualified)

Roland Marlier once wrote that there was nothing like a Belgian for getting round the rules—before getting his own collar felt for supplying drugs while on the anti-doping committee. There is indeed nowhere like Belgium for complicated politics and infighting.

Koppenberg, Belgium, April 3, 1977: One day you'll have to go to Oudenaarde. You'll go for the Ronde van Vlaanderen, probably, which finishes there. Before or after that, you'll sit in the glorious square of cobbles and Flemish architecture and enjoy a Maes or a Jupiler and reflect that, somehow, these people do things better. And you'll think that even more when you take one of the streets away from the square and find that there's an entire museum devoted to that one race.

Have a look in the window. Around ankle level, you'll see a cobble stone for every year of the race, each with that year's winner. But for 1977 there are two names. Roger De Vlaeminck is there for having crossed the line first but there, too, is the inscription in Dutch: "Moral winner: Freddy Maertens." It probably wasn't difficult to have it put that way. Freddy Maertens is the museum's curator and guide and his biographer, Rik Vanwalleghem, its administrator.

Maertens was a star from the day he abandoned his studies, with the permission of an over-dominant father who made it so much a condition that he devote himself to racing that he sawed his son's bike in half after he'd been seen talking to a girl. Nothing else: just talking. Freddy was the uncomplicated son of simple folk who had a small business by the coast. That trusting, open nature led Freddy to be talked into joining the chaotic but colorful Flandria team rather than the more professional Scic—pronounced like the French *chic*—in Italy. And it led him and his wife Carine to trust sharp-suited "advisers" who bled them dry. Or, as Pierre Chany put it more colorfully, "to trust the first idiot to arrive."

That simple approach to life, said Vanwalleghem, meant that in his first year as a pro "he rode as he had as an amateur: straight to the front, fire in his belly, opposition in his gun sights. He couldn't see that in the world of grown-ups there were other, higher interests in play. His naive joy in races and his fight for victory meant he didn't notice how many feathers he ruffled. He blundered without timidity into Eddy Merckx, the very emblem of cycling. And into Roger De Vlaeminck. And into everyone else of the established order."

He split not just those in races but also those who watched them. There was as little love between Maertens' supporters and those of Merckx as there was between the riders themselves. Years passed without the two men exchanging any more words than they had to. Maertens and Merckx have buried the hatchet. But the enmity with De Vlaeminck has settled into a smoldering resentment, not helped by Maertens' insistence that De Vlaeminck owes him money for the race in which, as the window display says, he was the moral victor.

The catalyst in a grudge that has lasted four decades was a short and bombastic team manager called Guillaume, or Lomme, Driessens. His history, as he tells it, was that he was a moderate rider in the 1930s—which is undeniable—who then realized his skill at motivating riders and managing teams—which is also true but not without those who disagree—and that he was responsible for the rise of Fausto Coppi, Rik van Looy and Eddy Merckx, a claim for which it's worth hearing the tale as the riders themselves tell it.

Driessens, who died aged 94 in 2006, managed many teams. He was one of those big men in a small pool that many disliked but nobody could ignore. He was a wheeler-dealer, trading riders and selling victories. By the mid-1970s he had drifted or gravitated to Flandria, the most consistent name in Belgium but one of the worst payers.

Driessens was delighted to have lured Maertens away from the Italians and immediately put him to work with an astonishing number of races, some in round-the-houses races of no appeal except to the brothers who sponsored the team, and a wearying round of public appearances and openings. One reason Maertens holds the record for the number of wins in a year is that he had to ride so many races.

That day in 1977 was, as De Vlaeminck put it, wet, windy and cold, "everything you needed to make a great Ronde." The course was the usual tortuous winding from Brugge to Oudenaarde, not far in a straight line but 256 kilometers the way the riders went. They included a hill in the middle of nowhere that started with a sharp right bend and went into a cobbled climb hard even to walk. Steep grass banks rise each side and trap riders in place. The surface, which has since been improved but is still hard and dangerous, is barely wide enough for three riders at a time.

It's called the Koppenberg, or Heads Hill. It's always been a concern for both riders and managers. It takes just one rider to falter and a dozen more will fall. Once fallen, they have to run to the top because it's too steep and bumpy to remount. In an ideal world, riders would use a bike with unusually low gearing, lower than would be useful for the rest of the race. And that year, to keep things fair, the team managers met before the race to set a policy. They knew that they wouldn't be able to drive up the hill—they were to bypass it and rejoin the race after the top—and they agreed what to do about bikes.

They "had agreed before the start that there'd be no bike changes at the Koppenberg, but Driessens didn't think that applied to him. He was the boss and he did his own thing," Maertens remembered. He had a love-hate relationship with Driessens, who bossed him about but who replaced the dominant father he needed. Only with his father's or Driessens' direction did he do well; the rest of his career was a disaster.

Jef D'Hondt, the team's equally colorful soigneur, therefore waited at the foot of the climb with another bike. Maertens was to say there was something wrong with the one that he was on and that therefore the change was legitimate. But it was an old trick and it convinced nobody, certainly not the international commissaire, Jos Fabri.

Maertens had fallen out with Fabri as he had fallen out with so many others. For a man with such a lovely personality, Maertens had acquired an impressive list of opponents. Fabri watched as Maertens rode his new bike up the Koppenberg with De Vlaeminck. Unlike the team managers, he was allowed to drive up the climb. Maertens and De Vlaeminck reached the top ahead of the rest, with Fabri behind them. Maertens began riding "as only Eddy Merckx could have ridden," said De Vlaeminck, who was clinging to his wheel.

It was then that Jos Fabri drove up alongside. "You can no longer qualify for first place [*gij telt niet meer winnen*]," he shouted, according to Maertens, who insists that Fabri never said he had actually been disqualified. By now the team cars were back behind the race. Driessens drove up beside his rider and shouted for him to stay in the race. And so Maertens kept going for 70 kilometers, "as only Eddy Merckx could have ridden", remember.

They came into Oudenaarde and, with 300 meters to go, De Vlaeminck got out of the saddle and sprinted, at two thirds the speed that Maertens could have managed, to a silent crowd. Maertens, tired and perhaps dispirited and worried about his disqualification, crossed the line turning the pedals slowly and passed De Vlaeminck, now surrounded by helpers, without a glance.

Maertens and De Vlaeminck disagree to this day about what happened after Fabri's intervention. De Vlaeminck says he didn't know about the illegal bike change. He also says he didn't hear what Fabri had shouted. But Maertens said he must have done because he then asked him to work for him and said: "I'll make it worth your while." That suited Maertens because he couldn't win first prize but he'd be better off with what De Vlaeminck paid with the second place added to it.

Maertens said: "I asked for 150,000 for me and 150,000 for my teammates. De Vlaeminck agreed. Before the Wall of Grammont, he asked me to get going. 'It's still 300,000 francs?' I asked. 'Ja, ja,' he said."

Nobody at the finish knew the deal that had been done but they did know who had made all the running and then been outsprinted at the finish. There's little honor in professional cycling but it's tradition, and politeness, that a rider who's been towed all day should feign a sprint and then tactfully lose. It's such a tradition that a fish dealer watching at the finish pushed through the crowd and screamed: "A beautiful Ronde…and you had to go and ruin it!"

Tom Boonen once referred to bike fans as "those crazy Belgians", an acceptance that anything can happen and that passions will flare and then die as quickly. And sure enough, the fish man regretted his words, brooded on them for two years and then called De Vlaeminck at home to apologize.

"The man didn't owe me anything," De Vlaeminck recalled, "but he gave my brother, Erik, 20,000 francs to pass on to make things good again. Quite a fishmonger."

De Vlaeminck acknowledges that he promised Maertens money but says he never said how much. He gave Maertens 150,000 while they were riding together near the coast. Maertens honorably gave it to his teammates. But he is waiting still for the 150,000 he says he was promised for his own services.

The result that afternoon in Oudenaarde was given with "X" in second place. Then Fabri told the papers: "The race jury has come to the decision that Maertens was the victim of a mechanical defect. The illegal bike change had no influence on the result of the race, which can therefore stand as genuine. As a humane gesture the jury has decided that Freddy Maertens, in recognition of the remarkable athletic ability that he showed for 70 kilometers, will not be taken out of the result."

And that, you'd think, would be the end of it. But there was more. First, the managers of other teams protested. They could also have changed their own riders' bikes before the Koppenberg, they said, and then their own riders would have done better and may well have stayed with De Vlaeminck. And De Vlaeminck wouldn't have stayed away, they said, and wouldn't have won a sprint, had Maertens not corrupted the result by selling his services.

That, Fabri and the other commissaires had to acknowledge, was a good argument. And they took Maertens out of the result again.

And the other little snag that intervened? Maertens failed the drug test. So did Walter Planckaert, who came third, and so did the Frenchman, Guy Sibille, for not turning up for a check at all.

It had been, as the fishmonger put it, "a beautiful Ronde." And then so much had ruined it.

18

Put Me Back On My Bike

It took a tragedy, a death and that sudden shock to jolt cycling out of its blindness. Blindness to a cancer that had taken hold and which some say has never been cured.

Mont Ventoux, France, July 13, 1967: "Put me back on my bike"…the last words that Tom Simpson never spoke that day in July, 1967. The tragedy happened, sure enough. But the words were a paraphrasing by the experienced and shambling reporter, Sid Saltmarsh, who was covering the Tour de France for *Cycling* and the pre-Murdoch *Sun*.

Cycling reporters trade anecdotes and help each other with background. They can't speak every language and nor do they have time or the access to all of the riders. In the press room at Sète, therefore, they crowded round Saltmarsh and asked for Simpson's last words. Saltmarsh hadn't been there at the time, though. As he wrote: "Only when we reached the finish did we learn that he had fallen, assuming it was a crash."

He had, though, spoken to some who'd been there and they said Simpson had fallen and that he'd insisted on getting going again. So he said: "They told them to put him back on his bike," and that was put into the first person and became not a summary but the truth.

Nobody then, in Britain, anyway, seriously thought that drugs may have been involved. There are still some who, forced by facts to acknowledge that he'd taken them, believe that he drove himself to his death through honest willpower and that doping was incidental. Drugs, anyway, were what foreign riders took. If good, honest British riders took them, it was only to make things fair again. When William Fotheringham wrote his biography, *Put Me Back On My Bike*, the legend was killed. He came across letters to George Shaw, a friend in Britain, in which he spoke of taking drugs, with the breathtaking comment that if ten pills would kill him then he'd take nine and win.

Few at the time saw the significance in the comment by Jacques Goddet, a man who knew much more of the riders' private lives than he committed to print, when he said: "He wanted victory too badly. We often asked ourselves if this athlete, who at work often appeared in pain, had not committed some errors in the way he looked after himself."

Of course, Simpson wasn't alone. Riders who'd crashed earlier that day from Carpentras to Sète had been refused hospital treatment until doctors found what they had taken and the effects had worn off. The whole field had gone on strike the previous year when officials insisted on applying a recently passed law and began testing riders at Bordeaux. News had spread and most of them disappeared before the testers got there. Simpson took part in the strike but he avoided the front line because he thought it unwise to draw attention to the problem.

The day the race crossed Mont Ventoux was an obvious one to seek extra help. Antoine Blondin, the Tour's most literary chronicler and here, perhaps, leaning a little too heavily on color, wrote of the Ventoux: "There are few happy memories of this sorcerer's cauldron. We have seen riders reduced to madness under the effect of the heat or stimulants, some coming back down the hairpins they thought they were climbing, others brandishing their pumps and accusing us of murder...falling men, tongues hanging out, selling their soul for a drop of water, a little shade."

Jean Mallejac of France collapsed there in 1955 and was still turning his legs in a coma after he'd been strapped on to an ambulance bed.

Jock Wadley, the editor of *Sporting Cyclist* who saw his job mostly as a way of getting out to see bike races instead of working, left his press car before the summit of Mont Ventoux and walked to the summit. There were fewer spectators in the days when cars were less common and it was still possible to stroll beside the course.

"I knew who would be coming up first because the transistors were blaring out the news that Jimenez had now dropped Poulidor and was alone in the lead. I knew, too, that the man in the yellow jersey, Roger Pingeon, was in a group of half a dozen which included Gimondi of Italy, Janssen of Holland and Lucien Aimar of France. I knew that Tom Simpson had been with this group until halfway up the fifteen miles climb but had lost contact.

"Then, just after Jimenez came by—in and out of the saddle and alternatively pedaling and stamping his way up the last 200 yards of the climb—above the shouts and applause of the crowd, the shrill whistles of the motorcycling gendarmes and klaxoning of impatient cars, above this terrific din I heard this from the transistors: 'Tom Simpson is now riding very slowly and is zig-zagging all over the road. He is in a state of great distress.'"

Wadley hitched a lift with another press car and the driver told him: "We saw him by the side of the road three kilometers from the top, being treated by Dr Dumas. It seemed to me that Tom was in the same condition as Mallejac in 1955."

Tom Simpson had had a couple of troubled years. To general surprise and not a little suspicion, he had outsprinted the sturdy German road-sprinter, Rudi Altig, to win the world championship near San Sebastian in Spain in 1965. But the supposed curse of the rainbow jersey was ready and that winter Simpson broke his leg in a skiing fall. The money he should have earned never came. Worse than that, he had investments to support and his agent, a swarthy Corsican called Daniel Dousset, had warned him that he'd be worth nothing at all in contracts unless he could do something of note. On top of that, his team, Peugeot, looked likely to drop him as leader; it had just recruited a promising Belgian called Eddy Merckx.

That day, July 13, 1967, therefore, Simpson set out to win the Tour de France, to push up his worth and to secure a place in the Salvarani team of another rider showing promise, the Italian, Felice Gimondi. He had at least to finish the race, to show he had completely recovered from his broken leg.

Mont Ventoux is a freak mountain that volcanic forces forced abruptly out of the surrounding Provence plain of gorse and the constant chirruping of crickets that Simpson disliked. It's a monochrome eyesore on the colorful Provence plain, one writer said.

It's no higher than other big climbs of the Tour but it held a special fear because the rise through the trees was airless and could, as

Blondin said, turn into a cauldron. And there was no relief when the race reached the Châlet Reynard, the bar that stands on the right where the route to the summit turns left and another road comes in from the right. There, suddenly, the trees end and the rest of the ascent is surrounded by bleak, volcanic lava from which the sun reflects mercilessly.

Simpson wrote in his autobiography: "It is like another world up there among the bare rocks and the glaring sun. The white rock reflects the heat and the dust rises, clinging to your arms, legs and face."

Maybe by now Simpson realized he couldn't win the Tour. There were better riders than him, riders who could survive a three-week race more dependably. Simpson by contrast had enormous strength and willpower but he was weedy with a concave chest. His closest friend, Vin Denson, used to speculate that it came from the generations who had worked in mines "with all the lack of air that they got down there."

Even his wife, Helen, conceded the point: "He had no chest and no shoulders. There was nothing to him, really."

Lucien Aimar, who was with him as their group climbed the Ventoux and to whom coincidentally Simpson owed £300 for a British appearance fee he hadn't yet passed on, said: "After ten days of racing, he was fading away. I came back up to him on the Ventoux after I'd flatted. Van Springel and Letort were with us. The heat was suffocating. I offered him a drink but he didn't hear me. He had a totally empty look and the extraordinary thing was that he tried to jump me. He took 250 meters out of me. I said to him: 'Tom, don't play the fool.' But he didn't answer. A moment later, he was on my back wheel. I heard a cry but I didn't see him fall."

The doorless white car of the British team was behind him. Simpson lay on the road, still on his bike, still lucid. "Get me up, Harry, get me straight," he said to one of the three mechanics, a Manchester bike-shop owner. Harry Hall had watched him riding slower and slower, as Wadley had heard on the radio, and he wanted Simpson to call it a day.

The team manager, a little, gray-haired man named Alec Taylor, was beside him. At that stage he worried not that Simpson was dying, which nobody knew, but that he'd be in too groggy a state to be safe on the fast and winding descent after the observatory at the summit. That morning he had asked Denson to warn two of the team's domestic professionals, Colin Lewis and Arthur Metcalfe, to take the drop carefully.

"For God's sake, concentrate!", Taylor shouted as Hall pulled Simpson upright.

"Me straps, Harry, me straps," Simpson shouted as Hall began pushing him on his way, and he bent to pull up the leather straps to bind Simpson's feet to his pedals.

Simpson pressed on but began weaving from side to side of the road. The right of the road was a upward slope of fallen rocks but the left was an unguarded drop into the valley. The support team was scared. And then, a kilometer from the top, around where Wadley had stepped out of his car for a walk, he came close to a stop on the edge of the fall into the valley. Hall and another mechanic, Ken Ryall, were with him before he went over the side.

Simpson was still pedaling. He stopped, upright on his bike but gasping. Hall, shirtless and tanned in the heat, put his arm under his chest and helped him pump for air. Simpson's fingers were locked to the bars and Hall and Ryall prised them off. They laid him across the road, head towards the stones. They pulled up his white woolen jersey with the pinned-on name of his sponsor and begin lifting and lowering his chest. Some reports have Taylor weeping and muttering, either there or when his death was confirmed: "The stupid bastard, the stupid bastard."

Pierre Dumas, the chief of the medical team, drove up alongside, alerted by a motorcycling gendarme who'd said there had been "a bit of a problem." In all the confusion, Denson rode past and assumed his leader had fallen but nothing worse.

A police helicopter began its way up the valley and hovered over the road before finding somewhere to land on sloping land towards the valley. Simpson's body was put aboard, loaded on a stretcher. The helicopter took off across the valley and headed for the hospital in Avignon. Dumas, who had put Simpson's head in an oxygen mask and pumped his heart through his chest, said later that Simpson was already dead on the roadside.

They emptied Simpson's pockets and tested his blood at the hospital. Both contained drugs. Barry Hoban, the next most talented man in the British team, has no friendship for those who suggest that Simpson cheated. To him, even though doping was by then against not only cycling's rules but the laws of France, Simpson was doing no more than any other rider. Doping was expected, common currency and hard to detect, helped by the lackadaisical way in which the sport looked for it.

"Tom was looking after himself in a way that a lot of people were looking after themselves," Hoban said. "Maybe you could accuse us, and I was part of that generation, of being ill-advised, but we were ill-advised by the medical profession from the knowledge that they had then."

Which is true as it stands but contains the ironic phrase "looking after himself." To take nine pills only because ten would kill perhaps falls short of "looking after himself", but it was the euphemism that riders used and the one which Goddet had employed.

Many debate the extent to which drugs killed Simpson but it's undeniable that he had taken them. Colin Lewis, who shared hotel rooms with him on that Tour, said Simpson referred to them as his Mickey Finns and that during the Tour he had paid a dealer £800 for a year's supply in a box six inches long, four inches wide and three inches deep.

The sum was around the annual wage of an office worker in Britain and what would have taken Lewis four complete years to earn from the retainer from his small British team.

That night the police raided the team, their rooms and their cars. "We knew there was going to be a hoo-ha about drugs," Hall said long afterward, acknowledging that he knew what was going on, "knew that we had to keep that side of things quietened down." Taylor and the team's two Belgian soigneurs were questioned much of the night by the police. The police arrested Hall and Ken Bird, the third mechanic, and held them at the police station in Sète. Bizarrely, the two waited to be questioned, got up, walked to their car—which had also been impounded—and drove off. They heard nothing more.

Most of the riders in that year's British team are still alive. The staff have all died, Taylor thirty years to the day after Simpson. What happened to Ken Bird is a mystery. He ran bike shops in south London and managed a domestic team in their name. And then he vanished. Nobody knows, or nobody will say, what happened. But just after I made a documentary about Simpson's death for the BBC, on the twentieth anniversary, he called me to say he wished he had taken part.

"I could have told you much more," he said.

"Like what?"

"Like what happened to everything when it was loaded on to a lorry."

He wanted to take me back to where events happened and he explained them in detail. But British libel laws were too strict then and they're too strict to repeat his story now. Which is a shame.

The granite Tom Simpson memorial on Mont Ventoux

19

Man of Steel

They make steel in Solingen, or did when the industry counted for something. And it took a constitution of steel to win the world championship there.

Solingen, Germany, August 22, 1954: Louison Bobet was obsessive. He is the only man in the history of the Tour to turn down the yellow jersey because it wasn't made of wool. The Tour, always stuck for money and more impoverished than ever when it restarted in 1947, had done a deal with Sofil, a company that made artificial yarn at a time when such things were exciting. It was the forerunner of Lycra and Gore-Tex and all the things we take for granted now.

Sofil hadn't been able to make a wholly synthetic yellow jersey but it had blended its thread with wool. Until then, jerseys had been made only of wool.

Louis Bobet, as he was still known because the family diminutive of Louison hadn't caught on, wouldn't have it. He had been influenced by meeting Fausto Coppi and his soigneur, Bruno Cavanna, and he and his own soigneur, Raymond Le Bert, had assumed the mixture of sense and baloney that ran through cycling in those days. And that insisted that no good would come of artificial fabrics because they didn't breathe properly and absorbed sweat.

The fact that nothing soaked up sweat more than wool, which became soggy and sagged after only a few rain showers, didn't matter. Bobet had been bothered by saddle boils, and was so for the rest of his life, so he had no plans to make things worse by wearing anything he didn't know. But there was also reasoning in it. "There was no question of hygiene," his frequent roommate, Raphaël Géminiani, said. "We used to wear the same jersey unwashed for four days." And if that made wool smell, it was nothing to how it made synthetic fabrics.

Jacques Goddet recalled: "It produced a real drama. Our contract with Sofil was crumbling away. If the news had got out, the commercial effect would have been disastrous for the manufacturer."

It may be that Bobet didn't know what he was being asked to wear when he accepted the jersey and only that evening did he decide to send it back. Goddet was having dinner when the news arrived. You can imagine the indigestion. By then it was too late to do anything about it. There'd have been Sofil staff in nearby hotels but Goddet had no intention of warning them. And they wouldn't have had an all-wool jersey even if he did.

Goddet abandoned his meal and went to Bobet's hotel. In those days everyone on the Tour slept in neighboring streets. "I remember debating it with him a good part of the night," he remembered in his autobiography. "Louison was always exquisitely courteous but his principles were as hard as the granite blocks of his native Brittany coast."

Or as Géminiani put it: "Bobet had a monstrous pride, a sort of cannibal before Merckx. He could never just abandon a race: he had to do it theatrically."

Goddet despaired. There was no alternative but to find Sofil's agents, to ask them to bring staff into their factory at night and to turn out another yellow jersey for the morning, their logo still in place but their artificial fabric absent. In the end the drama died. Bobet wore his all-wool jersey, nobody knew what had happened, and he didn't finish the Tour anyway.

This was the moody, proud and sometimes arrogant man who pulled on the reassuringly woolen blue, white and red jersey of the French national team to start the world championship in 1954. The Allies were still occupying Germany and French soldiers had made the journey to see him ride. The first man to win three Tours in as many years was an international hero. And he was about to become the first Frenchman to win the professional road championship in nearly twenty years. The last had been Antonin Magne in 1936—the same Magne who managed Bobet's Mercier professional team.

Les Woodland

And Magne agreed with critics that Bobet had neared the top of international cycling but needed more.

Magne was even more in the hokum world than Cavanna. He was a farmer from outside Paris who persisted in wearing his white milking jacket to races. He addressed all his riders not by the informal *tu* that everyone else used but the formal *vous*. And he expected to be addressed as Monsieur Magne. He lived in the past, with his own arcane rules. To the end of his career, when he managed Raymond Poulidor, he forbade riders to have zippers in their jerseys. And he diagnosed riders' ailments by hanging a suspended needle above their body to see which way it turned.

The actual idea that Bobet should dedicate himself to the world championship came from Charles Pélissier, a prolific winner of Tour stages thanks to his sprint, who was covering the Tour. Pélissier was interviewing Bobet for *Miroir Sprint,* a weekly magazine in a stable of publications associated with the communist party, then a movement for social advance and not yet tainted with its Russian alliance of later years. Pélissier listened to Bobet's account of the Tour and ended his audience with advice: "In your condition, there's nobody around who could beat you. Forget about the criteriums after the Tour, or most of them, and start training to become champion of the world."

Pélissier said Bobet didn't reply straight away. But Bobet would never have done that anyway. His sense of purpose forbade it. But he nodded thoughtfully and the interview ended with the usual cordiality. And then the suggestion matured over the days.

Solingen is a little south of the industrial Ruhr valley. It's been making steel since sword-makers settled there in the Middle Ages, later committing treachery by taking their secrets to England.

The world championship there was the third to be held in Germany. It began in the rain and it finished in the rain and it rained all the time between the two. It was what the French call a *temps de chien*—weather fit for a dog. Daniel Dousset, the agent who represented not just Tom Simpson but Bobet and just about every other prominent rider except Raymond Poulidor (who was with Dousset's minor rival, Roger Piel), talked to Bobet on the line at Solingen's Klingen circuit. He was on a percentage of Bobet's earnings and they, high after winning the Tour, would be even higher if he could win the championship as well. Both men recognized that the challenge came from Fausto Coppi, who had also said publicly that he was concentrating on the world title and who had not ridden the Tour and was fresher for it.

Coppi had the edge in strength and panache and, once clear, could never be caught. On the other hand, Bobet, in the words of the Tour's official historian, Jacques Augendre, could "at his best drop Charly Gaul in the mountains, win the Grand Prix des Nations in time-trial-ling and beat Rik van Steenbergen in a sprint."

"If I'm not world champion this evening then I never will be," Dousset remembered Bobet's telling him. It's hard to tell if rider number 30 was confident or doubting.

There were sixteen laps and, sure enough, Coppi attacked with 50 kilometers to go and shredded the hopes of half the field, who couldn't resist him. Nor could the hopeless early leaders, Robert Varnajo of France and Michele Gismondi of Italy. Coppi reached them with Fritz Schaer of Switzerland, Charly Gaul of Luxembourg, and three Frenchmen: Bobet, Jacques Anquetil and Jean Forestier.

It was an explosive mix: Bobet the joint favorite, Schaer the sprinter who had won the Tour's first ever green jersey the previous year, Gaul the climber, Anquetil the time-trialist who had no love for Bobet and was there to attack and not to defend him, and Forestier, not yet at his peak but *maillot jaune* and points winner in the Tour de France three years later.

Bobet attacked ten times and rid himself of all the other French. The two climbs, with the distance and above all the weather, were wearing everyone down. Coppi was shattered enough that he lost concentration on the wet descent and crashed into Gaul, bringing both of them down. Gaul didn't regain the other two, which put Bobet the hardman up against Schaer the sprinter.

Bobet waited for the Balhaüsen hill, the harder of the two, and attacked hard. Schaer stayed with him, clinging to his wheel. The two team cars were behind them, wipers fighting the rain. They had just passed the feeding station. Paul Delaye, the mechanic in the French car, was worried. He saw what the others hadn't and he wound down his window and peered out to confirm it, his hand cupped over his eyes to keep out the rain: the spokes were breaking in Bobet's back wheel.

There were fourteen kilometers to go. Bobet had been reluctant to stop but now there was no option. The rim had started rubbing the brakes and one more broken spoke would stop it turning at all. Some reports, by the way, say Bobet had flatted but it would be easy to assume that, the more usual reason to change a wheel. Delaye had a front and back wheel on his lap in the car. He threw the unwanted one towards the driver and stepped out of the car with the other before it had even stopped.

Schaer, of course, was delighted by this turn of events. Riders are never sure whether to profit from a rival's mechanical problems but that day Schaer's conscience didn't trouble him. The chance gave him fresh energy and he bounded off up the road. He had a minute's lead. Delaye pushed the large-flanged Campagnolo hub into the sloping rear drop-outs of Bobet's bike, ran pushing him as Bobet clipped his feet back into the straps, then took the broken wheel back to the car.

British *Pathé News* said there were 100,000 fans on the Klingen circuit that day. The French soldiers among them began to despair at their wasted day. But in the words of a French newsreel commentator, their man got back to Schaer "with a superhuman effort." One chronicler wrote: "For anyone but Bobet, the affair would have been over at that moment. But Louison didn't even feel the pedals and, despite a bike which had different gear ratios from before [the spare wheel didn't have the same size cogs] he succeeded in catching Schaer the last time the race went down Balhaüsen hill before dropping him a little further on."

Bobet, his face drawn and ghostly, crossed the line with 12 seconds' lead and just the slightest wave of his right hand. He had finished at 32 kilometers per hour. His head drooped, he undid his toe-straps and he braked to a halt. It took a long time to recover, not helped by unhindered crowds of well-wishers and the simply curious who mobbed around him. Someone found a tracksuit top and wrapped it round his shoulders and the sodden blue jersey. Bobet stood, let someone take his bike, wiped his face, then walked to the podium for his rainbow jersey and the sound of the *Marseillaise*. He had won the Tour and the world championship in the same year, the first Frenchman to do so since Georges Speicher in 1933, who'd had to be hauled out of a nightclub because he'd never expected to be selected.

Bobet spoke only a few words to reporters after the race. His helpers took him to his hotel and there he showered and lay on his bed, finally talking to whoever came to see him.

"You can't imagine how much I suffered to get back to Schaer after my wheel went," he said in his high-pitched voice, a phrasing suggesting that it was indeed breaking spokes rather than a flat tire that halted him. "I thought I had lost it. I thought I'd lost a title that I deserved. Not for anything in the world would I relive that chase."

So the idea that "Louison didn't even feel the pedals" was more romance than reality.

"*Mon dieu*, that was hard. You need to have suffered on a bike to understand."

Jacques Anquetil was barely out of his teens that day at Solingen, where he finished fifth. Just as Raymond Poulidor later haunted Anquetil, so Anquetil was haunting Bobet.

Raphaël Géminiani, whose affections were more in the Anquetil camp, said: "The current never passed between them. It was the eternal conflict between the aging champion and his challenger."

Finally the elder man realized his days were over and, with his flair for theater, stepped off at the top of the col d'Iséran in the Tour de France in 1959, pulled off his mitts and accepted a waterproof jacket. There was surprise not just at that but why he'd left it so long, considering what a hopeless path he was following.

"I'd never climbed the Iséran," he explained. "It's the highest road in Europe and I wanted to see what it's like."

There's a cycle-tourist in all of us.

In one of those oddities that repeat themselves throughout cycling, the pudgy man beside him who agrees to hold his bike is Gino Bartali, the star of Italian cycling before and after world war two. Bartali had been surpassed by Fausto Coppi and he knew how Bobet felt at being overshadowed by Anquetil. Bobet waited for a team helper to bring a pale brown raincoat and then he left, his last Tour behind him.

"He lacked humility," Géminiani remembered. "But that was Bobet. He genuinely thought that after him there'd be no more cycling in France." Orson Welles came to encourage him once. "You have the good fortune to shake the hand of Louison Bobet," Bobet told him.

Bobet lies now in the graveyard at St-Méen-le-Grand, the village in Brittany where his father ran the bakery, just a short walk from where the Louison Bobet museum is now. It displays trophies, letters, an all-wool yellow jersey from the Tour—and the rainbow jersey he won that day in 1954 in Solingen.

A 1955 French weekly sports magazine cover featuring Bobet

20

Of Triumph and Ashes

The curse of the rainbow jersey insists that nobody who wears it will be happy the following year. It never happened more devastatingly than on a car-racing circuit in Belgium.

Zolder, Belgium, August 10, 1969: The oddest things happen in world championships. They look open and uncomplicated, the fastest man winning. But there are unseen currents, private wars and allegiances, of which the world knows little. Part of it is that the races, unlike almost all others, are contested by national teams; the rest are for the glory of washing-machine makers, lemonade companies or anyone else prepared to foot the bill. And the allegiance between friends of fortune is often stronger than between those brought together for the day in a national jersey.

Part, too, is that some countries have barely enough riders to fill a team and others have too many. And then there is the rider who could never win the title, or who doesn't care deeply about it, who will help a rival if he's paid for it.

Sometimes, in this maelstrom of confusion and intrigue, *le troisième larron* can win. The third thief. He watches the other two bicker over the bounty and makes off with it himself. And so it was with Harm Ottenbros, a Dutchman unknown outside cycling even in his own country and called into the world championship team of 1969 only because he was available and, some suggested, because he lived right on the Belgian border and would ask less in gas money as a result.

Ottenbros beat Eddy Merckx. He beat the world. He could show the rainbow jersey of a champion to his children and then his grand-children. He could, for a beer, sit in a bar and relive the race time after time. Instead, it ruined Ottenbros so utterly that he wishes he'd never been a racing cyclist at all.

Harmin Ottenbros, known as Harm, was a 26-year-old who scraped a living carrying bottles for the great and filling the field in criteriums of significance only to locals. Holland had few of the big stars it would have later. Its main man was Jan Janssen, the defending world champion and winner of the previous year's Tour de France. It wasn't hard for the rest of the team to ride for him because there was no one else. But at the last moment he fell ill. The KNWU, the Dutch federation, couldn't find another name that big and so it moved everyone up the ladder and called Ottenbros to make up the number at the bottom.

To the south, Belgium had the opposite problem: overflowing riches. Merckx was rampaging—"When you know how much Merckx is earning in this race," the French champion Raymond Delisle said during that year's Midi Libre, "you lose the will to compete for just the leftovers"—and upsetting the old guard, especially Rik van Looy.

He and Merckx had the same relationship as Bartali with Coppi, Bobet with Anquetil: the old fading against its will to the new. Van Looy—"as a rider, exceptional; as a man, *niks*," Janssen said—had dominated Belgian cycling for years. The teams he led had one order: to get him over the line first. He grew up just when hot money from the Occupation burned in pockets and poured out in prizes in round-the-clocktower criteriums. Van Looy was the attraction and the big-gest earner and he let it be known with whom he was prepared to race and who not. In an era when Tour riders got the bulk of their earnings from appearance money, it didn't pay to upset van Looy.

He in his day had had to challenge Rik van Steenbergen, another rider who had trouble stomaching him. And now he was being rid-iculed by Merckx. His resentment was such that two weeks before the world championship he glued himself to Merckx's wheel in a race only streets from Merckx's home and then sprinted past to win. Three days later, both were sulking so much, Merckx from being beaten at home and van Looy from the crowd's whistling, that they watched

Les Woodland

each other so closely they slipped off the back at Denderleeuw and were lapped. A shouting match followed.

There was another race that afternoon, at Rijmenam, east of Mechelen on Belgium's language border, and this time Merckx sprinted out of every corner until van Looy could no longer follow. The two were suspended for eight days for not racing seriously at Denderleeuw. And two weeks later they were supposed to ride for each other and for Belgium in the world championship.

To many, spoiling Merckx's chances was more important than winning the race. And that extended into the Belgian team itself. No cycling nation has more infighting than Belgium and having the world championship in the country predictably produced a civil war. L'Équipe reported: "This world championship, just as we'd forecast, was held to ransom right from the start by the formula of national teams, by disagreements among the Belgians, and by the order of battle, which was to stop Eddy Merckx winning. For him, the best of all in terms of absolute talent, the problem looked insoluble. And it was. So the winner of the Tour de France, crushed by numbers, paralyzed by the hunting-wolves of the peloton left the race on the last lap so that his name never even figured in the results."

Among the hunting wolves was van Looy, who was on Merckx's wheel whenever he attacked, to help according to the crowd, to sabotage according to Merckx. So Merckx gave up and dismounted 500 meters before the grandstand to avoid his fans' eyes. He wouldn't talk to anyone but his manager, Lomme Driessens, for an hour and a half. When Driessens came out of his hotel room, it was to tell journalists that "what van Looy did today doesn't merit any commentary." And Merckx, when he did emerge, called van Looy his worst enemy.

The rest of the field had put so much into stopping Merckx that they had no follow-up plan. They rode round puzzled and, at the bell, a break had two minutes. Were they going to chase or were they not?

Even the new leaders were paralyzed. Roger De Vlaeminck was the strongest and he could ride away from the rest, especially as two were make-weights even in their own teams. But do that and he would take the Dutch sprinter Gerben Karstens with him and he would lose. But Karstens couldn't attack because De Vlaeminck would overpower him. There's no glory in coming second so each watched the other, powerless.

The minnows were delighted. Ottenbros was in the same orange as Karstens, and Julien Stevens—national champion the previous year and a stage winner in the 1969 Tour de France but little else—was in the same light blue as De Vlaeminck. And, unhindered by their own stars, they rode away. Now neither De Vlaeminck nor Karstens could make their own move without its sabotaging their own team.

The crowd now were in fairyland, the stars ambling like also-rans and the also-rans racing like stars. It came home to Stevens that he could be within minutes of being world champion. And Driessens had the same idea. Stevens had been such an outsider that he hadn't been part of the pre-race conversation of who would pay whom what, not beyond doing the dirty work of chasing breaks and so on. So Driessens handed up a bottle containing nothing but a note. On it was the bonus he was prepared to offer if Stevens won. And below that the sum that Stevens should offer Ottenbros to lose.

Ottenbros's memory is that the two didn't speak, that Stevens never offered a bribe. They rode a straight sprint and Ottenbros, sharpened by criteriums, won on the inside by centimeters.

"The nearer the finish line came, the more I had to tell myself I was just in a kermesse, although with a few more spectators than usual. I had to forget that I was riding for a world title because, if I'd realized that, I'd never have won," he said. He threw his head down like a track sprinter to cross the line and didn't look up for a couple of seconds. "It was an odd feeling," he said years later.

Pierre Chany barely hid his sneer: "The race needed a winner, and it was Ottenbros: Ottenbros, who finished the Tour de France in 78th place, three hours behind the yellow jersey.... He was escorted to the podium by just his team manager and two policemen."

The world of cycling turned against Ottenbros. Maybe they felt guilty for turning a world championship into a whipping session for the man who should have won. More likely, because proud men don't admit guilt, they felt an unknown had no right to their prize. The only rider to congratulate him was Franco Bitossi, who rode up alongside in the Tour of Flanders and said he admired what he'd done. Ottenbros was so moved that he gave him a rainbow jersey.

Riders combined to stop him winning even petty criteriums when he rode abroad. Often he was lucky even to get start money. He earned

€2,500 as world champion, no more than he had the previous year. Riders laughed at how poorly he rode hills and called him the Eagle of Hoogerheide, a reference to Federico Bahamontes, the Eagle of Toledo, and the impressive flatness of southwest Holland where Ottenbros lived.

"That nickname made me more famous than my world championship ever did," he says now with bitterness. "And yet I was the strongest rider on the day. Or do you reckon that I bribed all the other 190 riders? Don't forget that they all wanted to be world champion as well. I raced and they didn't. I can't be held to blame if the stars of the day didn't take their chance."

In Holland he was a hero one moment and then, abruptly, the fans deserted him, disappointed by the lack of further results. He felt he had let down his father, Jan, whose own successes he was trying to honor. And life got worse. He broke his wrist in the Tour of Flanders and could neither ride in his rainbow jersey nor defend his title. Then his team, Willem II, folded after a ban on cigarette advertising in sport.

"Believe me," he says, "I wasn't in the slightest bit sorry when my year as world champion was over and I didn't have to wear that jersey any more. I could just go back to being the unknown rider in village criteriums. But the old feeling never came back. I was never happy again."

He considered suicide. In 1976 he rode to the Zeeland bridge across a sea inlet called the Oosterschelde. And there, with Gerrie Knetemann, a rider of the new generation, he threw his bike into the North Sea. The pair watched it disappear. They shrugged, smiled at each other in embarrassment, and Ottenbros rode home on the top tube of Knetemann's bike.

Ottenbros' marriage broke up. He lost contact with his three children. He drove round France for two months, camping if he could, looking for where he'd ridden in the Tour, looking for what had once been. He reached Tours at the same time as the Tour. He didn't bother to watch. He moved into a condemned building in Sliedrecht and slept on the floor for two years with the fellow dropouts who'd become his world.

"I had money in the bank," he says, "but I never touched it. I wanted nothing to do with cycling and the self-centered life that had led to my divorce." Some say he lived a life of sex, drugs and abandon. It seems unlikely.

Eventually he had a go at sculpture but he didn't dare sell what he made for fear it would make him known again. He did voluntary work but never gave his name. He says he has forgotten much of his past. "I'd need to read the newspapers again to answer that question," he tells the few journalists who ask.

"I'm scared of being interviewed, scared the questions will revive memories and make me ill again." He lives now in a housing estate—a project, as they'd say in America—south of Rotterdam. His last sponsor was a carpet company, Kela, and it stood by him. It offered him work when he needed it. He glued tiles to walls and floors, fitted carpets. Now, he works with mentally handicapped children in his spare time. He has even taken up sculpting female nudes. His steel-rimmed glasses give him an artistic, studious air. Someone wrote he had the look and the talk of a philosopher, and it's true. He gets to the track at Alkmaar now and then, so you could see for yourself. But whether he'll talk about the past depends on the time and mood.

He still has his rainbow jersey. He keeps it in a closet, along with his medal and other souvenirs. He doesn't look at them. He does rides again, although more often on a motorbike. He turns up on television and other public appearances sometimes with other old riders such as Janssen, whose absence from the world championship led to his fall, and Jo De Roo. He asks just 35 euros an appearance. But most have no idea who he is.

"If I could live my life all over again," he says sadly, "I'd miss out the cycling bit."

21

The Devil in a Dress

Many a racing cyclist has been just a little odd. But none was ever as odd, or at any rate as unexpected, as Italy's Devil in a Dress.

Milan, Italy, June 1, 1924: It's something we've all dreamed of: somehow entering the Tour de France and getting away with it. And it used to be that Europe's biggest stage races were short enough of riders that that was the way that many did it. They called them *touristes-routier* at first, tourists of the road, and in the Tour de France they were happy to let them ride provided they caused no inconvenience. They put their suitcases on the train each morning, collected them at the finish and rode round town looking for a hotel. One, as exhausted as anyone else from a day's riding, performed acrobatic tricks in the street to pay for his food and bed.

But take the idea further? Could a woman ever ride the Tour de France? Or any of the other big Tours? Well, it's been done. Just once, but it's been done.

The woman's name was Alfonsina Strada and she rode the Giro d'Italia in 1924. The stars' teams had fallen out with the organizers and weren't going to ride. The country was going badly and bike sales with it and the factories demanded terms that the organizer, Emilio Colombo, couldn't meet.

The Giro wasn't in the dominant position of the French Tour and, even in its twelfth year, it wasn't strong enough to negotiate. If the big men wanted to ride, they'd do it on the Giro's terms because, the Giro insisted, it could afford nothing better. So the stars shrugged and said they'd go and ride somewhere else and the Giro, needing a field, opened its doors to whichever 90 riders wanted to ride. *La Gazzetta dello Sport* promised to pay their bills, their hotels and for their food. That was all they'd get because, unless they could afford it themselves, they'd have no managers, no masseurs, no mechanics and no team cars.

They wooed them with 600 chickens, 750 kilograms of red meat, 4,800 bananas and 720 eggs. They'd ride a long way to earn that food, but it was better than many Italians got in the 1920s and that and maybe some glory and prizes turned heads. And they'd get to see Italy in an era when few then had seen much beyond their own home.

Alfonsina Strada—a good name because Strada is Italian for "road"—had seen more than most. She was born Alfonsina Morini on March 16, 1891 in Castelfranco Emilia, near Modena. Her bike had allowed her to ride out of the town along the Via Emilia. The town and the road are still there but they've been bypassed now by the A1 *autostrada* to the south.

Alfonsina grew up in the via Moritata in a part of town where animals roamed in the road. Her family, like most of the town, was chronically poor. The legend grew as Alfonsina became famous that her childhood house was little better than a shack, with no windows. She never denied it and she may even have invented it. Along with the idea that no fewer than two dozen people lived there. It was part of the mystique.

Her father worked as a laborer on one-day assignments, taking what work he could. Her mother suckled other women's babies for money. It's probable she was their second child but it's less clear if she had ten siblings of which eight or perhaps all were brothers. No surprise, anyway, that she grew up a tomboy, dressing like them in cloth shirts that, legend again says, were too tight to prevent gossip in a rural Catholic society. And she raced against her brothers on her father's old roadster.

Old people called her "the devil on wheels" and crossed themselves as she passed. Women who might have been inspired to copy decided just the opposite. Exercise for women was harmful. The Almanac for Women in 1923 ruled that sport was not to "force the body to dangerous excesses and ridiculous exaggerations." The sight of women racing men in the 1890s was so shocking that the *Unione Velocipedista Italiana* ended all women's racing in 1894. In short, not only women but much of the country thought Strada an embarrassment.

But her success against her brothers persuaded her to try formal racing. There were no women's races so she said she was a boy, which at about 13 wouldn't have been difficult. She won a live pig, which did wonders for her family. Animals were not just food but currency in a barter society. Her father had paid for his own bike in chickens. The world had still to come to rural Italy. But Alfonsina Morini could go to the world.

By then she was five feet two inches tall, not as short as it is now, "athletic and powerful, crouched low over the handlebars, clad in trademark black wool jersey and black socks with her hair fashionably bobbed." She won nearly all the girls' races and many against boys. In 1909 that brought an invitation to the Grand Prix of St Petersburg in Russia. Nikolas II, the last czar, gave her a gold medal. It's worth remembering that because it overturns the usual telling of the story.

In 1911 she went to Moncalieri, now a southern suburb of Turin, and set an hour record, presumably an Italian one. It can't have been a women's record because she was never credited with her 37.192 kilometers because her performance, remember, was unladylike. So either it was unofficial or she bettered the men's distance. The most likely is that it was unofficial, although the details are hard to find.

At twenty-four her family decided she was to marry, to bring respectability and get her out of the house. She walked the aisle with Luigi Strada, a modern, open-minded and progressive type, another cyclist. His wedding present to her was a new bike. He suggested they move to Milan, where Alfonsina could train on the track while he offered advice. It worked out. Mrs Strada twice rode the Tour of Lombardy, finishing last and thirty-second in 1917—Philippe "Fat Dog" Thys of Belgium won—and twenty-first and ahead of several men in 1918. She also raced in the cities of northern Italy and in Paris.

This is where legend bangs head-on with logic. The story is that Strada wasn't confident she'd be accepted for the Giro and so she gave her name as "Strada, Alfonsin." The absence of a final "o" or "a" to her first name hid whether she was a man or a woman and that was said to be enough to fool the organizer and editor, Enrico Colombo, into accepting her. She was given the number 72 and, assuming the program entry to be a misprint, journalists began writing of her as Alfonsino.

Now, workaday reporters on everyday papers may have been fooled. But how likely is it that Colombo, who made his living from sport and edited one of the world's biggest sports papers and organized one of its biggest races, could have missed a woman who'd ridden the Tour of Lombardy, set some sort of hour record and been given a medal by the czar? Was that not the very stuff his paper reported? How many other Italians received medals from a czar?

How much more likely is it that he worried that his Giro, deprived of big names, would be a flop reflected in poor sales for his paper? That a woman taking part would bring sensation to a dull race? And if he could delay the news until after the start, it would perk up flagging interest if the unknowns he was forced to accept weren't up to the job. Just speculation, of course, but surely more probable than that he didn't know the identity of this rider 72.

Strada dressed for the race like the men, in men's clothing. Some have suggested that that was part of the camouflage. But she'd always been a tomboy and what else was she going to wear for a bike race? She wasn't going to wear a frilly skirt down to her ankles.

For four stages she rode well, 74th on the first day. The hour between her and the rider in front was nothing by the standards of the day. She came 50th of 65 between Genoa and Florence and clung on through Rome as far as Naples. But she was weak. She lost weight, despite the quarter of roast chicken, 250 grams of meat, two ham sandwiches, 100 grams of cookies and 50 grams of chocolate, oranges and apples that she and other riders were given each day. She wasn't sure she was strong enough to finish. And, on the day from l'Aquila to Perugia, the heavens opened, the wind howled, mud turned to treacle and rocks on the road protruded like deadly traps. Her waterproofs, and those of the others, were close to useless. Riders fell. Some abandoned.

Strada came crashing down. Her handlebars snapped and she stood helplessly—no service cars, remember—until a peasant snapped a broomstick to jam it into the jagged hole. She finished outside the time limit, one side of her bars steel and the other broomstick.

The judges wanted to exclude her. But Colombo let her go on for as long as she could last. She was good copy for his newspaper and people stood by the roadside to see her. Colombo paid her hotel bill, gave her money and provided a masseur, all of which suggests his interest from the start had been commercial. He felt rewarded at Fiume next day when his devil finished 25 minutes outside time after 425 kilometers but before a crowd that had waited to see her and carried her on their shoulders as she wept with exhaustion.

"This little lady's popularity has become greater than all the missing champions put together," said one report.

But even so, each night at the hotel, Strada had to wait until the men had had their bath. She wasn't actually in the race. She couldn't take her turn in the single bathroom that most hotels offered before riders who were still in the race to win. She passed the time mending tires.

The further the race went, the more people began looking for her, mobbing her at the finish and reaching out to touch her. "Touch me but keep your fingers off the bike," she'd tell small boys.

The race ended at the Sempione velodrome in Milan on June 1 and Strada with it although not, of course, actually in it. She was cheered as she turned on to the banking. The judges timed her as they had every day. She finished 28 hours behind the winner, Giuseppe Enrici, after 3,613 kilometers. But two men finished behind her. She was given her own lap of honor and she was feted by Benito Mussolini and by the king, Victor Emmanuel.

She never again rode the Giro d'Italia. It's not clear whether she didn't want to or if she was refused. Some say that, the dispute with riders and teams cleared up, Colombo no longer wanted the novelty of a woman in the race, or maybe he worried what the reaction would be from real professionals he had no wish to upset.

She cashed in by performing at circuses and by riding on rollers, judged terribly adventurous by those who'd never tried it. Her husband died and in 1950 she married the muscular sprinter, Carlo Messori, a dapper man who looked every bit a Victorian cad with his mustache twirled up at the ends. When she retired, she opened a bike shop in Milan, where she lived in the via Varesina.

Widowed for the second time in December 1957, Strada lived alone with her Siamese cats, still riding a bike but now in baggy pantaloons.

She was never happy again. She invented a married daughter in Bologna, denying that she was alone in the world. She grew weaker and sold medals and trophies to buy a scarlet Moto Guzzi 500cc motorbike. In September 1959 she rode to the Tre Valli Varesine race, then home in the evening. She got back pleased by the day but complained to her concierge that no one had recognized her.

The concierge heard her kick-start the engine and then a crash. She had knocked it off its stand. She reached to grab it but the weight was too much. She had a heart attack as she and the Moto Guzzi fell to the ground. Someone sent for a car and she was driven to the nearest hospital. But she was dead by the time she arrived. The only woman ever to have ridden one of the three major Tours had left the world at the age of 68.

Few remember her now. But she's not forgotten. Many may wonder at the name but there's a piazza named after her, the Piazzetta Alfonsina Strada, in San Salvatore Monferrato in the Piedmont region. The race passed through there when Strada rode the Giro and her last relatives lived in the town.

Alfonsina Strada

22

Scarlet Legs and Pink Jersey

All big races aim for sensation. But the Giro has a knack for finding it where it hadn't been expected: Charly Gaul, Alfonsina Strada and then...

Passo di Gavia, Italy, June 5, 1988: The days when races sent riders off into the wilderness with little more than an apple and a bottle had long gone. Henri Pélissier, an unpleasant gadfly from France but a man who spoke a lot of modern sense until he was murdered by his lover, put an end to that. What was the point in stages so long, so difficult, that riders survived rather than raced? What was the point in a stage so long that the bunch stayed together for protection and raced only in the last hour?

Henri Desgrange reluctantly saw his point and slowly reduced the length of his races. By the 1980s the grand tours had changed hands and attitudes with them. Where Gaul had been sent into the mountains with a wave and a promise to see him at the finish, the Giro in 1988 spent a long time dithering. The riders were in Chiesa Val Malenco, a ski station grateful for the publicity, around 1,500 meters below the Passo di Gavia, 2,618 meters high, the third highest pass in the Italian Alps. And the problem was that it was snowing, and snowing hard.

Word came down that fresh snow was knee deep at the summit. It was nothing new for the Giro to ride between man-high walls of snow. But the road had always been plowed clean. Fresh snow, like thick sand, is impossible.

Then came fresher word that the road was clear, that it was horribly cold but that it was safe. The truth was somewhere between the two but the organizers and commissaires didn't know which. They went into a huddle to decide what to do, while busybody managers and anyone else keen to get in the act pestered them for news or to offer advice. Close on two decades had passed since the race last went that way and nobody wanted to miss the moment. But…

In order, the stage was canceled, shortened, reinstated, canceled and then brought back to life once more. All this time the riders sat miserably and tried not to scare each other with forecasts of the terrors to come. When the stage did start, they were naturally unhappy. They rode slowly and angrily in the falling flakes and, when they got to a tunnel and some shelter, they stopped and refused to go any further. Tempers were now high. A spokesman was sought for the riders and the case explained: they couldn't go back because there was nowhere to stay and they'd have to go on because that was the only way to reach their hotels that night. If they'd do that, the least the race could do was give first choice of hotel to the teams of the first riders home.

The riders didn't like it but they could suggest nothing better. And nor could they agree among themselves. If they all refused to ride, there'd be no problem. If only some stopped then there'd be trouble from the managers and from those in the team who'd ridden on. And among those in the running for prizes, well, none of those was going to call it a day if the others didn't.

It's surprising how ill-equipped some of the teams were. Mike Neel, the manager of the small 7-Eleven team, sponsored by a chain of American convenience stores, organized a search for ski clothing. He handed out some before the start and more in a bag at the top of the big climb. Others didn't. Nor had the riders thought far ahead. Many were in short sleeves and shorts, the American waif, Andy Hampsten, included. Only when Neel drove up beside him did he get a woolen hat, a pair of waterproof gloves and a small scarf. The snow had been settling on his head.

"I brushed my hair, thinking I was going to wipe some water out, and a big snowball rolled off my head and down my back," he remembered.

The race rode on, grim-faced, staying together over the lesser climbs, then turning left at the Ponte de Legno to start on the southern side of the Gavia, on which all but the hairpins were said to be unpaved.

Les Woodland

Two Dutchmen, Johan van der Velde and Eric Breukink, led with two Italians: Franco Chioccioli and Marco Giovannetti. They were none of them also-rans. Van der Velde, lanky, long-haired and anemic-looking from close to the Belgian border, had been the best young rider in the Tour de France of 1980, only a year after turning professional; Breukink had been the Tour's best young rider in 1988; Chioccioli went on to win the 1991 Giro; and Giovannetti, an Olympic Games medalist in Los Angeles, won the Tour of Spain in 1990.

They were none of them happy. Van der Velde, in orange arm warmers but neither hat nor leggings, got to the top first but couldn't take much more. The road was clear, as the report had said, but it was wet with slush and enough ice had built on his rims that the brakes no longer worked and he refused to ride the most risky parts of the descent, getting off and walking instead. The descent was "deadly dangerous," said the Dutch TV commentator Mart Smeets that day.

That, and waiting at the summit for his team car to bring up warmer clothes, cost him 47 minutes. Chioccioli was no happier. He had the race leader's pink jersey but not the confidence of his manager. Rather than follow him up the Gavia, he had stayed behind Flavio Giupponi. Chioccioli shivered and slithered, his morale shattered and his team unable to help.

The one man to profit was Hampsten. Nobody had seen him as a threat for the overall Giro, although he'd won a stage in 1985 and twice won the Tour de Suisse. His talent was as a climber, not at winning long stage races. Yet that day he was in fifth place, 78 seconds behind the leader.

He rode, though, for the inexperienced and under-equipped 7-Eleven team, largely American and offering more enthusiasm than experience. The bunch mocked it as Team Slurpee, after a frozen drink that 7-Eleven sold. Experienced riders ordered them to stay at the back so they could knock each other off but nobody else.

Hampsten had been tipped off by a friend, Gianni Motta, who had won the Giro in 1966. He had taken to the Americans. He knew the Gavia and he knew nobody had raced over it for nearly 20 years. He had, he said, and he knew that riders and managers were underestimating it. Hampsten was a talented climber. He could make something of it. He could win the Giro. Hampsten remembered he smiled and said: "'That's really nice of you to say so', but he was, like, 'No, I'm serious.'"

Motta protested. "These guys, they think it's just another climb."

In that, anyway, the Americans were better prepared than most. The family of their doctor, Max Testa, had rented a ski chalet at Bormio, on the other side of the Gavia and the town where the stage would finish.

Davis Phinney says in his autobiography: "For years, Max had been wearing us out with talk of this obscene climb, this glorified goat track, with its ominous headstones—memorials to loved ones who had left the road, and this earth, in that order. He spoke of the back side of the mountain, a perpetually chilled valley seldom penetrated by the sun."

Testa had also spoken of a point at which the road would narrow to a single lane as it passed through a bunch of pines before becoming unsurfaced and then, as a sign would point out, rearing to 16 percent.

Hampsten recalled: "All my competitors were watching me. They knew I was going to attack." And he attacked, crossing the summit and starting the descent, as scared as everyone of frozen snow and black ice. "I kept my Neoprene gloves on the whole time because I figured that if my fingers went numb, I'd never get them back. At the top I struggled into a plastic rain jacket and that's when Breukink caught me. On the descent I had just one gear because the thing was starting to freeze, so I feathered the brakes all the way down and stayed in 53×14.

"The descent was a maddening number of turns and hairpins. I remember thinking: 'Never look down, never look down.'" But he did look down and he felt horrified that his legs were red from the cold and that his shins had a length of ice. "I was looking for road signs and marshals. Everything was fairly blurred together. I couldn't look for potholes, rocks, or obstacles. I was only concentrating on figuring out what was a curve and what was a gentle bend. And I was only putting on the brakes if it was a curve."

Breukink, whom he'd passed, was still less comfortable and took his feet off the pedals several times to keep his balance. He reached Hampsten before the finish in Bormio, from where a road also leaves to climb the Stelvio to the Austrian border, then pushed on.

He came by so fast on Hampsten's right, that the American couldn't react. Hampsten lifted himself out of the saddle, made an effort, then let the Dutchman go. Breukink would take the stage but Hampsten was going to lead the Giro, the first American in the leader's jersey of that race. Not that Breukink was confident; he looked repeatedly over his shoulder for a glimpse of the man he'd just passed. He rode the rise to the finish on his larger chainring, powering along out of the saddle, hands on the drops of the bars, then lifted both hands in a victory salute above his sodden blue Panasonic jersey.

Hampsten followed 7 seconds later.

Breukink remembered: "It was once in a lifetime you have a stage like that. At the top, it was really a major blizzard. It was difficult to see. The snowfall was very heavy. On the downhill, you were really alone, because you didn't see a car behind, there were no fans on the road, you couldn't see anything in front of you. I've never been so cold in my career. Even one hour and one and a half hours after the stage, you were still shivering."

Hampsten said: "After the race I was just an emotional ruin. I remember I went up to the podium to try to do the TV interview and I just left. I couldn't handle it. I went back to the car and hyperventilated—the car was nice and hot—and sat there. Emotionally I was on fire. I cried. I dried myself off a little bit and put on some more clothes. And after ten minutes I was okay."

Next morning, *La Gazzetta dello Sport* wrote of a "day the big men cried."

Hampsten kept his new pink jersey all the way to the Vittorio Veneto. He retired in 1997 and lives some of the year in Italy, where he and his wife, Linda, restored a farmhouse in Tuscany. There, he runs a bike-touring company. A fairly gentle one, he admits.

"I teach people about the four-course lunch. So many of my clients are used to grabbing a sandwich on the go, but when you're in Italy, you don't do that. It's great watching the Type A personalities. It's usually about the second or third day when they say: 'Wow! I get it. I'll have some wine with my lunch.'"

He also said: "When I went back to the Gavia with a friend, I realized there are dozens of turns on the descent that I really don't remember, nor do I fully understand how I got down them at all."

Johan van der Velde retired in 1988, was jailed for theft—he acknowledges being a kleptomaniac and friends had to check what was missing each time he visited them—to support his drugs and gambling. He was addicted to amphetamine and began hospital treatment to cure him.

Erik Breukink came third in the 1990 Tour de France and, after retiring in 1997, he became a team manager and television commentator.

23

Around and Round

Now, of course, you wonder that anyone went to watch. Who'd pay to see cyclists riding round and round until they fell asleep? But they did—and it created the sensation of winter six-day racing.

London, England, November 24, 1878: On the British Monopoly board, Islington is one of the cheaper squares. It was all it merited when the game reached London in 1935. Islington, in northern inner London, has gone up in the world since then but there's still a mixture of shabby houses and smart addresses to walk through on your way to the Business Design Centre.

It used to be called the Agricultural Hall and it illustrates how the area has changed. In the 1860s it was near enough to the country-side that cattle could be driven through its roads to agricultural shows that could draw 135,000 visitors. The hall was available to anyone who wanted to hire it and it was big enough for circuses, military band concerts, even chariot races. At one exhibition, a crocodile escaped and alarmed everyone with its running speed—they can get to 30 miles per hour—as visitors fled. In 1864 a keeper was pushing straw into a cage of lions when one grabbed his arm and the rest moved in for a bite of their own. "It was not," a newspaper reported, "until the brutes were nearly blinded with the blows inflicted on their eyes that they were induced to relinquish their grip."

One of the oddest events there was a walking marathon. An American, Edward Payson-Weston, and an Irishman, Daniel O'Leary, bet each other £500 that each would be the first to walk 500 miles. They were only 22 miles apart after 135 hours, "only" in this case being relative, so they declared it a draw and set off again to see who'd drop first. Weston did and O'Leary went home with the money.

Later there came a walking race with 23 on the tiny track at the same time, and either life was quieter then or the idea of excitement was different because the turnstiles admitted 20,000 people. And from that came the idea of a bike race. If so many would pay to see a race at walking speed, thought a couple of long-distance road riders called Fox and Etherington from the Temple Bicycle Club, imagine the profit in putting cyclists on the track. A tired walker just gets a chair and sits down; tired cyclists crash and bring down everyone else as well. They did that a lot but Fox and Etherington stopped its happening too often—their riders were on high-wheeled penny-farthings, remember, rather than far more stable chain-driven bikes, which weren't invented until the following year—by insisting riders spend 18 hours off the track each night.

The race was to be run under Wolverhampton rules, riders were told, a phrase that came from the domination of cycling by the Midland city's tracks, and which went into detail about the way riders were to overtake and what the judges should do if they smelled corruption.

The *Islington Gazette*, which missed announcing the event, caught up afterward. "A bicycle race was commenced at the Agricultural Hall, on Monday last, for which £500 is offered in prizes for a six days' competition, the money to be allocated thus: £100 for the first man, £25 for the second, £15 for the third, and £10 for the fourth."

The promoters were hedging their bets: that was a lot less than for the International Pedestrian Match Championship of the World, which had a first prize of £500 and half the gate money. It was enough, though, to attract Bill Cann, billed as the Long Distance Champion of the North because he came from Sheffield, which is only the North in the eyes of a Londoner, and a prominent Frenchman called Charles Terront.

Terront, being foreign and, still worse, French, was viewed with suspicion by the rest. He was riding in London because his manager was Herbert Duncan, the Englishman in Paris who'd helped bring about the Buffalo track there.

For all that the home riders disliked each other, they disliked Terront even more. They went as far as handing him a bouquet of flowers, the sort of thing they were sure would appeal to a Frenchman, which they'd sprinkled with sleeping powder. Politeness would commit him to sniffing it, they thought.

Terront hadn't fallen with the last rain, as the French say, and he did no such thing. He also took to leaving the stadium to eat at a café in the street rather than risk his food being adulterated. That meant he spent more time away from the race than he wanted but he would at least finish it if he could.

Most of the British riders were solid working-class lads, laborers, factory workers, unknown within their fledgling sport let alone outside it. Terront, on the other hand, was France's first sports star. Robert Penn wrote that he had "riches, a memoir published in his lifetime, many female admirers and a reserved seat at the Opéra in Paris. His success made him an icon for successive generations of working-class Frenchmen who sought the mansion on the hill through cycle racing."

In 1891 Terront won the first Paris–Brest–Paris race, after 71 hours and attempts to sabotage his bike. He had learned a lot from the treachery of those he rode with in London.

There were twelve starters that day in 1878 and they saw no point in rushing to the track for the start. If they were going to race for six days then another hour or so would make no difference. They'd join in when they wanted, riding between ornate columns and beneath balustrades. It was going to be hard going: pace the available area now and it works out at around 35 by 130 meters. The track was advertised as seven and a half laps to a mile, or 234.7 yards or 214.6 meters round, but there's little reason to think it was measured that accurately. That puts the result in doubt, at least so far as the distance was concerned, but that hardly matters because there was a winner and the crowd got enough sensation to be pleased. Even if it was pleased easily.

There's an idea of how it looked from a report in *The Field*: "The arena, where the horses have been in the habit of displaying themselves, is boarded over as evenly as the floor of a dancing saloon. At each corner of the inclosure [sic] a huge tub of flowers is placed." That was an earlier circuit, laid for anyone to use, but the six-day track may not have been that different.

The *Islington Gazette* said crashes were frequent but showed that the action was less so: "At seven o'clock Markham fell heavily and ten minutes later the Frenchman came on the track and rattled away in fine style, he at the time being seventeen miles and a half behind the leader, Phillips. The men kept well together for some time after this, but at twenty minutes past nine Markham again came to grief, Andrews falling over him. About half an hour afterward Phillips and White fell heavily, and in a short time Phillips had to give up all idea of participating further in the contest, his example being followed by Markham after he had completed 78 miles.

"Just before five o'clock Stanton took some refreshment whilst riding and in throwing the vessel back to his attendant he swerved slightly, and Evans being close on him a collision occurred, both coming down heavily."

By the end, word had spread outside London and even the *Liverpool Mercury* was interested. Up to a point, anyway.

"On Saturday night the match was concluded in favour of Cann, who since the retirement of Stanton from the contest, had held the lead. Nothing of importance occurred during the day, the most noteworthy event being the completion of 1,000 miles by Cann at forty-two minutes past eleven in the morning, Edlin completing the same distance at thirty-one minutes past three in the afternoon. At seven minutes to eleven, the competition was concluded."

Bill Cann, the winner, may have been Long Distance Champion of the North, whatever that may have meant beyond pure publicity blurb, but he'd done no training for London. Romance says Terront should have won after all the shenanigans he'd had to overcome, but he didn't. He came fifth of the seven who finished, ending 160.5 miles behind the winner. Much of that must have come from having to run from the stadium to eat at a café.

Fox and Etherington presumably made a profit, especially with the betting there, even if they at first had to lower the price of tickets. But *The Field* was sniffy: "Fat cattle, monster balls, popular concerts and horse shows have followed in rapid succession and now a 'bicycle race' is the object of public interest.... There is no doubt that the spectacle called a race was got up with a sole view to profit, and in all probability, it answered excellently well but whether such an exhibition will prove a permanent source of profit we will not venture to predict."

Others certainly looked and sniffed money. There were more races in Britain and, in America, an Englishman called Tom Eck thought he too should have a go. He organized a six-day race, ten hours a day, in Minneapolis in 1887. There'd been other long races, just as there had in Britain, but Islington and Minneapolis were the first in each country to have no scheduled stops.

Encouraged by what must have been a profitable venture, he aimed higher in 1891 and booked Madison Square Garden, in New York. There, Bill "Plugger" Martin rode 2,360 kilometers in 142 hours of racing. It proved a sensation. Just as six-day racing died in Britain, as *The Field* had predicted, it boomed across the ocean. Americans, it seemed, were even keener to see spectacle and gore.

It was an era which brought dance marathons and pole squatting. Riders rode in a trance, some colorfully said to have gone temporarily crazy. But the entrants insisted because there was money in it. The Irishman, Teddy Hale, won $5,000 for winning in 1896 and thought it worth it even though he was "like a ghost, his face as white as a corpse, his eyes no longer visible because they'd retreated into his skull."

The six-days were week-long doping laboratories and the spectacle on the track showed it. The *New York Times* said. "Riders go queer in their heads and strain their powers until their faces become hideous with the tortures that rack them…. [It is] not sport, it is brutality…. It is likely some of them will never recover from the strain."

It was the sign for the law to act. Six-day races would be allowed but only if those taking part spent half the day off the track. That, lawyers felt, would kill the spectacle and the phenomenon would die of itself. Nobody could be accused of banning a sport which attracted thousands, gates increasing with each report of a rider going "queer in the head."

But that was to reckon without the ingenuity of men who saw their livelihood threatened, specifically Bill Brady, who promoted plays on Broadway and managed boxers as well as organizing bike races. Riders may have to spend half the day off the track but that didn't mean there could be no racing in the other twelve hours. Put riders into teams of two and one could sleep and the other ride. And so speeds went up, the grisly side of the sport went down, and the spectacle brought in crowds bigger than ever, including show business stars and millionaires who flamboyantly offered huge bonuses whenever the action flagged.

And what ended the boom? Well, not lack of enthusiasm, that's for sure. The public wanted it. But the Depression meant they couldn't afford it. Not in enough numbers, anyway. Riders chugged round to half-empty and once even to entirely empty stadiums. The sport which had once entranced a nation never returned to the USA.

It survived in Europe, helped by the move to racing only in the evenings and weekday afternoons that was pioneered in London in 1967. But the days when the stars of the Tour de France rode six-days to cash in on their fame are long past. Six-day riders now are track specialists, faster than the roadmen who preceded them, but—just as at Islington—their names not much known within the sport let alone outside it.

Doesn't stop its being a heck of a night out, though, a six-day race.

THE SIX DAYS' PEDESTRIAN RACE AT THE AGRICULTURAL HALL, ISLINGTON

Above and next page, contemporary illustrations of early 6-Days, both walking and riding

Les Woodland

THE LONG-DISTANCE BICYCLE CHAMPIONS AT THE AGRICULTURAL HALL.

[SEE "SPORTS AND PASTIMES."]

24

Fall of a Handsome Man

Triumph and tragedy follow each other so swiftly. But rarely so swiftly, so mysteriously as with the Pedaler of Charm.

Agen, France, July 15, 1951: He was one of those men you felt you knew, knew you wanted to know. He was blond, handsome and intelligent. Where others glared only at the wheel ahead, he looked around at the countryside and took an interest in old buildings. He'd been known to reach into his pocket at the end of races, sometimes before he'd crossed the line, and take out a comb and a sponge soaked in eau de cologne to end his working day with elegance. And now and then he blew kisses to pretty girls who turned out to watch him pass.

Hugo Koblet seemed a man of permanent psychological poise, smooth in personality and style. René de Latour said of him, perhaps a little too unctuously: "Koblet had not an enemy at all. His ready and kindly smile came from deep down inside, and one knew from the start that this was a genuine, gentle man with a natural warmth of character." Even in an era when journalists rarely spoke ill of anyone in cycling, that's quite a tribute.

More, de Latour added: "Hugo Koblet was the quintessence of style. Even when the battle was at its fiercest, his pedaling was beautifully smooth. To see him in action was a 'make believe' that cycling wasn't really hard at all."

And yet the man's most glamorous moment wasn't a beginning: it was the start of the end. Within a year he would be a shadow of himself and a little later he'd die in an unexplained car crash, his life a mess of debt and riddle.

There have always been a handful of Swiss riders at the top of world cycling. In the 1950s, they both had the initial K: Ferdi Kübler and Hugo Koblet. Other than they both spoke German—Koblet therefore rhymes with goblet—there was no comparison. Kübler was dramatic, extravagant, rough and rowdy, fury on his bike. Koblet was elegance dispensed with honey. Kübler relived each day's race for hours in a torrent of inelegant words. Koblet preferred to lie in a bath with a radio and a newspaper. The singer, Jacques Grello, referred to him once as *le pédaleur de charme*, and because it was close to the truth, the name stuck.

No surprise, then, that they didn't always get on and that their rivalry in a small land brought an unusual streak of cruelty. Kübler tells of a moment on the San Bernardino pass during the Tour of Switzerland. Kübler had no water. Koblet reached for his own bottle, made to pass it to his rival, then tipped the contents on the road with a laugh.

"A folly of youth," Kübler said much later, a folly for which Koblet had the grace to apologize.

Often Koblet could be more subtle. The Frenchman, François Mahé, was giving him a hard time in the mountains of the Tour of Switzerland in 1951. Unable to fight him any other way, Koblet took his hands off the bars, pulled out a comb and began attending to his hair. Mahé was so demoralized that he gave up and dropped back.

Koblet's last glory came on the eleventh stage of the 1951 Tour de France in a year of short stages that showed the head organizer, Jacques Goddet, was moving from the epic era to the modern. From Brive on the edge of the Massif Central, to Agen, on the river Garonne, was 177 kilometers. Of those 177, rider number three, darkened by the sun, as smooth as Anquetil, rode alone for 135. He eased away on a small hill and defied the greatest names to make any impression.

The historians Patrick Fillon and Laurent Réveilhac wrote: "Imagine the Italian team, with Fausto Coppi, Gino Bartali and even Fiorenzo Magni (despite a broken elbow); the French team with Louison Bobet, Raphaël Géminiani, Pierre Barbotin, Lucien Teisseire; individuals like the Belgian, Stan Ockers, the Dutchmen Wout Wagtmans and Wim van Est, the Frenchman, Jean Robic, all united to avoid an

Les Woodland

unbelievable assault on their pride, relaying each other without the slightest easing and seeing, with rage and humiliation, that they were making no impression on the Swiss metronome. And worse, he sometimes even gained on them."

Koblet wore the red jersey of Switzerland, with a collar, the Swiss white cross on his chest, and a spare tire looped round his neck and back. On his left arm, just below his elbow, he had looped a pair of aviator's goggles, which had become his trademark. He had won the Giro the previous year, the first foreigner to manage it, a humiliation that the Italian Press didn't take kindly. The man whom Italy *thought* should have won it, Fausto Coppi, had crashed and he already knew he wasn't going to win the Tour either. The death of his brother, Serse, had hit him badly and he was in prolonged mourning.

At first, nobody took Koblet seriously. He could be left out there to die slowly and there was no need to waste energy on chasing. This was only a bridging stage, between one set of mountains and the next. The Pyrenees were just ahead and it was there the race would be decided, not on a road to a city known for its prunes but little else.

Legend says the bunch chased immediately. But it didn't. It was only when Koblet got to four minutes that the alarm sounded.

Pierre Chany recalled: "That Koblet achieved a real exploit, I don't contest. It was a formidable break. But don't tell me, even if it spoils the legend, that all the riders behind him had their foot hard on the floor [were going flat out] straight away. The truth is that the Italians didn't chase immediately. Seeing the Italians weren't chasing, Bobet kept something in reserve. Géminiani didn't respond straight away either. Do you really think that Koblet could have stayed out there for 135 kilometers if Coppi, Bartali, Magni, Bobet, Géminani, Robic, van Est, Brankart and Ockers had really been taking turns chasing? No, impossible!"

Chany was there on a motorbike, watching first the bunch and then Koblet, going backwards and forwards between the two. And he was there when the bunch finally took Koblet seriously.

"What *is* true," he said, "was that the climax, spread over two hours, was grandiose. Coppi, Bartali, Bobet and all the others I mentioned, more and more nervous about what was happening, relayed each other faster and faster. And at the same time, but two minutes ahead of them,

Koblet was advancing like a metronome. He wasn't losing anything. He was advancing! It was chaos! And what an athlete! Every turn of the pedal was strong and perfect."

Koblet finished 2 minutes 35 seconds ahead of this angry, red-faced mob, on top of which he collected a one-minute bonus. And next day, a day off in Agen, he tucked into ham, french fries and mayonnaise. When someone suggested it wasn't a meal that cyclists usually allowed themselves, he said: "Allowed? *Everything's* allowed after yesterday!"

But why go into an attack which nobody else thought could succeed? Well, it's true that the best time to make an impression is when the others would rather not race. Brian Robinson showed that in 1959 when the race was so sleepy that it let him win by more than twenty minutes.

But Robinson was no threat. Only a rule that any rider in the first ten couldn't be thrown out had saved him from being eliminated when he finished outside the time limit with stomach cramp. He lost so much time that day that even allowing him twenty minutes made him no risk. Koblet, on the other hand, was a *client*. But why make that effort just before some of the hardest days of the race?

One of the most colorful explanations, not often cited, holds that Koblet was in pain from haemorrhoids. He'd called in a doctor at Brive in the hope of a solution. Instead, the *toubib* told him only an operation could cure him. And that meant the end of the Tour. Another doctor was called and he had an answer: a cream of aspirin and cocaine, the first to lessen the inflation and the second to numb the pain. It wouldn't last long but, cocaine being cocaine, he'd feel exhilarated while it lasted. Everything would be possible.

And so, to believe that story, Koblet was on a cocaine high. And drugs were nothing new to cycling and least of all to Koblet. The film of his life, *Hugo Koblet: Pédaleur de Charme*, makes no bones. His decline was due to "doping abuse." And the decline came suddenly. In 1950 he won the Giro, with five stages and the mountain prize; in 1951 he held off the world from Brive to Agen; and in 1952 he abandoned the Tour of Switzerland and the Tour de France, complaining of a mysterious infection. His blood lacked red corpuscles yet the medicine he took sent him to sleep. His kidneys hurt.

By 1953 he struggled in the mountains. Now and then he showed hope but more often he slid off the back.

"He could be seen crying on his bike," said Philippe Brunel.

Jean Bobet, brother of Louison, lamented: "We saw him in 1953 getting an odd sickness above 2,000 meters, then above 1,000 meters. We saw him unable to get over even the tiniest hill and we were witnesses to his disappearance. His face grew older and his personality sombre."

He could have ridden a winter of six-days, where he was one of the most popular and best paid stars. But instead he married a beautiful 22-year-old model, Sonja Bühl. Just when he most needed money, he spent it wildly. Not only on Sonja but on any girl who took his fancy, and there were many of them. Now the tax people were also after him. Koblet began to see the end. "I'm not going to live to be old," he told his friend and former team manager, Alex Burtin. "I wasn't made to grow old, so I have to profit from it now."

He raced a bit longer and then went to South America to represent Pirelli and Alfa Romeo. It didn't work. He came home depressed and bitter. His marriage began to fall apart. He moved into an apartment next to a gas station that a fuel company let him run through kindness and appreciation of what once he had been. It stood close to the Oerlikon bike track where he had first raced.

On November 6, 1954, he got into his white Alfa Romeo and began driving. An attempt to get back with Sonja had failed. He drove towards nearby Möntchaltorf. The road was dry and Koblet pressed the pedal as he reached the hill at Esslingen. Nobody knows for sure what happened next. A carpenter who lived there, Emile Isler, said he saw Koblet slow after passing a tree, turn, pass it a second time, turn again and then drive into it.

The police reckoned he had been driving at 120 kilometers per hour, some say faster. They found him in the wreckage, still alive but unconscious and with his right foot torn off. He died in Uster hospital four days later.

Sonja met Isler and asked his opinion. For him, Koblet had committed suicide. Others have different opinions but all the versions end the same way, with Koblet dead at the wheel. The law gave Sonja the right to all that he left. But she declined, because to accept would mean having to settle his many debts as well.

Koblet was only 39. The doctor who operated on him was called Kübler. And the pear tree against which Koblet crashed was later cut down. Because it produced so little fruit.

The beautiful Hugo Koblet

Les Woodland

25

Forgotten Pain

The story of how a Tour de France can be won, can change hands by just 8 seconds after 3,000 kilometers of racing, is well known. The loser was devastated—but it brought him a new life.

Paris, France, July 23, 1989: Laurent Fignon was the master of the educational anecdote. Why, for instance, did riders keep pedaling into the back of a vast pile-up that even juniors and novices could see? How did the field tolerate the boredom on the long, flat days down the Atlantic coast?

Fignon was full of stories that brought questions to life, the sort of question you might not have thought to ask but were glad to have answered.

The answer to the first is that riders keep heading for the mayhem and a certain fall because they can't see beyond the three or four riders ahead of them. "And when the helicopters are low over you, you can't hear the brakes or the sound of crashing, so the first thing you know, you're in the pile-up yourself and wondering how it happened."

And the second?

"I remember one day I was riding at the front with the others and we were bored as heck on the long flat roads, just riding along, when we started having a competition to see whose team car would get up to us fastest. So one by one we'd put our hand up and the directors in the red car would radio that we wanted the car, and we'd say: 'Oh, Cyrille Guimard, 22 seconds. Not bad. Now you have a go.'"

It may be that Laurent Fignon would have got his commentating job on French television because nobody readily turns down an expert with that experience. That, for example, is why stations took on Laurent Jalabert and, less successfully, Richard Virenque. But Fignon's case was special because he had never been deeply popular with French spectators. Like Jacques Anquetil before him, he was rarely demonstrative. If anything, his round, John Lennon glasses and his long, often severe face, brought memories of your most disapproving schoolteacher. Only the ponytail softened the image of an *intello*, an intellectual in a sport in which it doesn't always pay to be one.

Fignon's nickname, The Professor, came from that sour-faced image and, more flattering, because he was a good deal brighter and better educated than many who rode with him. It's been a while since boys from humble backgrounds chose cycling, as others before them had turned to cycling, as a way to escape a life in the fields, the mines or a factory. But it remains the case that cycling is still no Sorbonne on wheels. One account said he was the only French rider in the Tour of 1989 to have passed his *baccalaureate*, the series of examinations which open the way to a university education and in which it's obligatory to pass the first: philosophy. Fignon had that superior education: he studied to be a vet. And he collected old books, especially Hetzels.

Of that day in the Champs-Elysées when he lost the Tour de France to Greg LeMond by 8 seconds, he said: "To tell you the truth, there are many things my mind has blocked out. At the finish, for instance. The only thing I remember now is that, at the moment I collapsed on the ground after crossing the line, I couldn't believe that I could have lost. Everything else has been erased, and perhaps it's best that way."

He complained at the time that his whole career, with its two Tours de France, the Giro d'Italia, two Milan–San Remos and the Flèche Wallonne, had been reduced in the public memory to...coming second in the Tour de France on the day it reached Paris.

That was the afternoon when the last stage was a time-trial over 24.5 kilometers from Versailles in the west to the Champs-Elysées in the center of Paris. Fignon was the race leader and favorite to win. Tradition held that the yellow jersey wasn't attacked on his day of glory, but tradition was impossible in a time-trial. Gloves were off.

So much off that his challenger, the American, LeMond, kitted his bike with what looked unfamiliar then but are now known widely as tri-bars. They'd first seen life in triathlons, which explains the name, and looked so odd at first that *Cycling* in Britain misunderstood and took them for aids to relaxation, for which the softy triathletes were mocked.

The time-trial into Paris was the third of the race and only LeMond had tri-bars, which gave a more streamlined position. He had used them in the other two as well. Which brought two problems. The first was that they broke an international rule on how much contact a rider could have with his bike and which stipulated just one conventional handlebar. The second was that the race referees, the commissaires, had never had to apply the rule and they missed it.

Thierry Cazeneuve remembered: "From the first minute of racing, LeMond was the better. Very bunched up on his machine, his head wrapped in an aerodynamic helmet, elbows tucked in and his hands grasping the bands of his bars, he could use all the power he had. With each turn of the pedals he leaped more than nine meters, and each of these fantastic leaps followed the one before in perfect harmony. By comparison, Laurent Fignon looked clumsy, his body too raised, and he clearly couldn't roll his big gear. Nevertheless he finished third, 58 seconds behind LeMond and 25 behind his young friend, Thierry Marie. But he had lost the Tour by 8 seconds. What drama."

The streamlined bars gave LeMond four or five seconds' advantage in each kilometer, according to Frédéric Grappe, a prominent sports scientist. And that was enough to take him from second place and, by 8 seconds, into the final yellow jersey. The picture of LeMond's uninhibited yelp of joy as he stood by the line to wait for Fignon, the only rider to start after him, at two minutes, is one of cycling's classics. It occupied half of *L'Équipe*'s front page beneath the single word *Inoubliable!*—Unforgettable.

Another factor was that streamlined helmet. Those were also little known at the time and Fignon rode instead in the traditional helmet of leather bars now widely dismissed as a hairnet, his blond ponytail flowing behind him.

Fignon said: "Cyrille told me he'd give me the time differences. I started normally and straight away I'd lost 2 seconds in a kilometer. I accelerated, I went flat out, flat out, and it was still the same. And when Cyrille stopped giving me the time gaps, I understood. But I still kept going flat out. What else was I supposed to do?"

Cazeneuve wrote: "Now consider the other scene: Laurent Fignon crossed the line and collapsed to the ground to cry for a long time, and in silence, huddled up on himself, oblivious to the commotion. The only thing that brought him out of his nightmare, and then only after a long time, was the loving hand of Nathalie, his wife."

That day Fignon rode the fastest time-trial of his career, even with a urinary infection that made it painful to sit and restricted the time he could warm up on rollers before the start. But the bewilderment, the misery, never turned to bitterness. "It's true, yes, that if LeMond didn't have those bars, I'd have won the Tour by more than two minutes. It turns out that a commissaire let him start with them. I see that more as an individual error than an injustice. Frankly, I've had worse injustices and more painful ones.

"And despite it all, I rode at 52 kilometers per hour that day. I can't see that I could have done better, although, yes, I'd have won if I'd had those bars."

L'Équipe asked him in 2004 if he often thought of that day. He said: "I can't do otherwise, because people talk to me about it every day. They get the gap wrong—some say 9 seconds, 6, 5—but they talk about it. The fact that I'm still around [at races, on television] twenty years later is because that defeat is stronger in the public memory than my victories."

Cyrille Guimard, who had both riders in his team from 1982 to 1984, said: "Greg was a fighter, with this ability to surpass himself in the biggest races. Laurent had a very assertive nature, which you could see in the way he refused to play to the public that cheered him. People saw him as haughty."

Fignon agreed that he'd never courted affection. "Only winning interests me," he told an interviewer. "I had to turn down interviews, not give autographs, but I always did it politely."

He did, though, spit at a television cameraman that year, on the train going to Paris for the time-trial. He didn't like a station called Canal 5, which he judged sensational. "I was having a hard time with my medical problem and I was concerned, worried, and they never stopped hassling me with their camera. And so, yes, I reacted. The guy started a court case against me but the judge ruled that it was all part of the risks of his trade."

In 1988 and off the back of the Tour, he flung water at reporters he thought were taking an indecent interest. The Tour fined him 1,000 francs.

Now he stood on the podium, publicly humbled, his face turned to the ground. That day in Paris was the beginning of the end. He never completely recovered and he never won a big race again. What he *did* win was hearts, in a way the similarly cold Anquetil never did.

He was helped, too, by business failures. Word had it that he put his own money into buying the rights to Paris–Nice from Josette Leulliot, who had inherited them from her father. She hadn't made a success of it and Fignon thought that he could. It was June, 1999, and he had just turned forty.

"In the world of cycling, there are hundreds of guys looking for a team to ride for, but how many do you know who have invested the money they earned back into the sport?", he asked. He said, too, that doors opened for him at potential sponsors but that one company president had said: "I know you; you're that man who lost the Tour de France by 8 seconds."

"No, I'm not," Fignon said, as he was so often been forced to say, "I'm the man who won it twice."

He ran Paris–Nice in the name of Laurent Fignon Organisation, from his home at St-Maurice, 200 meters outside the Paris postal area. It didn't work out and the ASO, the company behind the Tour de France, took over instead.

In 2010 he knew he had cancer. He already had an appointment to speak to *Paris-Match*, what the French call a "people" magazine. And because he was open about it, insisting there was nothing shameful about cancer, *Paris-Match* printed the story and messages arrived at St-Maurice from around the world. Pleasing for him but annoying for a man who never liked writing text messages or using e-mail.

Lance Armstrong, himself a cancer patient in the past, suggested tests in New York. Fignon flew there, only to be confirmed as having stomach cancer. He and Armstrong were due to be in the Alps, where Armstrong was training, to meet another photographer from *Paris-Match*, the cancer survivor and the cancer sufferer together. It never happened. Fignon needed another operation.

"I'm not scared of death," he said. "I just don't fancy it."

He died on August 31, 2010, just fifty.

26

Drama in the Deluge

He was the swashbuckler of his time, a man who saw himself as a pirate even if he was no taller than Peter Pan. And even though he didn't live for ever.

Les Deux Alpes, France, July 27, 1998: Michel Bloch wrote: "Marco Pantani had everything: panache, talent and style. The public loved him. He was the great champion of the second half of the 1990s."

The little bald Italian, with unstuck ears and the sort of face you find on a marionette, came to the Tour de France in 1998 in the shadow of the race's greatest scandal. A Belgian soigneur with a long face and hollow cheeks had been found at an unexpected customs post to be carrying enough drugs to dope a regiment. Willy Voet on July 8 was on his way from Belgium with a plan to drive to a ferry port in France, then across England and Wales to take another ferry to Ireland. There he would deliver the drugs to the Festina team as it waited to start the Tour de France in Dublin. It was to be one of those rare Tours that would finish in August, and for a long time there was doubt that it would finish at all.

Distress and alarm spread through the race and it was already in a nervous state when more French police became involved, raiding riders' hotels and finding drugs at that of the Dutch team, TVM. By then many riders had already left the race. The rest sat down on the road next day and went on strike to protest against police action which they judged heavy-handed. Pantani sat cross-legged, a blue bandanna on his forehead and a lost, even vacant look on his face.

By the last days of the race, barely 100 riders were left racing and the entire Festina team had been expelled. Jan Ullrich, the German who had won the previous year and who was himself embroiled in doping allegations later, was leading the race once more. Pantani wanted to lead instead, but his opportunities were fewer. Above all, he was too lightly built to challenge the solid German on the flat or even on minor hills. There were only two mountain stages left and he had to risk all and win or blow.

Ullrich knew he was at risk in the Alps but he didn't have to worry deeply. He was a solid climber, although a grovelling one as he slogged a gear higher than looked comfortable. His style wasn't to leap away but to hold his pace until he wore his rivals into exhaustion. On top of that, Pantani was ten places down, always a threat but by now a footnote to an animated Tour. He had lost a lot of time in the time-trial in the Corrèze, the hilly, poor and sparsely populated region of the central west. He tried to attack Ullrich in the Pyrenees but neither won the stage nor made much impression. He took 20 seconds from the German but still had four minutes to make up. Much of that he picked up on the plateau de Beille, moving to fourth and on the last climb catching the unhappy Swiss, Roland Meier, who thought he'd built enough lead to be invincible. So now Ullrich had to take Pantani more seriously.

That morning dawned foggy. It dawned wet. Incessant, icy rain. The day barely dawned at all. As Feargal McKay wrote: "It was one of those days when you look out the window and just want to go back to bed. The sort of cold, gray, drizzling day when you hate the weather for not having the courage to either piss down or piss off." Or, as another writer put it: "It felt like forty years ago. All it needed was for Charly Gaul to come surging through it all to win. It was the day that Marco sensed would be his moment of personal glory. Everything was too sombre and dusk-like for legend *not* to be created."

The stage had three big climbs. It crossed the col de la Croix-de-Fer (Iron Cross pass) and then the Galibier, from the Télégraphe side. That done, it finished at the station of Les Deux Alpes. If Pantani needed a hint, it came in *Dauphiné Libéré*. "It's today or never", it said on its front page as riders woke with the thought that in a few hours they'd be riding the north side, the more difficult, of the Galibier.

Pantani wasn't sure. Normally he attacked on the last col of the day. But this was a special case and he was prepared to go earlier, to crack

Ullrich then or later. The trouble was that he didn't know the mountain well enough, not that side, to know where to attack. Nor could he speak French to ask any of the locals. He put the question to Alfredo Martini, the national team manager, who was there to watch. And Martini went to Charly Mottet, the French climber who'd become assistant director with the Tour. Mottet was well respected in Italy.

Mottet suggested the suddenly steep section, with its hairpins, at Plan-Lachat. It's easier now than it used to be after the building of a new road but it's still horribly hard. Pantani followed him to the letter. Six kilometers before the top, where the scenery is at its grandest, he accelerated repeatedly in the way that only true climbers can. He'd attack out of the saddle and ease up, attack while staying in the saddle, then rise to attack *en danseuse* all over again.

Luc Leblanc tried to follow and Pantani even freewheeled briefly to let him catch up, to help him in some way. But both men hoped for too much. Pantani despaired of his company and went off alone. Ullrich was confused. The actor hadn't kept to the script. Ullrich had made the normally safe bet that Pantani would wait for the last climb. And what he gained there, Ullrich could take back in the last time-trial. Now not only did he see clearly for the first time just how ambitious the Italian was but he was put to his limit even to keep the lead tolerable.

The weather was so dreadful that TV pictures repeatedly turned to electrical sparks and flashes. When they *were* there, the lights of following cars reflected on the road and on the falling rain. The cloud was too low for the usual helicopter to reflect pictures from the motorcycle cameramen and, instead, pictures were making the longer and less effective journey to a circling aircraft. And that in turn was having to fly higher than usual, at 27,000 feet, to avoid the mountain tops.

Laurent Jalabert, the French hope, said: "The cold was killing me. I knew the stage would be tough, but I didn't realize how tough. I couldn't recover and my muscles wouldn't respond. My teeth were chattering on the descents and I felt my circulation had stopped." He bade farewell to his hopes on the Télégraphe, the smaller peak that lies on the side of the Galibier itself.

Pantani rode that day as though the mountaintops weren't there. Where Bahamontes, Gaul and all the greats had held the brake hoods or the flat top of the bars, he rode on the drops like a time-trialist. And when he wasn't a time-trialist, he was a sprinter, rising from the saddle and forcing the bike forwards.

Another rider, Pavel Tonkov, explained: "It all comes down to an exceptional power-to-weight ratio, which permits him to suffer much less than other riders, especially on the steeper climbs. Unlike Ullrich, say, or Indurain, who rely on their power, on their ability to grind riders down, Pantani can accelerate violently and repeatedly." That was helped by his being 1 meter 70 (5 feet 7 inches) and weighing only 60 kilograms (132 pounds).

Those too weak to follow were weakened further by the rain, ever colder as the altitude increased. Riders went off the back every few seconds. Ullrich didn't but he was in distress. And he had no team-mates to help because they'd all been dropped.

Pantani stopped to take a white waterproof jacket and a bottle of energy drink at the top. By then he had reduced Ullrich's lead from 3 minutes 10 seconds to 2 minutes 30 seconds. He pressed on, using the width of the road on corners down to the valley. Desperate now and grimacing as he always did, felt his front tire flattening. He daren't ride it further on a wet road which twisted round hairpins. And yet his team car would be slow to reach him.

All the time, Pantani raced on along the valley road and then up to Les Deux Alpes. It was the first time the Tour planned to stop there. Again Pantani rode on the drops, now without his rain jacket, either in the saddle or dancing his tiny weight on the pedals. He spent more time out of the saddle than sitting on it, his bike fitted with yellow tires, yellow stem and yellow saddle like a forecast. On his head, his blue bandana with its dark contrasts, pulled over his scalp like a cap, and on top of that, the arms pointing downwards, over-optimistic sun glasses with a yellow frame.

Back in the darkness, Ullrich powered up in chase on his white bike, his gear larger, his style consistent but inelegant by contrast, using the passing cars whenever he could to gain a moment of slipstream. He was struggling to manage his deficit on Pantani but also to fend off an American challenger, Bobby Julich.

"Ullrich is in the process of losing the Tour de France but perhaps Julich is in the process of winning it," said the commentator on France 2 a little optimistically.

A thin line of spectators who'd been up on the mountain for hours stood in plastic coats and yellow cycling capes to pick out what they could from the gloom. That day, only those sitting in the warm at home were getting the full picture—on television. By the plateau which marked the start of the final kilometer, Pantani had taken more than seven minutes out of Ullrich. He dropped back into the saddle only five meters from the line. He had the yellow jersey. And Ullrich had an impossible deficit of 8 minutes 57 seconds.

L'Equipe wrote: "Today was the day that providence sent Marco Pantani to the Tour de France."

Sam Abt wrote in the *International Herald Tribune* that he was "the first Italian in 33 years to win the Tour de France. He is also the first bicycle racer since Miguel Indurain in 1993 to win both the Giro and the Tour in the same year. The only riders to have done it are the big stars: Coppi, Jacques Anquetil, Eddy Merckx, Bernard Hinault and Stephen Roche." That, he said, qualified him as a *campionissimo*—a champion of champions.

That evening at his hotel Pantani had a call. It was no secret where he and his team were staying and few callers got further than the switchboard. But even the hotel receptionist knew this one was different. It was Gino Bartali, by now 84 and in hospital. He'd followed his ride on television, he told Pantani, and wanted to congratulate him and say how much he admired him.

"Victories like this do everyone a power of good, even me," he said.

Pantani's problem certainly wasn't physical. It was mental. He was embarrassed by his weediness and highly sensitive to ears which stuck out enough for others to call him Elefantino, or Dumbo. Lance Armstrong, never the subtlest of men, deliberately referred to him that way in a television interview after they'd fallen out. Pantani was hurt for weeks.

He was also one of the few riders to employ a publicist, to promote his image. Together they recast him as The Pirate, in which guise he wore a bandanna and a snappy beard and mustache. But, as a British writer said of him, the truth was that, beyond the talent, there was just a little guy trying to strut and push shoulders against bigger men.

But sadder than that was the irony of 1998. It was the year in which the police raided the Tour, in which riders went home or on strike to protest against heavy-handed investigations and the prying nature of journalists. It was the year in which Pantani breathed life into a race which many said had died and which the colorless Miguel Indurain had dominated and after which Pantani said his win proved that the Tour was possible without doping.

"I've never had anything to do with doping," he said once. "You can rule it out completely. I'm clean."

It was a lie. The Giro threw him out for having souped-up blood and he left angrily denying it and escorted by police. The national anti-doping agency began investigating more deeply and Pantani responded by barricading himself in his home. He came out only at night, oddly dressed, stunned by barbiturates and then cocaine, and dressed in a wig and odd clothes. And then, after a comeback, then more drama on and off his bike, he just gave up. He died on Valentine's day, 2004, sprawled half-dressed on a hotel floor after an overdose. He left a note that said: "No one has been able to understand me, not even in cycling, not even in my family. I've ended up alone."

And alone was how he died.

27

Sacrifice by a Sad Man

It's one of the greatest tales of youthful sacrifice or, alternatively, the exploitation by a father-figure of his child. But maybe it wasn't quite either of those.

Col de Puymorens, France, July 20, 1934: Many tales surround René Vietto, a sad-looking and sad-natured little climber from the Mediterranean city of Cannes. Many are wrong. Cycling in the 1930s was still in its epic period, in which riders and journalists contrived to create a picture which would sell newspapers and enhance appearance contracts. Journalists needed heroes in the days before television showed the truth and cyclists who were heroes, or at any rate had a tale, could draw paying crowds to round-the-houses races which made up much of their income.

There was tragedy and triumph indeed for René Vietto, but not everything is as it seems.

Vietto is always described as a bell-boy, an elevator operator in a swanky hotel, the Palm Beach, in Cannes. Or was it perhaps the Croisette Palace? Or, failing that, any hotel? But historians who searched employment and tax records say there's no mention. The story also tells that he surrendered his chances in the Tour to help his leader, Antonin Magne, and that he did it happily. But long afterward, when it no longer mattered to the fortune he received in appearance money, he said he had done it because he'd been told to and that it had been "a hold-up."

The picture that accompanies the story shows Vietto, with his brush haircut and his fresh twenty-year-old face, sitting on a stone wall, miserably waiting for a team car down in the valley to bring another wheel. His bike is shown, the number 38 clipped to the frame, the rear wheel on the verge and its empty front forks on top of the wall. Vietto sits with one foot on the ground, the other drawn to his chest. But he is not alone, as the picture suggests. It has been edited to increase the drama, to increase the legend and sales. Far from suffering in silent solitude, he has a crowd next to him that includes the future editor of *L'Auto* and the future organizer of the Tour de France, Jacques Goddet.

And finally it's not true that he was as chirpy as he looked. In old age, although not as old as he looked, he told a television interviewer: "Monsieur, I have had suicidal tendencies all my life." He talked with his head turned down, rarely looking at the camera, never smiling. He lost all his money through bad investments and ended his working days as a pig farmer. The few people who visited him were more than he wanted. He was a difficult man, hard to like.

The story of the front wheel is complicated. Vietto and Magne were on the col de Puymorens, a pass in the Pyrenees which rises to 1,931 meters and takes 25 kilometers to climb. The Tour was in its fifteenth stage and Magne had tried in vain to drop his challengers. The leaders then set off down the other side toward l'Hospitalet.

Tour riders in those days still rode wooden rims, first because many preferred their lightness and more forgiving ride, second because Henri Desgrange banned metal rims for fear they'd overheat through constant braking on descents and that tires would roll as the heat melted the glue that held them. Going down, Magne crashed and his front rim broke. Vietto was with him, the domestique who had begun to outclass his master but a domestique nevertheless. Magne told him to remove his own front wheel and give it to him. There were no service cars following the leaders, only a truck or a car far back down the road.

Vietto's wheel would not fit Magne's front forks. Hub widths weren't yet consistent. And, although he set off, he stopped several times to get it right and in the end asked for a second wheel, this time from another member of the team, Georges Speicher. Speicher was the world champion and better placed in the Tour than Vietto. He had also won the Tour the previous year. Still more, he could ride down mountains faster than many dared and certainly faster than the lightweight Vietto.

Speicher had ridden up the mountain behind Vietto and Magne and stopped when he saw his leader stranded. It was he who took Vietto's

Les Woodland

wheel, which would fit his bike—they were all three in the same national team but not on the same makes of frame or equipment, which was significant then—and left Vietto to wait for the team car.

Just what happened on the mountain is made hazier by there being few reporters there. Much of what you read of bygone Tours was written on the stories of tired and breathless riders at the finish, some of which were themselves only hearsay, to which reporters added whatever they thought sounded reasonable and dramatic. Legend has it, therefore, that Speicher had handed over his whole bike, that it was too large for Magne but that Magne heroically rode it to the finish.

If the crowd didn't realize then that Vietto had sacrificed his chances for his leader, that's what they could read later. The papers were full of it, especially *L'Auto*. Vietto was crying "hot tears" of despair according to one photo caption. But Vietto had never been in a position to win the Tour. He was too far back on Magne. As the Dutch writer, Benjo Maso, says: "He couldn't do much more than climb, with the result that at the foot of the Pyrenees he was around 35 minutes behind."

Or as another historian, Richard Yates, says: "René's 'generous and sporting sacrifice' had ruined his chances of overall victory, or so it was claimed, and later the story was to be further embellished to the point where most people came to believe that the only reason Vietto had lost the Tour was because of his act of generosity on that first day in the Pyrenees. The power of the Press was such that they had not only turned a previously unknown provincial rider into a national hero overnight, they had also imposed their own interpretation on the overall result of the Tour."

Bill McGann's *The Story of the Tour de France* tells that even though Vietto had won twice in the Alps, he was close to half an hour behind Magne as the race left them. Vietto's wait for another wheel was only a fraction of that. By the finish that day in the Pyrenees, he was only 4 minutes 33 seconds behind the winner, Roger Lapébie.

Speicher, on the other hand, was more of a contender and it was he who sacrificed his chances, however unwillingly and however briefly. But that's not the way the legend tells it. Vietto was now a poor suffering kid exploited by a wily and selfish man who'd already made his name. And Speicher was a party animal who frequented night clubs, so he didn't fit the image either.

Look at the full, uncropped picture of Vietto on the wall that day and you see *L'Auto*'s reporter, Jacques Goddet. He's given away by the pith helmet, shorts and long socks that were his trademark. He had seen what had happened but had chosen not to report it in the daily column that he wrote under the pen name of l'Ami Bini. No matter that Vietto could never have won the Tour.

By that time, as Maso also points out, riders recognized that legends were what made them gods and they had a mutual interest in not telling the truth when it suited them. Speicher was a world champion and a Tour winner, a big enough draw already. He let Vietto have his moment and never spoke of the incident.

The historian, Jean Roussel, says: "Vietto's real 'sacrifice' came the next day when Magne's chain came off coming down the Portet d'Aspet. Vietto had attacked in the first hairpins and, hearing about Magne's problems, turned round, climbed back up the mountain and gave his bike to his leader." But he writes sacrifice in quotes because first, he says, Vietto knew he couldn't win, and second because any hope that might remain would vanish on the flat. He just didn't have the strength, and when he trained to get that strength, he put on weight that hindered him in the mountains. And maybe, just maybe, he knew the commercial value of his actions.

Roussel adds: "Vietto's 'sacrifice' has entered the realm of what we now call story-telling, which is to say the art of telling a tale rather than actual history." Or, as he put it in French, where the phrase works better: "*Pas l'Histoire, mais 'une histoire.'*"

As Benjo Maso explains: "Riders like Coppi and Bartali received really very little as salaries from the factories for which they rode and they earned their money mostly from start fees. How high those fees were depended not only on their successes but also on the color with which they were described. So they had to inspire journalists to write lyrically, and that they did through lone breakaways and spectacular attacks."

In this they all contrived to the mutual good. If Hugo Koblet could win at Agen after riding half the afternoon alone then he would gain but so would everyone else, because they would then be paid more to ride against him. They weren't inclined to lessen another rider's achievements because it reflected on their own.

The legend of *Roi René*—King René—therefore became unstoppable. But false. Vietto won the stage from Tarbes to Pau by six minutes, or in other words he made up about the time he had waited for another wheel. And in Paris he finished the Tour 59 minutes 2 seconds behind Magne, which is hardly the place of a man who could have won.

The Tour finished at the Parc des Princes and the man they wanted to see wasn't the taciturn Magne but the "cheated" Vietto. The two had to ride their celebratory laps of the track together. There were banners reading: "*Vive* Vietto, moral winner of the Tour."

Goddet's boss, Henri Desgrange, was furious. He had printed Goddet's story but never supported it. He distanced himself, writing pointedly of the time gaps, saying Vietto had lost at most eight minutes.

"A legend was born and now nobody dares attack it," a French journalist sighed.

Vietto cashed in on his name, the story and his reputation. Good riders could earn seven times their salary if they took all the appearance contracts they were offered. The success of the French team and the glamor that surrounded them, especially when France was going through a complicated political scandal, bound the nation for a summer. Towns and villages put together road and track races to bring in the stars they had seen only as blurred faces.

Above all, they wanted to see Vietto. What he had done, especially the second time, was generous. But it was also new. The previous year and in all the Tours before that, it would have been against the rules. The Tour of 1934 was the first in which teammates were allowed to help each other that way. The sensation was therefore all the greater. And, right or wrong, sensation it has stayed.

Vietto claimed publicly that he could have won the Tour. But he knew that his lost time came not from his sacrifices but on the flat and on rough roads that shook him about. He moved to northern France to train on cobbles, to learn the technique, and he rode much more on flat roads to build his speed. Why do that if neither rough roads nor speed had been the cause of his defeat?

"Still," writes Bill McGann, "the French love a gallant man and Vietto was that. He became a hero and to this day is remembered with fondness for his sacrifices."

His memorial, strikingly like Tom Simpson's, is at the col de Braus above Nice.

28

Hey, Look at Me, Look at Me!

What's the link between a man "all dressed up like a Union Jack" and the world's biggest bike race? Read on...

Thionville, France, July 10, 1999: Screaming Lord Sutch was a household name in Britain. It's a shame his memory isn't more widely recognized. The self-styled Lord Sutch—"Screaming" was accurately added in a brief moment of pop stardom—stood repeatedly in British national elections. The more the country sought to exclude him, the more determinedly he dressed eccentrically and stood behind the more sober candidates as the results were announced.

When Mick Jagger sang, in *Get off of My Cloud*, about a man who shows up "all dressed up like a Union Jack," he was complaining about Sutch's uninvited intrusion into his dressing room.

Lord Sutch's interventions on behalf of first the Teenage Party and then the Monster Raving Loony Party were much valued by a nation tired of the heavier side of politics and in the end he became a national treasure, tolerated and sometimes even admired by more conventional politicians.

The nearest cycling has come to him is Mario Cipollini. No rider before or since has turned up at races dressed like a gladiator, posed openly naked or held nude girls beside his bike, declared that he'd have been a porn star had he not taken up cycling, or so aggravated officials by making phone calls to friends while racing that they brought in a rule to stop him.

There have been more prolific sprinters. Freddy Maertens didn't just win the Tour of Spain in 1977: he won thirteen stages and left only eight to everyone else combined. It's a record for a major tour that's never been bettered and may never be. That same year he won seven stages of the Giro, and might have won more had he not crashed. But Maertens never had the self-publicizing talent of Mario Cipollini. So it's Cipo the world loved when he won four consecutive sprint stages in the Tour of 1999. Nine fewer than Maertens in Spain, but...

The 1999 Tour was a difficult one, not because of its mountains but a collection of events unlikely to be repeated. It was the first after the Festina doping scandal, and it started under such a cloud of suspicion and discontent that spectators painted huge hypodermic needles on the road, jeered at riders and threw anything they could find at cars taking the now notorious soigneurs to the finish.

It was remarkable, too, for there being no winner. There was at the time: it was one of Lance Armstrong's seven victories. But the list of winners now shows a dash, a line, after he was stripped of all his victories as the sport's greatest drug-taker. For the same reason, three stages in 1999 no longer have a winner.

It was the year no Frenchman won a stage, the first time since 1926; the year a Frenchman, Christophe Bassons, felt obliged to abandon the race after treatment he received for writing in a newspaper that drug-taking hadn't ended despite assurances after the Festina revelations. That had been shown that spring when the flamboyant but troubled Belgian, Frank Vandenbroucke, winner of Liège–Bastogne–Liège, was implicated in a doping scandal around Dr Mabuse—the nickname of former French rider Bernard Sainz, later jailed for his activities.

As Florian Joyard wrote in *Vélo*: "[For] a number of riders, life continues as before. Marco Pantani on the eve of his final victory [in the Giro] in Milan; Javier Ochoa and Nicola Loda, sent out of the Giro for hematocrit levels above the 50 per cent tolerated; Sergui Honchar, winner of the time-trial at Treviso in the last Giro, thrown out of the Tour de Suisse, also for his hematocrit level; the news of positive tests for amphetamines (nothing changes) of Laurent Roux in the Flèche Wallonne, without mentioning the eleven Italians thrown out of the amateur Giro."

And on top of that Willy Voet, the soigneur whose arrest on the Belgian-French border started the Festina scandal, published a book in which he detailed the way he said he had treated prominent riders.

Super Mario, as he was known after a computer game of the period, therefore came as a flash of color. It got so that people expected it of him and he was happy to oblige. He wore shorts of a different color day after day in the Tour of 1997, matching the green jersey, the yellow jersey and then the American flag for the company that made his bike. It brought him a fine each time but the cost was worth the publicity for him and his backers.

He would have ridden a green jersey labeled "Peace" in Ireland in 1998 had officials not told him to take it off. And in 1999 he summoned—there's probably no better word—reporters to a reception in the middle of the Tour in which he dressed in a toga as Caesar. Beside him was a striptease dancer billed as Cleopatra. Next morning, his whole team turned up in silver jerseys stamped with the words of Julius Caesar: *Veni, vidi, vici* (I came, I saw, I conquered). It honored his four stage wins. Fines showered upon them but the good, for Cipollini, had been done. For the moment, anyway; the stage started and he fell off in the rain and went home.

William Fotheringham recorded: "His shoe ads created the biggest stir, as he was depicted being fed grapes by topless models, and dressed up as Superman alongside a bodypainted nude. In a sport that has lengthy traditions of celibacy, he makes much of his liking for *amore*. 'Ejaculating costs you all of 100 calories, no more than a bar of chocolate,' he once said."

He rode once with a picture of the bosomy film star Pamela Anderson on his handlebars, although he said: "This gigolo image has been built up a little, for sure, although it's based on the truth. It has been exaggerated in the media. After all, I'm a married man with a family. I admit it, I'm a narcissist. I love being the center of attention. Even as a child, I wanted to be recognized. But if being a narcissist means trying to develop your own abilities, and creating a future for yourself, I can't see the harm in it."

He won the fourth stage into Blois by beating Erik Zabel and Stuart O'Grady, and he won next day at Amiens, then at Meubeuge and finally at Thionville. Four in a row, the first time it had been done since Charles Pélissier in the last days of 1930.

"This really is unbelievable stuff," he gasped. "The sort one dreams about."

But as so often, glory silently announced a fall. In Cipollini's case, literally. In 2000 he was adjusting his jacket as he rode, using both hands, when he crashed and hit his face on the road. It took 30 stitches to hold it together.

By then his sponsor, Saeco, a maker of coffee machines, had started growing tired of him. He wanted two years more and at €600,000, it was said, and Saeco would offer the €500,000 it was said to be paying already and only one more year.

When Cipollini insisted, Saeco told him to ride the Tour of Spain and start earning his salary. So he rode, punched Francisco Cerezo, a Spanish rider, for insulting his mother (professional riders have different conversations from ordinary cyclists) and got sent first to a police station and then home to Tuscany. As *Cycling* put it: "Like the Tour de France, [he] has never finished the Vuelta, although he has always managed to make his departure something of an event."

He was only just getting over that when he heard he hadn't been invited back to the Tour for 2000. The official reason was that his team, and therefore he, hadn't been good enough. Or, as he said Jean-Marie Leblanc had phrased it: "He said he didn't have confidence in the team after the first week." The flat stages, the sprinters' stages, therefore.

Cipollini, by then dressed in zebra stripes of the Domina Vacanze travel company, pinned his hopes on a reprieve and late selection through sympathy. The main selections were outside the Tour's hands but Leblanc had the right to pick four other teams as he chose. Instead, he picked the unremarkable Delatour team, albeit a young French one that could gain from the experience.

Italian fans were furious. A roadside poster read: "Go Mario! Leblanc is crazy." But look at his Tour record and you see he never once finished the race. There is at the least an expectation by organizers and referees that those who start should also intend to finish. It had always been the case that sprinters had a hard time in the mountains and some climbed off and went home a shade earlier than decency permitted. But Cipollini didn't even put up a pretense.

There are two points here. The first is that race organizers put up prizes in good faith, that riders will follow the spirit as well as the letter of the race. And the second is that a rider who intends to ride only half the race, and not the hardest part, is running a half-marathon where the rest are in it for the full stint. He can afford to be more reckless with his energy, he can use different tactics, and the mental strain will be less.

If all that didn't occur to the Tour's organizers, it occurred to everyone else.

It may never have occurred to the man himself, though. He saw himself as much an entertainer as a contender. "I think they've always had their money's worth when I've ridden," he said angrily. "I've won twelve Tour stages in the last few years and I've brought a bit of color to the boring first week."

There started a long sulk, which included refusing to enter Paris–Roubaix, "because it's organized by the people who've closed the door of the Tour on me." They probably shrugged in Paris and muttered that there was little chance of his wanting to enter anyway and none at all that he could play a part, still less win. But it caused bad blood at his sponsor that year, Acqua e Sapone, where the boss of the team, Vincenzo Santoni, was trying to sweet-talk his team back into the Tour.

The Tour, had it even been considering let him back in, was now less convinced than ever. Cipollini said his exclusion put him in a shadow as an accused dope-taker, which he said he had never been but was why others had been left at home. The day the Tour started in 2001, he was so upset that he spent the night at the Billionaire discotheque in Porto Cervo, Sardinia, where he clamped a cigar in his mouth and bopped with celebrities and other sportsmen. Only the most intimate press were invited, as Zsa Zsa Gabor once put it.

That night, for the first time, Cipollini said he was leaving cycling. He said it again several times over the years and in 2004 he rode the Tour de France again. And once more didn't finish. The triumph of his four consecutive stage wins had turned to tragedy.

Screaming Lord Sutch

29

Battling Shoulder to Shoulder

The oddest things can influence a race and cast a life. Who'd have thought that a closed gate could cost a Tour de France...but make a man richer?

Puy-de-Dôme, France, July 12, 1964: Raymond Poulidor is a genial, ambling man with a puffy face and the slow speech of a Limousin, someone who lives in the green, hilly land around Limoges. For a decade, he and Jacques Anquetil followed each other in the Tour de France, alternately Captain Hook and the crocodile, each waiting for the other's fatal slip.

Anquetil was cast as the city slicker, although his origins were as rural as Poulidor's, and the emblem of France emerging from stifling traditionalism. Poulidor, the son of farmers just as Anquetil was, personified the slow path of tradition and reassurance. You favored one or you favored the other and which you picked said as much about you as the riders themselves.

Two events illustrate their difference. The first is that by the time Anquetil—the younger of the two—had ridden for France and won a medal in the Olympics in Finland, and then won the Grand Prix des Nations, Poulidor hadn't even taken a train to the next town. The second is that Poulidor stayed with the same team throughout his career, much of it under the taciturn and traditional Antonin Magne while Anquetil changed teams and ended up with the flamboyant Raphaël Géminiani, a man with sufficient personality that Charles de Gaulle lent him a jet to get Anquetil between two races.

(For accuracy, I should point out that Géminiani has never denied it and nobody has disproved it. At Géminiani's urging, Anquetil was flying from the Dauphiné Libéré to start the mammoth Bordeaux–Paris hours later. De Gaulle appreciated Anquetil "because he made them play the *Marseillaise*.")

Such was Poulidor's following in the slow-moving French countryside he personified that Magne said: "I know farms in the Limoges area where his picture hangs between Bernadette Soubirous [the fourteen-year-old saint who saw the Virgin Mary at Lourdes] and the picture of the family's late grandfather. As Pierre Chany summarized: "The Tour de France has the major fault of dividing the country, right down to the smallest hamlet, even families, into two rival camps. I know a man who grabbed his wife and held her on the grill of a heated stove, seated and with her skirt held up, for favoring Jacques Anquetil when he preferred Raymond Poulidor. The following year, the woman became a Poulidoriste. But it was too late. The husband had switched his allegiance to Gimondi. The last I heard, they were digging their heels in and the neighbours were complaining."

It occurred to Poulidor and certainly to Magne that the crucial climb of the Tour of 1964 may not be in the Alps or Pyrenees but on an extinct volcano outside the tire-making city of Clermont-Ferrand. The climb is called the Puy-de-Dôme, a puy being a dead volcano. Géminiani had grown up at Clermont-Ferrand and he knew this striking cone with its road spiraling round it like a helter-skelter.

The road is there because ancient Gauls built a temple on the summit of their Puéi de Doma. The Romans replaced it with a temple to Mercury. Then history and the neighbors forgot it until, in 1873, it was uncovered when work began on a weather laboratory. The scientists built a railway to get their equipment to the top. That was replaced in 1926 by the road that in 1952 greeted the Tour for the first time.

Magne remembered that summer well, especially how decisive the Puy had been. Coppi had minced the field as he climbed round and round it for five kilometers at seven per cent and then a long time at thirteen. By the top, he had distanced Jean Robic by 1 minute 20 seconds and Stan Ockers by 3 minutes 22 seconds, all from a single attack.

Magne told Poulidor to ride up the Puy, learn it and decide what gears he needed. What neither man remembered was that the road is private. There was a gate at the bottom that opened only occasionally to let club riders emulate Coppi but when Poulidor arrived it wasn't one of those days and his journey was wasted. He drove up but he hadn't ridden up before the Tour got there.

As a result, he struggled with a bottom gear of 42 x 25. Federico Bahamontes, who came second that day, had 42 x 26. "And to think you were talking about using 42 x 24," Magne chided as the two drove back down to Clermont-Ferrand after the stage. "You even came to recce the hill before the Tour."

Poulidor took a while to reply. Then he said: "No, Mr Magne, I didn't recce the climb."

"But you told me…"

Poulidor that day was 56 seconds behind Anquetil. If he could win by 27 seconds, the 30 seconds' bonus would give him his first yellow jersey. And it wasn't a vain hope: he had been the better climber throughout the Tour and higher overall. And it had to be the Puy because there were no more climbs after that. There was a closing time-trial, in which Anquetil had an undeniable advantage, but get the Puy right and Poulidor could wear a yellow jersey as far as Paris, even if he had to hand it over when he got there.

Two other riders had eyes for the Puy that day. The first to attack was Julio Jiménez, balding, bobbing and grimacing as he climbed gracelessly, out of the saddle, leaning his weight first one side and then the other as he plunged on his pedals. He was chased by Bahamontes, curly-haired, taller, more slightly built, more elegant but characteristically moving his hands around the bars every few moments.

Anquetil could have chased them. But he didn't, first because the Spaniards couldn't win the Tour; second because they were better climbers and he would have blown in the attempt, third because Poulidor would come with him and four men together complicated his strategy, and fourth, letting the Spaniards get away meant one of them and not Poulidor would pick up the winner's bonus.

Anquetil rode by the mountain wall and Poulidor the outer edge by the precipice. Poulidor wore a cap, Anquetil was bare-headed. They heard each other's breathing, sometimes felt the other's hot gasps on their bare arms. They refused to look at each other, so that at times they banged elbows.

Goddet followed on a motorbike as the race threaded through what the police estimated as half a million spectators. He recalled "the two, at the extreme of their rivalry, climbing the road wrapped like a ribbon round the majestic volcano, terribly steep, in parallel action." One of them had to crack. It was Anquetil. He gave out spectacularly, getting lower on his bike, his elbows jutting like the davits of the lifeboat he desperately needed. They said you could balance a glass of water on his shoulders without losing a drop, but that day he bounced up and down like an amateur, legs less turning than forcing the pedals. Chany wrote: "His face, until then purple, lost all its color; the sweat ran down in drops through the creases of his cheeks." He was only semi-conscious, he said.

Anquetil, the man who could drop nobody but whom nobody could drop, intimidated true climbers by being there and refusing to go away. He never bothered to cross a col first, let alone by himself; all that mattered was the control of others.

"I've always been convinced," Goddet said, "that in these moments that supreme player of poker, the Norman [Anquetil] used his craftiness and his fearless bluffing to win his fifth Tour. Because, to me, it was clear that Anquetil was at the very limit of his strength and that had Poulidor attacked him repeatedly and suddenly then he would have cracked."

Jiménez crossed the line first, rounding a bend at the summit, looking over his shoulder for last-moment danger from Bahamontes, then slackening his toe-straps before acknowledging cheers with a single raised arm. Bahamontes followed a few seconds later, riding on the drops. But by then all eyes were on the bend that both men had rounded. Poulidor and Anquetil would be coming round it. Word had it that Poulidor had dropped Anquetil but nobody knew by how much.

Then Poulidor came round the bend by himself, shattered, riding on the drops, struggling for every second. "For a moment I thought I had won the Tour," he said. A shout went up that Anquetil was coming but it wasn't him: it was Vittorio Adorni, who'd passed him on the last, terribly hard ramp. And then, twenty meters behind, Anquetil, his head repeatedly falling downwards in a way familiar to every cyclist who has ridden further and faster than his energy allowed.

Les Woodland

Helpers held him upright as he rode into the crowd beyond the line, protesting with his arms that he didn't want that help. His cheeks were hollower than ever and his eyes bulging. Géminiani recalled: "I'll never forget what happened when Jacques crossed the line. Close to fainting, he collapsed on the front of my car. With barely any breath left, exhausted, but 200 per cent lucid, he asked me: 'How much?' I told him 14 seconds. 'That's one more than I need. I've got 13 in hand', he said.

"In my opinion, Poulidor was demoralized by Anquetil's resistance, his mental strength. There were three times when he could have dropped Anquetil. First, at the bottom of the climb. Then when Julio Jimenez attacked. Finally in the last kilometer. The nearer the summit came, the more Jacques was suffering. Poulidor should have attacked: he didn't. Poulidor didn't attack in the last 500 meters—it was Jacques who got dropped, and that's not the same thing."

Poulidor never did get his yellow jersey and he didn't win the Tour. There were two stages on the last day, one of 119 kilometers from Orleans to Versailles and then a 27-kilometer time-trial from Versailles to the Parc des Princes. It was France's national holiday, July 14. Rival fans teased each other and mingled with the curious who, having nothing else to do that day, had come for the spirit of the *fête*. The Parc was full.

Poulidor, as tradition demanded, started last but one, just Anquetil behind him. In an era when managers depended on Radio Tour they shouted time gaps from car windows to riders who had no ear-piece radios. Poulidor had no news of Anquetil for the first two minutes—the gap in their start times—and then not until someone had timed him. All he could do was ride as hard or harder than he dared.

At the top of the côte des Gardes he was five seconds better than Anquetil, the time-trial specialist. He rode the cobbled street to the track, turned right through the wooden doors of its tunnel, then right for the last few hundred meters of the Tour. And then he waited. In his heart he hoped he had won. In his head he knew that he hadn't. His five seconds had vanished when the course reached the gentle slope down to the Seine. Anquetil rolled himself into his skiers' crouch and turned his biggest gears. He entered the track to a roar and a shower of sweat from his yellow woolen jersey. His last ride in the Tour that year was over in 37 minutes 10 seconds—21 seconds better than Poulidor and 55 better over the month, of which 20 were the bonus for winning in Paris.

The crowd cheered his name but France has remained uncertain ever since. Bobet, the previous hero, looked happy when he won. Bernard Hinault, who came after Anquetil, looked the satisfied thug who'd just roughed up the opposition. But Anquetil was as unemotional with a bouquet as he was with a bike. He rarely lifted a hand when he won, seeing it as his job rather than a moment of happiness, and a shyness and reluctance to show emotion meant the most the crowd got was a flickering smile and the sight of his back as he walked away. It was that battle not just of wills and muscle but of personality and the self-image of France that for many people makes July 12, 1964, on the Puy-de-Dome, the most gripping moment in Tour history.

The two avoided talking for many years. They posed together as publicity and convention obliged and they were pictured kissing cheeks on the cover of *Paris-Match*, the affection, however formal, sufficiently out of character that it was worth the front page.

But there was no affection. "If Poulidor had taken my jersey [on the Puy-de-Dôme], I'd have gone home that night," Anquetil said. He could never understand the way he was treated. "He always comes second, usually behind me, and still they shout more for him than for me. If he loses, he doesn't have to find excuses. But, if I come second or third, then I've failed. They call me a calculator, a strategist, even if a miscalculation has just made me lose."

In the end, he went on too long. It was a job, not a romance, and he sought no happy ending. The French grew tired of him and he raced last not in France but Belgium, to general indifference. In death he was recognized again for what he had done. He died of cancer at 53 and lies now beneath a marble stone shaped as a black book in the graveyard at Quincampoix, the village near Rouen where he grew up.

He and Poulidor were friends at the end. The last time they spoke was in Rouen in 1987. Anquetil turned in his hospital bed and said: "Raymond, I feel bad now. But believe me, this is nothing compared to how I felt on the Puy-de-Dôme."

Poulidor has since then made a living out of being Raymond Poulidor, making appearances, taking part in commercials for pensions and insurance, following the Tour—in a yellow shirt—for whoever will pay him. He confesses cheerfully that he is more celebrated and better paid as a man who didn't win the Tour than ever he would be if he had.

To this day, "to be a Poulidor" means to have tried but never succeeded. Today's politicians were teenagers that day in 1964 and remember how the country divided and papers, radio and television spoke of little else. They are occasionally asked, not from a love of the sport but as an indication of their personality, which man they favored. Some say. Others, tactfully forgetting the passions of their teenage years, insist they were divided. Lionel Jospin, the prime minister until 2002, answered: "I was a big fan of Poulidor but it got on my nerves the way people celebrated the way he kept coming second. It went against my winning instinct."

In such a way he avoided upsetting those to whom the memory is dear while stressing that he himself was a winner, the man to take France to the *maillot jaune* that Poulidor never had.

Jacques Anquetil's grave at Quincampoix, France

Les Woodland

30

Round and Round on an Old Bike

The world's best rider should hold the world's most glamorous record. But what if it means going to the other side of the world, putting a reputation at risk? What if even your wife isn't wholly convinced?

Mexico City, October 25, 1972: A Canadian woman in one of Amsterdam's orchestras said once that she loved humming the singalong bits of Wagner operas but that she detested playing his works. Asked if that was because they were demanding on an orchestra, she said: "Yes, because you have to sit on that damned chair for ten hours."

Something similar applies to hour records. Because they are prestigious, they are tough to beat. And because they entail going round and round a track for an hour, they are among the dullest to ride. Many riders have been colorless enough to rise to the task. Ferdinand Bracke of Belgium beat the record in 1968 and nobody accused him of being over-exciting. If anything, he simply looked ill. Only four journalists watched him break the hour record in Rome—the rest were at the Tour of Lombardy, which they thought more exciting—and one of those lived in the city anyway and the other had compiled his schedule.

Maybe it wasn't surprising. Pierre Chany, who went there reluctantly and only at the last moment, remembered: "Bracke seemed even more pessimistic about his chances than I was." He was so pessimistic that his manager, Gaston Plaud, insisted Chany stay with him in his absence for fear that he'd shrug and go back to his hotel.

In fact the most thrilling story about him is that he faced Hugh Porter of Britain in the final of the 1969 world pursuit championship and, realizing Porter started slowly, rode as though the distance were only half as long and caught Porter partway through. Porter was deeply offended and spent 30 minutes complaining to the editor of *Cycling*, who kept saying: "Hugh, it was a pursuit: he caught you."

There have, though, been colorful winners. Two have significance: Eddy Merckx and Francesco Moser.

Merckx, in October 1972, could have sat at home and put on his slippers and watched quiz shows on television. He had won the Tour and the Giro, Liège–Bastogne–Liège, Milan–San Remo, the Tour of Lombardy, Dauphiné Libéré, Paris–Nice and the Tour of Belgium. His superiority the previous season was such that in the Super Prestige Pernod, a forerunner of the World Cup, he had twice as many points as the second, third, fourth and fifth riders together.

Why bother with more? Because, probably, it was there.

Claudine Merckx said: "When Eddy decided to try for the record, after a lot of deliberation he said: 'I want to do it.' He was taking a huge risk. I'm sure he said to himself: 'You've got to beat it. You can't let yourself lose it.' He was putting his whole reputation at risk. In Mexico he could either prove himself or make a fool of himself."

The Augustín Melgar Olympic velodrome is, at 2,240 meters, as high as the highest Tour climbs, and its thin air is a problem and a bonus. A problem because while the percentage of oxygen is the same at any height, there's less total air the higher you get and therefore less oxygen; a bonus because, the air being thinner, there's less of it to push out the way. Cyclists have long understood that air resistance is the hill that never ends but not until Mexico, first in the Olympics in 1968 and then in two successive hour records, did this become spectacularly clear. As Professor Maurice Ménard, the former director of the Institut Aértonautique at St-Cyr, south of Paris, points out, a powerful cyclist would be capable of only 91 per cent as much power as at sea level—but he'd be pushing aside only three-quarters as much air.

World running records dropped in Mexico for every distance less than 400 meters; many of the jumps, vaults and throws were bettered; and the cause was so well understood that Mexico sold empty metal boxes labeled *"especial para batir récords."*

What was harder to calculate was how much the thin air in a distance event would hinder a cyclist compared to the benefit of the thin air. There had been no individual races an hour long at the Olympics. Merckx trained on the track at Ghent to perfect his riding style and on rollers in his garage, breathing from low-pressure air bottles that would, he hoped, get him used to Mexico. Two doctors stood with him as he pedaled, one of them was hurt when a bottle exploded.

Merckx's business manager, Jean van Buggenhout, and his father-in-law, the former six-day winner Lucien Acou, flew to Mexico on Tuesday, October 17, to set up camp. Merckx followed five days later, with sponsors, masseur, doctor, several journalists and Jacques Anquetil. They arrived just before midnight on Saturday, jet-lagged and tired after ten hours of travel. On Sunday and Monday, it rained. But for all the waiting frustrated him, he was getting used to the altitude. On Tuesday, October 22, he woke at 5:30am. The sun wouldn't rise for another hour and a quarter but from his balcony even in the darkness he could tell it wasn't raining. He went straight to his breakfast and, around six, left for the track to train behind a pacing motorbike. He learned the track, felt happy with the air, decided that the attempt would be next morning before the wind rose.

More than that, he decided with his team manager, Giorgio Albani, and with Acou, that he would try for the five and ten kilometer records and decide only then whether to continue. Nobody, including the two dozen Belgians who'd come to watch, expected he'd pull up once started.

And so it was. A little before nine o'clock, having warmed up in woolen leggings beneath his shorts and the brown-and-black sweat top that showed the name of his sponsor, the Molteni food company, he collected the bike made for the record by Ernesto Colnago, who had flown to Mexico to be with him. The frame was steel, which was still the standard, but the components had been made of Duralumin and titanium, both drilled and pared down, and metal ball bearings had been replaced by plastic. It weighed 5.9 kilograms, less than later rules allowed.

Merckx, who is bilingual, spoke French to his entourage. Someone reminded him not to start too fast, to keep to the schedule drawn up for him by the journalist René Jacobs, editor of the annual review, *Vélo*, which had forecast a finish in 48.800 kilometers. There'd been mild disagreement between rider and adviser, Merckx feeling Jacobs wanted him to start too fast.

He wiped a cream into his nose that would help him breathe more easily and sprayed the front of his neck. He put on his crash hat and a helper carried his bike, which had been propped against a chair, on to the track behind him. The crowd clapped politely rather than with enthusiasm.

The gun fired at 8:56 and he pushed away with his left leg, accelerating out of the saddle for much of a lap, then crouching low over his bike and concentrating on keeping close to the sponge pads that kept him from riding within the line which defined the track's distance. He missed the five-kilometer record, beat Ole Ritter's record for 10 kilometers and then rode faster than any man had before him.

On each of the 148 laps, Jacobs rang a bell. Merckx would be over the line if he was ahead of schedule, but the bell would ring before he crossed it if he was lagging. Colnago stood with a spare bike on his shoulder, turning to face Merckx wherever he was on the track. He calculated that the greatest risk of a puncture would be in the first 30 minutes; after that, the tires would pick up rubber from the track and grow harder.

Things got harder at 35 kilometers and Merckx's head started to hang and now and then he grimaced. Albani shouted: "Eddy, go easy!" in Italian and Merckx answered: "*Faticato*" (tired). But when the gun fired to end the hour, he had ridden 49.431 kilometers, beating Ritter by 778 meters, the biggest beating the record had received since Oscar Egg in 1913. He slowed down, rode over the sponges he'd so carefully avoided for the last 60 minutes, and rolled on slowly as the electric lights on the scoreboard printed one by one the letters that read *Nuevo Record*.

Having called Jacobs' schedule too ambitious, he had exceeded it by almost a kilometer and a half. He said it had never been easy but that he had never felt himself fading.

"But I won't do it again," he said. "People told me that, to beat the record, I had to go to Mexico because I wouldn't even feel the pedals. Well, I promise you that I felt them, the pedals."

Les Woodland

Even so, he felt he had concentrated too much on the intermediate records, that he had started too fast. But he'd been nervous, he said, and couldn't resist letting rip.

He walked slowly across the grass of the track's center, helped at each elbow, talking as he went. When he reached the middle, he half-emptied a plastic bottle of drink, turned, raised both hands and acknowledged the excited enthusiasm of the crowd. And then he took the trophy that was handed to him and raised that with straight arms above his head. The crowd whooped.

There was a party that night but he didn't stay much longer in Mexico. He went to a reception at the Belgian embassy, took a trip to the Mayan temple at Teotihuacan, then flew home to the Zaventem airport in Brussels to meet the crowds that had gathered there. Press comments rivaled each other in their excess. They glorified him but found a "but..."

But the price was going to be ten years off his life...

But he could have ridden still further had he controlled his speed at the start...

But he wouldn't have been as good at low altitude where Anquetil, Coppi and Bracke rode...

But he could have won six tours if he hadn't drained himself permanently at Mexico...

To which the answers were (a) I doubt it but I'll have to see, (b) Yes, perhaps, but we'll never know, (c) Perhaps not, because he developed 366 watts in Mexico and the same distance would have needed 436 at sea level, and (d) If I were going to win a sixth Tour, it would have been at the start of my career and not at the end.

Les Woodland

31

Round and Round on a New Bike

Merckx's hour record created more than a sensation on the day. It created nostalgia and, in the face of change, a feeling that things had gone too far. And the sport decided that, yes, it had.

Mexico City, January 19, 1984: Merckx never kidded himself his record would never fall. But it took a revolution in bicycles and in physical preparation to do it. And then both the rider and his bike brought a change to the rules to be sure that it never happened again, not at least without being in a separate class.

The rider was a handsome Italian called Francesco Moser. He was a dominant figure from the middle of the 1970s into the 1980s. He won the 1977 world road championship, the 1984 Giro, and six classics. His looks earned him the nickname of Dreamboat and his elegant pedaling style, which belied the power behind it, completed the impression to Italians that he was half man and half god.

He wasn't as good as Merckx, though, and he wasn't universally loved or even respected. "I try never to be in the same room as him," said Laurent Fignon, who never hid his contempt when his name turned up in television interviews.

In January 1984, Moser was already 32 years and seven months, more than five years older than Merckx had been and he was now going down rather than up in his career. He hadn't thought much about the record until the idea was put to him by Paolo Sorbini, the founder of Enervit, a maker of sports drinks.

"He loved a challenge," Moser remembered. "In the summer of 1983, we held a meeting at my home, with my team sponsor, Gis, my team and the Enervit people. We realized it was possible. I was 32 but I was good at time-trials. We created a good group for the project, with specialists for the bike, for the training, for my diet and my clothing."

He wasn't the world's best on either the road or the track but he was good at both. He was world pursuit champion in 1976, a race of minutes rather than an hour but which showed he had the speed. And he'd won Paris–Roubaix in 1978, 1979 and 1980, which showed he had the endurance and the toughness. By 32 he may well have had a little less of both but the base was there.

When he went to Mexico, he took disk wheels, which have solid sides in place of spokes. They were novel but they hadn't been perfected; they could be twice as heavy as conventional wheels. Their advantage was in reducing frontal air resistance and, far more, having no spokes to turn and slice through the air. As Mike Hutchinson, author of *The Hour*, pointed out, Newton had long observed that weight once shifted needed no more effort to keep it going than anything lighter. So Moser's wheels were a handicap only at the start. He didn't have to ride them up hills and so the weight didn't matter.

The disks were the clearest technological change, he said, because "otherwise there was not much about his equipment, apart from lots of shiny chrome, to set him apart from his predecessors." That intrigued Ian Cook, of the physical exercise lab at the University of Limpopo in South Africa, and he set out to find where the advantage lay, especially for a rider at the end of his career.

He expressed it dryly in a scientific paper: "The more recent sea level rides of Chris Boardman and Ondřej Sosenka and Merckx's 1972 altitude ride amounted to an approximate three percent improvement over Bracke's 1967 sea level attempt. In contrast, Moser's 1984 altitude ride was six per cent better than Bracke's 1967 ride. Clearly, some extraordinary measures must have been employed…to improve the world hour cycling by an astounding 3,058 meters—altitude, specialized clothing and bicycle equipment and *artificial manipulation of physiological parameters. Four days later, at the same venue, Moser raised the mark even further to 51.151 kilometers per hour."*

The italics are mine.

Hutchinson, a talented amateur rider against the clock in Britain, picked up the feeling when he wrote: "While in most of his career he was a hero, somehow Moser's hour-record rides...mean that he is unfairly remembered as a super-dull, scientific rider who got to the hour record by a sort of legalized cheating. Much of the cycling world felt that his records had as much to do with his coach, Francesco Conconi, as they did with Moser. Indeed, Conconi wrote one of the world's most extravagantly boring books about Moser's record attempts, and it's clear whom he regarded as the senior partner."

Conconi is indeed an interesting character, a professor at the University of Ferrara in Italy. There he researched the best ways to trace doping but he was better known for finding drugs that, at best, weren't yet outlawed. He and his colleague Michele Ferrari became the most prominent doctors in cycling circles of the 1980s. Conconi is credited with introducing the blood-souping drug, EPO, to cycling. Allessandro Donati, a campaigner against drugs in sport in Italy, said the athletics association there had asked Conconi to tell him about a project he was working on. Donati listened, thought it unethical and refused to get involved. The authors, Ivan Waddington and Andy Smith, write in their book about doping at high level: "Most striking was that the anti-doping laboratory in Rome, which had been duly accredited by the UCI, was being used for a totally different purpose: to establish how long it would take for traces of these drugs to disappear from the athletes' urine samples."

EPO created red blood cells, and made every lungful of air count for more, in a way that couldn't be distinguished from the body's own work. It wasn't new: Pierre Dumas had come across Gastone Nencini's receiving transfusions of blood and therefore being extra corpuscled in the Tour in 1960. Then Björn Ekblom, a doctor at the Swedish Sport and Gymnastics Institute in Stockholm, tried it more scientifically on volunteers in 1972 and found their oxygen uptake increased by nine per cent. EPO was different only by doing it artificially.

Moser denied using EPO. He also told *Gazzetta dello Sport* that he hadn't had blood transfusions either, a story that changed when *L'Équipe* reported him as saying: "I wasn't the only one nor the first to use blood transfusions to improve my performance. I was told that Jacques Anquetil had done that and that was well before my time.

The method was being used everywhere. It was my own blood. And I wasn't the only rider doing it. EPO, that is a whole new thing. It is dangerous and unnatural."

And then *Il Sole 24* confused things further by quoting him as saying: "Blood transfusions weren't banned them. Did I have them? I've never said; others have made insinuations that I did. The real innovations were the training, the use of a heart meter, the climbing intervals, the bike and the aero bars."

It's hard now to know how much was known in the wider cycling world. But those in the inner temple understood enough. Bernard Hinault, never bashful, dismissed Moser with: "This record doesn't impress me. Moser prepared scientifically and received the fruits of his efforts." Anquetil, too, said he wasn't impressed: Merckx's record was old, he said, the Belgian could have ridden better on the day, and Moser had "prepared well."

Merckx, who had beaten Moser in every time-trial they'd ridden, is quoted by Owen Mulholland as saying: "For the first time in the history of the hour record, a weaker man has beaten the stronger." Now, to be fair, whatever Moser may have done, if anything, was no more than almost every rider of the era, including Merckx (who was caught doping numerous times) and Anquetil (who spoke openly of the need for doping and took 15 milligram doses of methedrine three times a week, according to Pierre Chany, his confidant). Attitudes and expectations were different, tests were sketchy and easily cheated. Moser had found a way to go faster, whether it was through blood transfusions or better training.

Blood doping was banned after the American cycling team used it at the Los Angeles Olympics in 1984. But by then EPO had arrived, even if it wasn't yet easily available. The UCI knew that well. It was already working on the problem. What alarmed it more in the short term was the way bikes were changing shape, the way they feared technology would before long count for more than the rider, and perhaps that a sport which needed specialist bikes, useless for anything else, that cost thousands of euros, was hardly going to attract young kids and their cash-strapped parents. Not when soccer needed only a pair of boots.

Things came to a head when Moser rode a rear wheel 101 centimeters across when he tried again for the record at Stuttgart in 1988. You couldn't even buy a machine like that.

The UCI ruled towards the end of 1996 that records after Merckx's could stand but that they would count for little. What mattered now on was the so-called "athlete's record." The conditions were that wheels must have 16 to 32 spokes and be of equal diameter between 65 and 70 centimeters; the frame had to be triangular with round tubes no thinner than 2.5 centimeters; the handlebars had to be of classic shape, no more than 50 centimeters wide and no less than 34 centimeters; a rider must wear a helmet but only for safety and without additions for streamlining; the track could be no higher than 600 meters; and that a test of the rider's blood and urine was obligatory.

Merckx had ridden at a higher altitude than 600 meters but the attempt had met all the other conditions.

Moser, of course, didn't like the new rule, which without saying so labeled his ride as freakish. "The UCI has tried to stop the progress of technology," he wrote in a guest editorial in *Vélo*. "No other sport has done that."

And speaking of improvements to his own record, he said: "Chris Boardman did 56 kilometers in an hour on a highly technical bike and then, several months later, achieved 49 kilometers per hour on a conventional bike. And we're pretending that it's this second record that counts? Merckx rode on what was called a traditional bike but not of the least similarity to what Desgrange rode, and nobody said a thing back then. They allowed progress and now they're putting a complete stop to it."

The significance of Moser's ride, therefore, was less what he achieved—a record which both officials and fellow riders dismissed as not worthy of the record—than what he brought about. In his triumph were the roots of his tragedy.

And anyway, the UCI went back on its original ruling and said that any bike allowed more widely under the rules would be fine. That meant that Jens Voigt, one of the most likable men in cycling but far from either Merckx or Moser, could take the hour record in 2014.

In Moser's victory were also the roots of the hour record's fall from glory.

32

A Welcome Shot
Of Capuccino

Some riders are dull, a few are cautious and just a handful are casually reckless—and get away with it. For a while, anyway.

Sestriere, Italy, July 18, 1992: There are riders who race to a formula to the point of making a race predictable or even dull. Lance Armstrong attacked on the last mountain, Miguel Indurain crushed everyone in the time-trials. But Claudio Chiappucci—"Capuccino or whatever his name is," as Greg LeMond said in a TV interview before apologizing— attacked anywhere. It didn't seem to matter.

Few riders had as many cycling genes in their blood, certainly not without being themselves the sons of champions. But Chiappucci had a further difference. His father, Arduino, had fought alongside Fausto Coppi in northern Africa and both probably shared the relief of many unpersuaded Italian soldiers when the British took them prisoner.

The British knew nothing of cycling and had no idea who was in their hospitality. They kept their charges out of trouble by giving them small but time-consuming jobs. Coppi was told to cut hair, a job for which he had plenty of time but little talent. Not that that mattered to a British soldier called Len Levesley who, unable to fight because of polio, nevertheless needed a haircut.

"I was stretcher-bound and there wasn't a lot I could do for myself," he said, "so one day I asked one day if someone could cut my hair for me. They said they'd send for an Italian prisoner of war to do it for me, because in war time you grabbed anybody you could when you wanted something done. And I waited and then a few minutes later the tent-flap parted."

And there, tall, hawk-like and out of place, stood not just "an Italian prisoner of war" but Fausto Coppi.

"Oh, I should think it took me all of a full second to realize who it was," Levesley laughed, relishing the moment even as a 91-year-old. "He looked fine, he looked slim, and having been in the desert, he looked tanned. I'd only seen him in cycling magazines but I knew instantly who he was. So he cut away at my hair and I tried to have a conversation with him, but he didn't speak English and I don't speak Italian. But we managed one or two words and I got over to him that I did some club racing. And I gave him a bar of chocolate that I had with me and he was grateful for that and that was the end of it."

Coppi probably went back to his pal, Arduino Chiappucci, with whom he shared a plate and knife and fork, and told him in a bored way that he'd met an English soldier who recognized him. Levesley, on the other hand, went home and told all his friends and ever after they addressed him as Holy Head.

Arduino Chiappucci's son was born on February 28, 1963. The father encouraged the son to race, and lived just long enough to see him turn professional. He died the day after his son's first professional race, at Laigueglia, in 1985. It took his son four years to win his first race.

By then, cycling had become not the colorful jousting of stars with distinct personalities, about whom journalists could write flamboyant stories which nobody, least of all those concerned, would deny. Cycling had become a profession of leaders and followers, the leaders paid as millionaires and the teams dedicated not to excitement but the preservation of their stars. In Benjo Maso's words, "the hope of a victory becomes often overshadowed by the fear of a defeat."

The 1990s were the Miguel Indurain years. Journalists at *Procycling* who struggled to find a nickname to make him interesting, in which they failed, called him Big Mig. He was big and his name was Mig. That was as thrilling as it got. He won time-trials, the dullest and most mathematical part of any race, and he won the Tour.

So the reporting world became grateful for Chiappucci. He and three others careered away on the first day of the 1990 Tour and won by ten minutes. Chiappucci took the yellow jersey despite being the least known of the four and the one whose name had to be checked against the program. It was "Capuccino or whatever he calls himself", LeMond said with obvious irritation in a television interview, having been attacked while halted by a flat tire, which wasn't against the rules but nevertheless offended ethically.

LeMond grew increasingly crosser because he could barely make an impression on the man. Chiappucci so delighted in having the yellow jersey that he still had seven minutes on LeMond as the race left the Alps. And LeMond was the previous year's winner. In fact it wasn't until the last time-trial beside the man-made Vassivière lake in the Limousin that the Italian lost it.

"You just had no sense what he would do," Maso said of him. "He'd sprint on flat stages on every hill that could give him points for the mountains competition. He attacked especially on flat stages, pointlessly putting his energy at risk because the peloton had every chance of catching him.

"He was even more colorful in a stage through the Alps from St-Gervais to Sestriere in 1992 when he attacked 180 kilometers before the finish and without team-mates around him to lend support. It not only won him the stage but he drove Indurain to one of his rare errors: when the Spaniard tried to bring the Italian back on the last climb, it was more than he could manage and he sank lightly because of it."

The finish at Sestriere, just inside Italy, had been in the Giro back in 1911, included to mimic the Tour de France, which had its first mountain stages the previous year. It next went over there in 1914, a day so chaotic because of the weather that nobody thought to record who'd been first at the top. Over the years, thanks to Giovanni Agnelli, a founder of the Fiat car company and a senator in the government in Rome, Sestriere had developed into a ski station.

It was there in 1952 that Coppi won by seven minutes, soaked and battered by the wind. Traffic jams built up as fans who'd followed the stage by radio determined to be at the finish to see a man beyond heroism. He led the Tour by half an hour and Jacques Goddet had to double second prize to keep the others interested. The Tour was riding there in 1992 to celebrate the 40th anniversary.

Chiappucci kept his plans to himself. "That stage to Sestriere, I prepared for months in advance," he said years later. "A Tour de France stage in Italy. I wanted to win that stage." Without fuss, he and two teammates, Mario Chiesa and Fabio Roscioli, rode it over two days after the Giro, spending the night at another ski station, Megève. Riders raced a lot more in those days and the three men found a spare day only with difficulty.

But he gave no sign as he led the peloton over the day's first climb, the col des Saisies. It was a beautiful day "under a piercing blue sky with air that could bring back the dead," according to Gianni Mura in *La Repubblica*.

Chiappucci attacked at the bottom of the Cormet de Roselend. He was two hours into the stage. The nine who went with him included Richard Virenque, yet to reach his best, and an older Irishman better known for sprinting, Sean Kelly. They started the descent with two minutes on the chasers. Together they reached the Iséran, in most years the *toit*, the highest point, of the Tour.

And there Chiappucci attacked hardest. Virenque struggled to stay with him but gave up after repeatedly getting close and then dropping back, "playing the accordion" as French cyclists call it. Chiappucci made sure he didn't reach him; Virenque's team-mate, Pascal Lino, was race leader and even Virenque, ever a man torn by self-interest, couldn't be guaranteed to do anything but hinder. Chiappucci rode through snowdrifts and reached the col two minutes ahead. The chasers had shredded and LeMond was dropped by almost twenty minutes. He finished the day with seventeen other riders outside the time limit, 130th and almost fifty minutes down. That especially pleased Chiappucci, who had never liked him.

The minutes peeled away: from three and a half minutes at the summit, Chiappucci had only two when Sestriere was still fifteen kilometers away. Indurain chased and Chiappucci struggled. But he still had a minute in his pocket as he crossed the line, head tossed back, eyes closed, both arms raised.

"You've driven us all crazy!" was the headline in *Gazzetta dello Sport* next morning.

Gianni Bugno was guarded: "Chiappucci's break is great but hard to believe in."

Les Woodland

Spectators were bewitched. Just as with Coppi, many had driven to the mountains with their radio on. But riders, like Bugno, were more skeptical. Things like that, by riders who'd taken years to win a single race, happened for good reason. Eric Boyer told *L'Équipe* in 1999: "It was that critical moment when Italian doctors were one step ahead. The three letters E-P-O weren't mentioned much, or at least we didn't yet know what they meant." He asked a doctor about it. "Use it and your blood will turn as thick as mashed potatoes," he said. Boyer remembered: "It was the first time that anyone said to me that a medicament was immediately dangerous."

The mystery endured. On the tenth anniversary, *Vélo* asked: "What is the legacy of this day? Did it bring in a new era, polluted by a miracle drug? Did it symbolize the start of the EPO years?" It answered its own question by referring to the Italian as "the bionic man."

But the bionic man declined quickly. Within a few years, *Procycling* was writing: "It's hard to remember the days when the original *Diablo's* boastful cockiness was taken seriously. His star has been extinguished as dramatically as it burst into life." In 1997 he was caught in doping tests, the year the UCI introduced blood tests. He was banned from the Giro and then thrown out of the Italian world championship team.

Chiappucci rode to Sestriere with a heart meter strapped to his chest. It was sufficiently unknown at the time that he had to explain to reporters and even other riders that it was "like the rev counter in your car." Heart meters were the tool of Francesco Conconi and Chiappucci was indeed one of his clients. Chiappucci's blood tests were among 33 that a judge looked at before announcing Conconi "morally guilty", not convicted because the statute of limitations had expired.

As with Moser, the situation was contradictory. In 1997, Chiappucci told a prosecutor, Vincenzo Scolastico, that he had been taken EPO since 1993. And then he said he hadn't.

Either way, Jef Bernard, one of Indurain's teammates, reckoned that "Sestriere symbolized the arrival of the heavy artillery."

33

A Balloon Head
Floating in the Clouds

Paris, September 6, 1931: "To fully appreciate the merit of the ride, one should visualize for a moment the strain of a 300-mile drive (in one day) in a modern high-speed and comfortable car. Opperman has amassed more than half again this mileage and added it to the terrific and concentrated physical effort of 24 hours awheel.

"Setting off with an assisting breeze, he shortly afterward ran into heavy rain and hail, which was so dense at one stage that he had to dismount for a quarter of an hour to see the road ahead of him. In the course of the record, he broke seventeen intermediate records and tremendous crowds throughout the ride paid tribute to his performance.

"He...broke the world's record by 37¼ miles and, including stops, put up the amazing average of 21 miles per hour. That Opperman was able to annihilate such an outstanding figure [the previous record was attributed to Cyril Hepplestone of Britain at 468½ miles] must put the ride in the category of being the greatest of his long and brilliant career."

So wrote the *South Western Advertiser* in the western Australian city of Perth in 1932.

It's so hard now to imagine a country, any country, which could be so interested in a bloke on a bike. And yet that same day the news was the front-page story, with pictures, in *The Sun* in Melbourne on the other side of the country and was topped by a call to read the full story on page two.

Opperman was a lean man with large dark eyes, dark hair brushed upright, thin lips, protruding ears and one missing tooth below his left nostril. He was obviously no stranger to Australian sports fans—how could he be otherwise with coverage like that?—because he'd been celebrated the previous year, 1931, for sticking it to the distant and self-satisfied Europeans in their capital of cycling.

The *Daily News*, again in Perth, reported from Paris on September 6: "Hubert Opperman, the Australian champion cyclist, won the Paris–Brest–Paris race (750 miles), breaking the course record, his time being 49 hours 23 minutes 30 seconds. 'It is the hardest bicycle race in the world,' said Opperman, after his victory. 'Many people think the Tour de France is the toughest test, but there we had trainers and masseurs who were not provided in the present contest.'

"Opperman was among the first five to enter Paris. He beat the Belgian, Louyet, by two lengths. A thousand people waving flags acclaimed the victory for the first time gained by a non-French rider."

Opperman wasn't the first Australian in Europe. Don Kirkham and Ivor Munro rode the Tour de France in 1914, finishing seventeenth and twentieth. Reggie MacNamara had long been one of the toughest on the six-day boards. But Opperman was the first of the best, already good enough for *L'Auto*, organizer of the Tour de France, to name him Europe's most popular champion in 1928, ahead of the tennis player, Henri Cochet.

Paris–Brest–Paris began in 1891, when Pierre Giffard, editor of the era's biggest sports paper, jokingly said he would promote a race to the end of the world and back. You need to know that Brest is in Finisterre, which does indeed mean "the end of the world." In those days newspapers depended on the races they promoted to stimulate their sales. The longer the race, in an era when few people had been beyond the next town and asphalt had yet to be invented, the greater the interest, the more people would want to know and the more they'd buy another paper to find out what happened next.

These days it is an endurance event for amateurs who try to finish in 90 hours or less. In 1931, though, it was a classic, albeit an extraordinarily long one—Opperman won in 49 hours 20—and this one was harder than ever. A history says: "1931 was an epic PBP race, arguably the best of all. Run in wretched weather, it was fought tooth and nail by men of iron. After various breakaway attempts, chases and counterattacks, the race ended in a desperate sprint among five exhausted racers on the banked boards of the Buffalo velodrome in Paris!"

The starters—women and foreigners weren't allowed—included ten on tricycles, two tandems and a penny-farthing. There were 28 in the real race and 150 in the *touriste* class. They signed on at the Mauco café in Paris and set off from the Pont Noir on a leafy road lined with crowds near St-Cloud, where the world's first bike race had been held. Maurice Garin, winner of the first Tour de France, fired the gun. Rain fell and a westerly wind rose, pushing into their face. Far from being pole-squatting for the obsessive and slightly odd, the starters included Nicolas Frantz and Maurice Dewaele, former winners of the Tour de France. Frantz was the only rider in the field to have a derailleur: just two speeds, but it meant he avoided having to stop and turn his wheel at the start of hills.

Opperman said years later: "The hours and kilometers slipped by and we were into the first night. The rain ceased for some minutes, only to commence again with re-doubled fury. From the wheels, the water streamed constantly on bare legs which, grease-plastered like Channel swimmers, threw off the icy shower. The sombre clouds brought darkness at an early hour and soon the following cars were playing their powerful lights on the shiny surface of the macadam road. The road twisted and dipped, and despite the efforts of the drivers, the field would constantly plunge into icy darkness, causing a frantic brake-grabbing and shouting from the riders until the blessed illumination lit up the highway again to disclose some riders off the road, some nearly into hedges, some at a standstill and others with feet sliding— ready for any emergency."

The roads were so rough that the vacuum flasks that teams carried for hot drinks during the night fell and broke. "And that's where we had the advantage," said Oppy, who was riding as an individual. "The managers of the other teams had each about five or six men to look after. And each of those riders broke just as many flasks on the cobblestones as I did. Naturally, they ran out of flasks pretty quickly, and for the latter part of the race, when their bodies were crying out for the hot liquid, they had to be content with soups and coffees which had cooled."

It took more than 25 hours to reach Brest. "Once we'd turned there, riders were all over the road with fatigue. Once I had to fend off Frantz when he fell asleep."

Six abandoned on the first night, including Jef Demuysère, who'd finished second in the Tour. Others dropped out when they got to Brest, including the tiny climber Benoît Faure, who went into a café and fell asleep on a bench. More spectacular, Émile Joly called at a farm for water and set off again in the wrong direction. His team manager, Pierre Pierrard, couldn't convince him he was riding back the way he'd come.

Pierrard explained in Paris that Joly was no longer seeing straight, that he was incoherent from tiredness and that he no longer knew what he was doing. Nobody in those days spoke of massive drug doses. Pierrard said it had taken three men to stop him—by throwing a tent over him.

"When he came round, he no longer knew whether he was in France or at home in Belgium," Pierrard said.

Winning Paris–Brest–Paris wasn't unalloyed joy for Opperman. He'd ridden there and back in the striped jersey of the Alleluia bike company, only to hear in Paris that the company had failed and that he wouldn't be getting his bonus.

Opperman was born on May 29, 1904, at Rochester, a town of fewer than 2,000 people in Victoria. His father, from Germany, worked at whatever he could: as a butcher, miner, lumberjack and chauffeur. His mother was British. Hubert worked at what he could from the age of eight and sometimes earned extra money by delivering newspapers by bicycle. He started entering races and, at seventeen, in 1921, he won a Malvern Star bicycle for coming third.

Malvern Star was the trade name inherited by a former Salvation Army officer called Bruce Small when in 1920 he took over a bike shop in the Melbourne suburb of Malvern for the price of £200. Small was a rootless man, attending fourteen schools before his education ended at thirteen. His family was perpetually on the move. He played tenor horn in Salvation bands from the age of six and was solo euphonium player in the Territorial Staff Band of Victoria for 22 years.

He had read of Opperman and Opperman now knew about Small. They did a deal. Opperman would work for Small's business where, with bonuses, he could expect to earn half as much again as in his job as a government messenger. He would ride Small's bikes and he could win cash openly instead of, supposedly, getting racing trophies while having money slipped to him on the side. Small would look after Opperman's career.

Opperman credited Small with keeping him going. When he begged to ease up, Small told him to keep on. "And how right he was," Opperman said. "To stop when in the throes of a flat period is fatal. So on I had to go, a balloon head floating in the clouds, legs as long as chimney stacks and pushing the pedals in weary circle. But hammering into my brain there was one comfort and stimulant: 'This is for Paris–Brest, for Paris–Brest, for Paris–Brest.'"

Small fed him soup, raw egg, tea, black coffee, minced steak, chicken, milk and honey, rice cakes and raisin sandwiches.

Opperman won the Australian road championship in 1924, 1926, 1927 and 1929, and rode the Tour de France in 1928 and 1931, finishing eighteenth and twelfth. Fifteen stages of the Tour in 1928 were team time-trials as long as 387 kilometers. A team of Australians and New Zealanders had been sent thanks to the donations of newspaper readers, with the idea that they'd make up their numbers with Europeans. But the Europeans never materialized and the Australians were out-numbered and out-classed.

René de Latour wrote: "Even if I live to be 150 years old, I shall never forget the sight of Opperman being swept up by the various teams of ten super-athletes, swapping their place beautifully. The Australians would start together, Bainbridge would do his best to hang on, but the passing years had taken more of his speed and he would generally go off the back after 50 miles or so. Then if it was not Osborne it was Watson who would have to quit at the 100-miles mark. And almost daily, Oppy would be left alone for the last 50 miles."

Alcyon, the best of the French teams, usually started ten minutes behind the Australians. Its dictatorial and eccentric manager, Ludo Feuillet, was so impressed that he gave Opperman tires and food and ended by taking him into his team. There, he won the Boule d'Or, a 24-hour race paced by tandems on the Buffalo track in Paris. Distance races and solo rides suited Opperman better than the tactics and repeated accelerations of conventional races.

Small had expanded in becoming agent in Australia for the British company, BSA. Opperman now had a sponsor in Britain, where long-distance time-trials and records were most of the country's cycling.

The only racing Britain itself allowed was on the track and individually against the clock on the road. Just as Small had wanted to promote Malvern Star in Australia, so BSA and other companies in Britain wanted the publicity of exceptional rides to prove the superiority of their bicycles, all of which were much of a likeness.

BSA wanted Opperman to attempt the record from Land's End to John o'Groats, 866 miles south to north on the longest journey possible in mainland Britain. The record stood to a British amateur, Jack Rossiter, in 2 days 13 hours 2 minutes. Opperman accepted and sailed to England to prepare and see the route. He even joined Rossiter's club, the Century in north London. And he was shocked. There were none of the open spaces of Australia and few of the clear highways of France.

"I wondered how on earth I was going to get through. There were all these winding roads to negotiate, and you know what did it? Here was I, an Aussie, trying to take Jack Rossiter's record and his own club organized 250 helpers who went out to wave and cheer me on. It was fantastic."

Opperman set off from the hotel at Land's End at 7am on July 16. "Bruce [Small], of course, had ambitions: to take the 24 [hours] on the way, and go for the 1,000 [miles] as well. Well, we did the 24 with 431.5 miles, which was about 15 miles better than the standing record, and then I got sick. I couldn't hold anything down and gradually my lead slipped. Finally I got a doctor out of bed and he was as calm as could be, gave me a stomach mix, put me to bed for an hour and I was right.

"That was right up in the Highlands, at Beauly, and Bruce said: 'Forget the 1,000—just get to the finish.' I've never had anything so hard, except that 1928 Tour. The road went through the wildest parts of Sutherland. There was heavy rain and the surface was ruts and shingle for the first 25 miles, which took two hours." Despite all that, he beat Rossiter by a little less than ten hours, having startled the purist British by getting out of the saddle on hills. And he ignored the British tradition of "ankling", turning the pedals with an exaggerated rotation of the feet. His time: 2 days 9 hours 1 minute.

BSA worked him hard and presumably paid him well, even though the sport's arcane rules forbade publicity before the ride started. He beat the record from London to York, for 1,000 miles (3 days 1 hour 52 minutes) London–Bath–London, Land's End–London and London–Portsmouth–London, plus a handful of tandem records despite his inexperience. It was all from a different era, of course, and to us now it has a whiff of moth balls. But they were the monuments of the day.

The war put an end to it. Opperman joined the air force, tried racing again and finally retired in 1947. Two years later he was elected to parliament. He had no time for trade unions and thought the socialist party little different from communists. Nevertheless, he campaigned as "Opperman for the Working Man" and, as a minister, relaxed Australia's whites-only immigration rules. Bruce Small became a property developer and also went into politics, under the slogan "Think Big, Vote Small".

Opperman became dangerously overweight. He and his wife, Mavys, moved to a retirement estate where signs forbade cycling. He died of a heart attack just before his 92nd birthday—turning the pedals of an exercise bike that Mavys had told him not to ride.

Bruce Small went from making twelve bicycles a week to owning six factories, a wholesale business and 45 shops with 1,000 more selling his machines. In 1958 he bought land on Australia's Gold Coast and built Paradise City, founding the vacation area of Surfers Paradise. He died of cancer on May 1, 1980, and there is a memorial to him in Elkhorn Avenue in the city he founded.

BSA floundered in the 1950s and was sold to Raleigh in 1957. Raleigh, once the biggest bike company in the western world, closed its factory in Nottingham in 1999 and in 2003 stopped assembling bicycles in Britain. It was sold in 2012 to a Dutch company.

34

Grinta, Pure Grinta

It's easy to think that the epic years of cycling were back before the world war, when races started in darkness and finished at dusk, when men raced 400 kilometers a day on roads of rock and dust. A surprise, then, to find the tradition lived on decades later.

Bologna, Italy, June 13, 1956: The national speech radio station in Britain has a weekly obituary. It's called *Last Word* and you might imagine it's as cold and colorless as the inside of a coffin. But its charm is the variety and the telling of those whose lives are worth recounting, be they good or bad. Cyclists don't often make the list but one who did is Fiorenzo Magni. The contributor invited to talk of him said one word explained everything: *grinta*, he said, grit, determination. And Magni had lots.

He wasn't that lovable a man. Other riders were cold toward him because of his right-wing leanings and his supposed collaboration when Mussolini and the Germans between them ran Italy. And they laughed, because Magni was hardly a handsome man, when he introduced a beauty cream, Nivea, as his team sponsor.

But for one thing he could never be faulted: *grinta*.

In 1956, Magni was already an old man as cycling goes. And his lined face and long-retreating hair made him appear older than his 36 years. But he wasn't to be underestimated. This was a man who won the Tour of Flanders in 1949, 1950 and 1951, leading Belgium to despair. He won the Giro three times, wore the *maillot jaune* in three of his six Tours de France and won the national championship.

That year, 1956, he wanted to win the Giro and call a day on his cycling while he was at the top. The problem was that he crashed on the twelfth stage going downhill after Volterra, in his native Tuscany. He broke his left collar bone.

"Few doctors followed big bike races then," Magni said, "but they agreed: Magni needed a sling, perhaps even some sort of plaster. And above all, he couldn't carry on racing. At the hospital they said I should put on a plaster cast and quit. But I didn't want to. Since the next day was a rest day, I told the doctor to do nothing and that we should wait and see. The day after, I asked the doctor to put on an elastic bandage instead of a cast."

Next morning he went to the start, as anxious as the rest of the race was interested.

"Just before the stage started, I tried to ride my bike on a climb and I noticed I couldn't use the muscles of my left arm to pull on the handlebar very hard. So my mechanic, Faliero Masi, the best mechanic of all time, cut a piece of inner tube and suggested I pull it with my mouth. That was a great idea!"

Masi was one of two mechanics. Ernesto Colnago was the other, recruited in gratitude for the day Colnago, an unknown cycle-shop mechanic, spotted that Magni's leg pain that day came from his steel, cottered cranks being out of alignment. Magni and Masi had a long connection, because Magni was the first rider of note to win on a Masi frame, around 1924. Colnago is better known now but Masi had the romance, not least because in 1952 he opened a shop beneath the Vigorelli track in Milan and supplied frames, labeled with other companies' names, to Merckx, Anquetil, Maertens, Bahamontes and Reg Harris.

Masi pulled the latex tube out of a punctured tubular tire and handed it over. Magni wasn't sure. Who would be? But the timed climb to Madonna di San Luca was only three kilometers. It would be tolerable, just, and it would be over thankfully fast. And what choice did he have?

He rode like that until stage sixteen. After consecutive days of 270 kilometers, he came to a 230-kilometer stage from Bologna to Rapallo, through the Apennines. And he crashed again, falling on his arm on the same side as the broken collarbone.

"I didn't have enough strength in my left arm and I crashed after hitting a ditch by the road," he said. "I fell on my already broken bone and fainted from the pain. The ambulance came to bring me to the hospital. In the ambulance they gave me water and I got back on my feet. When I realized that I was being taken to the hospital, I screamed and told the driver to stop. I didn't want to abandon the Giro!

"I mounted my bike again and restarted pedaling. The peloton had waited for me, so I arrived in Rapallo in a relatively good position. I had no idea of how serious my condition was, I just knew that I was in a lot of pain but I didn't want to have X-rays that evening. During the days that followed I could hold my own."

He was in awful pain, although to be truthful, Magni *always* looked in awful pain. He had what nineteenth-century doomsayers used to call "bicyclist's face."

The stages that followed included the dreadful day through the snow, won by Charly Gaul, that you've already read about. Despite all that, Magni finished the Giro second, 3 minutes 27 seconds behind Gaul but three minutes ahead of the third rider. He didn't win but, to him, it remained his greatest victory.

Only then did he learn what had happened in that second fall. He had broken the upper half of his arm.

"The day after the end of the Giro, I went to an institute that specialized in bone injuries. And they gave me a dressing-down! They said I had two fractures—I thought I had only one—and forced me to put a plaster cast on. The next day I went to my machine shop and asked my mechanic to cut the plaster cast away with the special scissors he used for sheet metal. That way I could start training again. Well, my shoulder is a little crooked now, but that's that."

The machine shop he referred to was part of a motorcycle dealership, Fiorenzo Magni srl, that he started in 1951 when he realized his racing life wasn't going to go on for ever. "I trained in the morning and worked for my company in the afternoon. I could have continued racing for many more years, but my managerial commitments started to keep me too busy. So, after 1956 I decided to quit racing, even though I had the strength to continue."

By then the motorbike business had expanded to a car dealership in Monza, a town northeast of Milan where he lived and where, on October 19, 2012, he died in hospital. His legacy was his bravery and extraordinary courage. But there was, too, a murkier side. Magni hadn't been alone in supporting the fascist dictator, Mussolini, and the order the dictator tried to return to Italian life. He, after all, was the man who metaphorically made Italian trains run on time.

But there was another political force in the country: those who had never wanted a dictatorship and, beside them towards the end of the war, those who realized they'd backed the wrong side. It's impossible now to determine Magni's role in the war and the internal politics that went with it. It's known that he joined Mussolini's National Fascist Party in 1943, but neither the word "fascist" nor the movement behind it had the opprobrium that they hold now.

By 1946, with Mussolini now dead, fascism denounced and Italy having changed sides, Magni was put on trial with 23 others for allegedly fighting partisans, opponents of Mussolini, in the so-called Massacre of Valibona in the Apennines. The story, uncontested, is that a British prisoner of war released in September 1943 teamed up with an Italian sergeant-major to form an inexperienced militia of several nationalities to seek out and fight fascists.

They lived in the hills, as the French Resistance did, and slept where they could. In January 1944, they chose a barn at Valibona, seven kilometers from Magni's home. Unusually, nobody had been put on guard duty. Just before dawn, 50 fascists arrived from two directions. The gun fight lasted two hours, with deaths on both sides, and ended with the hotchpotch army scattering. There had been other and probably worse skirmishes before, and certainly more deadly battles. But this was the first clash of partisans and fascists in the area and it split local loyalties and politics for decades.

An over-romantic story often told says the partisans were forced to lie on the ground as the buildings around them burned. One looked up and recognized his cycling hero standing over him. And from that identification, Magni was charged. What is more likely is that a man of Magni's status would be recognized anywhere and his movements were always well known. Witnesses said they had seen him there and some said he had been one of the main killers, even boasting about it.

Documents produced in December 1945 put Magni in a group of fascists notorious for violence and which had worked beside the Germans in Tuscany.

Magni faced 30 years in jail, perhaps the death penalty. The trial opened in Florence in January 1947, without him. He had fled justice and police throughout the country were told to arrest him on sight. Meanwhile his lawyer defended him in his absence.

He called on Alfredo Martini, the manager of the Italian national team and described in court as a former partisan, to testify in Magni's favor. Legend says Magni was cleared on Martini's evidence, Martini being a socialist unlikely to defend an admitted fascist if he weren't innocent. But Martini said only that Magni "seemed a very good person until July 25, 1943." There was no mention of what he had become after that date. And Gino Bartali, who had avoided fighting in the war by exploiting his friendship with the Pope and taking shelter in the Vatican, refused to testify even that much.

Fascist evidence was dismissed as propaganda, and letters produced to suggest that Magni fought *with* partisans near the northern town of Monza in 1945 were so at odds with other evidence—and with records in archives in the USA—that they counted for nothing. In the end, Magni was cleared less because he was innocent than because the court couldn't decide he was guilty. Many denunciations followed in the press. Magni was never welcome again in the area.

He was booed as he won the Giro in 1948. Crowds shook fists and hissed and heckled throughout the final stage to the Vigorelli. He was the third man of Italian cycling, after Coppi and Bartali, and since neither Coppi nor Bartali had won, it followed that it was Magni's fault. Any idea that Magni was as worthy a winner as anyone else, especially given his record, was dismissed because of his reputation as a fascist. Magni wept as he stood in the track center and heard the crowd insult him and throw fruit as only an Italian crowd knows. The next year, only one Italian journalist bothered to watch him in the Tour of Flanders.

It was his toughest moment until the Giro of 1956. By then Italy had recovered and moved into a more modern era. It hadn't forgotten but, especially thanks to an amnesty, it had forgiven. Fiorenzo Magni could call himself a hero again.

35

Into the Mists of the Gods

On a single, dismal day in the mountains, a man alone set fire to a stage of the Tour. What nobody knew was that he was also setting fire to the Tour and to cycling itself.

Hautacam, France, July 10, 2000: The mountains had disappeared. The Pyrenees are mysterious, often hidden by air convection until you're right under them. But that day the clouds came down from the peaks seemingly to the top of the lampposts.

The Tour was in Dax, a town of rugby, bull-fighting and an appealing way of rolling the *rrr* in words. The town is on low, rolling land which edges the Atlantic. To the north are the Landes, tediously flat commercial pine forests that for a century had provided the most boring stages of the Tour, for riders and spectators alike. To the south, the mountains rise to separate France from Spain.

Lance Armstrong's team was in one of those identical, efficient but charmless business hotels that encircle towns throughout the world. They preferred it that way, to the extent of always using the same hotel chain whenever they could. They didn't care that they could wake in the morning without any clue where they were, that the room was the same as a week, two weeks before. That was what they wanted. Minimum change, minimum stress, minimum remembering directions to the bathroom or which side the telephone was.

The day's stage would take them and the other survivors over the Marie-Blanque, Aubisque, the lesser Soulor, down into the valley and then up to the cross-country ski station of Hautacam. Jacky Durand, winner of the Tour of Flanders eight years earlier and still the only Frenchman to have won in 60 years, knew he had no more chance of winning than almost everyone else. But no matter: no stage was too petty or too intimidating to go off ahead of the race alone or with a few others.

"I've spent my whole career knowing that I'll never win the Tour," Durand said, now an informed and amusing television commentator, "so I rely on my media value. If I do something, it gets in the papers. Sometimes, 100 kilometers of riding alone in the Tour de France has more significance than a win in another race."

His lone attacks became such a feature of the 1990s that one year *Vélo* published a monthly "Jackymetre." In 2001, it showed he had raced 16,524 kilometers and led for 2,270 of them. No surprise then when Du-du (the nickname means "teddy bear") pushed off through the gloom after 30 kilometers, staying out ahead with a changing cast for the next 155 kilometers.

Sometimes those *échapées matinales* can work. This one did for Javier Otxoa. The Basque region straddles the Pyrenees and Otxoa lived on the Spanish and more tumultuous side, an area with an independence movement that had been murderously violent. He and Nico Mattan, from a much flatter area of Belgium but one equally with an independence movement, were together alone as they reached the start of the increasingly barren Marie-Blanque.

Otxoa was the better climber—at 62 kilograms, 7 kilos lighter than Mattan, and at 1 meter 72, 9 centimeters shorter. It surprised no one that he dropped the Belgian going up, nor that Mattan came back beside him going down. Bigger riders climb worse but descend better. But they also expend more energy going up, so Otxoa shook him off for good on the Soulor, a lump on the side of the Aubisque, and reached the foot of Hautacam with nine minutes. And there he groveled, losing time not only through his own legs but also through the pandemonium that had broken out behind him.

It would have pleased any rider in the field to have won at Hautacam but it inconvenienced few that it was Otxoa, who finally crossed the line with only 42 seconds left of the nine minutes he once had. Behind him, those who counted had waited, watching each other, knowing that Armstrong often attacked on the last climb. Which he was going to, but to which he was beaten by Marco Pantani.

The Italian attacked, and Armstrong and the bespectacled and maladroit Swiss, Alex Zülle, scrambled to go with him. They caught him 13 seconds later, all three men out of the saddle. And from that moment the day belonged to Armstrong. Zülle, sensing the desperation but picking the wrong moment, came by almost straight away to Pantani's right.

Armstrong came back to Zülle on Pantani's wheel. "Normally, Armstrong will attack here," said the commentator on French television, "unless he's changed his method and if he's got the physical capacity." And sure enough, 2 minutes 15 seconds after Pantani started the move, Armstrong rose out of the saddle and rode by both him and the Swiss.

It was a test of each man's thighs, how long he could stay out of the saddle without lactic acid burning intolerably. The first to crack was Zülle. He dropped back into the saddle and slipped off Pantani's wheel seconds later. Armstrong now led Pantani, turning the slightly larger gear, looking one way over his shoulder and then the other. He signaled for the Italian to pass him, to share the work. It didn't work. Aggrieved, Armstrong pushed the pace several times, then finally dislodged his one remaining rival.

Ahead and out of sight, Otxoa was getting weaker and weaker, his shoulders rolling as he pushed. He had never won a professional race, he rode for a little-considered team, and he was getting news now of what was happening behind.

Armstrong squeezed to the left of Mattan, then caught the other survivors 50 meters in front of him. They included Richard Virenque, whose group had lost two minutes in six kilometers. A moment's pause to recover on a back wheel and then Armstrong rode by them, not attacking, just returning to his original climbing speed.

It doesn't look so extraordinary, now that we're accustomed to faster pedaling speeds in the mountains, but that day the talk was all of how Armstrong had turned the pedals at up to 100 times a minute. More obviously remarkable in retrospect is how long he stayed out of the saddle. As Zülle found out, and every Sunday rider knows, that takes exceptional blood flow through the muscles, to get fresh sugar in and, more important, to get the burned fuel out. Exceptional blood flow is coupled with exceptional ability to take oxygen from the lungs and slide it, through a process called osmosis, into the blood. For some, looking back, it was a clue.

That wet afternoon he won the Tour de France to the candle reflections of the car lights that followed him. He finished within sight of Otxoa, not relenting until the line, to take the fourth and final yellow jersey of the Tour. Pantani finished, gasping, 5 minutes 10 seconds later. Jan Ullrich, his other rival, had been pushed back three and a half minutes.

The author, Olivier Alvarado, wrote: "This dusk finish sounded like a death bell. After this climb of Hautacam, cycling would never be the same. The victory of Javier Otxoa, from whom he'd taken ten minutes, had been relegated to a footnote. That day was exceptional…Armstrong was exceptional…stupefying. But the doubts had begun."

A code of secrecy surrounds the inner workings of professional cycling. Even decades later, most professionals won't speak of what are euphemistically known as tricks of the trade. But riders change teams and bring news of what went on before. And there are rumors, and sometimes words are carefully chosen to say little but reveal a lot. Riders will say a rival's performance was exceptional but add nothing. The silence, the abnormal reticence to add details to praise, says a lot. You get it, too, in coded press comments, such as: "His ride today surprised even his team-mates." In other words, they didn't think he was up to it and that it could be worth seeking the explanation.

And that's what France 3's journalists did. The station is one of two that provides coverage of the Tour to stations all round the world. When the race isn't on France 3, it's on its sister, France 2. On July 18, spotting a helper leave Armstrong's team hotel with a black plastic bag, then extravagantly putting the bag into a car and driving off rather than leave it for the trash, they asked themselves why. And they followed. In the bag, they found 160 syringe boxes, equipment for blood transfusions, blood-stained pads, and empty medicine boxes including some marked Actovegin.

Actovegin is made, with veal's blood among other constituents, in Norway by a company called Nycomed. It helps blood carry more oxygen and, like EPO, gives extra whoomph to each lungful of breath. It had been banned in France since 1992 but it was available across the border in Germany, from where it had been used in soccer, especially for games at altitude such as in Mexico.

It didn't, however, appear on lists of drugs banned in sport. Not until the following December, when the UCI said it was blood doping. By then, it had spread through cycling, as Philippe Gaumont explained in his tell-all, *Prisonnier du Dopage*. That winter, Armstrong said: "We are completely innocent. We run a very clean and professional team that has been singled out due to our success.... Before this ordeal I had never heard of [Actovegin]."

Next summer, in the riotously expensive Georges Cinq hotel that overlooks the finish of the Tour on the Champs-Elysées, Armstrong stared at reporters and said: "I have never used illegal products, whether it's EPO or any other illicit substance." The lie was in mentioning EPO, which couldn't be detected at the time but which later tests showed he had taken in generous proportions, and the words "illegal products" neatly covered Actovegin.

He wasn't, of course, alone. His undoing was his bare-faced lying, his hypocrisy and, it later emerged, his bullying of team-mates, let alone rivals, and any journalist who dared to suggest there were doubts. And in Europe, they did. There, the story of plucky cancer survivor which had counted for so much in America was admired but considered with skepticism.

"So do we now have to have an operation for cancer to win the Tour de France?" asked Lucien Aimar, a former Tour winner no stranger to doping.

As one blogger wrote: "Never to take the 'no comment' route, instead he always claimed he was above it, saying simply 'What am I on? I'm on my bike, busting my ass, six hours a day,' when really he could have said nothing."

July 1999: "I have been on my deathbed. I am not stupid. I can emphatically say that I am not on drugs."

January 2001: "The simple truth is that we outwork everyone. But when you perform at a higher level in a race, you get questions about doping."

January 2004: "I have never had a single positive dope test and I do not take performance-enhancing drugs." (This was a lie; he had been found positive but then excused in his first Tour.)

August 2005: "I have never doped. I can say it again but I've said it for seven years."

July 2010: "As long as I live, I will deny it. There was absolutely no way I forced people, encouraged people, facilitated. Absolutely not. One hundred per cent."

And so it went on. Until it began falling apart. *L'Équipe* produced dope-check forms and the results of tests to prove that Armstrong had not only taken EPO but had taken it noticeably frequently. By then a test had been perfected. And still he denied it, branding *L'Équipe* a tabloid while knowing his American audience wouldn't know it was a respectable broadsheet with the power to expose his cheating, which it did on its front page under the headline "The Armstrong lie."

Only when former team-mates lined up to condemn him, frustrated by his lying and his role in their life, did he falter. And precisely, he stumbled when those team-mates, including his greatest ally, George Hincapie, were called to give evidence in court. Lying to journalists was one thing, risking jail for perjury was another.

Well, the result is well enough known. Armstrong confessed on television, was stripped of all his Tour wins and much else and was banned for life from all sports. Finally he showed humility: "All the fault and all the blame here falls on me. I viewed this situation as one big lie that I repeated a lot of times. I made my decisions. They are my mistakes, and I am sitting here today to acknowledge that and to say I'm sorry for that."

Had he not been such a bully, a fraud and above all a hypocrite, he would have been judged no more severely than many another rider of his era or, indeed, of all eras. As that blogger wrote, look who else was there. The top nine that day were Otxoa, Armstrong, José-Maria Jimenez, Virenque, Marcel Beltran, Fernando Escartin, Roberto Heras, Christophe Moreau and Joseba Beloki.

"Don't forget Pantani, Zülle and Ullrich. Where are [all] those guys now? How many of them left the sport on their own terms? How many were forced out? How many of them got caught doping? How many of them were implicated in scandal? How many of them admitted using EPO? How many of them are dead?"

The answer is that all of them were implicated except Escartin, although he too has been linked with the controversial doctor, Michele Ferrari, who advised Armstrong.

Armstrong rode hard, he lied even harder and he fell harder still.

36
And the Last Shall Be First

You'd need a heart of stone not to feel at least something for the last rider of the Tour de France. All that way for nothing. Except that, sometimes, there's something...

Puy-de-Dôme, France, July 18, 1969: Arsène Millocheau was the first. Or, rather he was the first to be last. He finished the 1903 Tour de France a whopping 64 hours 47 minutes 22 seconds behind Maurice Garin and became the Tour's first last man. Divide that by 24, the number of hours in a day, and you find it's more than two and a half days. Which, on a race of only six days was at the very least remarkable.

Arsène, or Florentin as his mother preferred to call him (Arsène was his middle name), was born in Champseru, a nothing sort of town right in the middle of France. He's unknown there, which seems unfair. Surely there's time to celebrate a man who lost ten hours on the final stage alone and, before that, fifteen hours between Lyon and Marseille. They rode 374 kilometers that day, it's true, but Millocheau lost more time that stage than Hippolyte Aucouturier took to win it.

Millocheau was a bright-eyed man with well-fed cheeks and the sort of wide mustache that demanded to be twizzled. He never rode the Tour again after 1903, although he never stopped riding his bike. At 54, still lean, his mustache much trimmed but blessed by a generous silver goatee, he rode Paris–Brest–Paris in 1921.

Nobody now celebrates the *lanterne rouge*, as the last man came to be known years later. For a long time, though, he was as well known as the race leader. Tradition demanded he carry a red light on his saddle and there was even a prize for him, the slowest man to Paris. On that he could be sure of more criterium contracts than riders who'd finished an hour or two sooner. Everyone wanted to sympathize with the under-dog and, cruelly perhaps, wonder whether he'd be dropped on the first lap. Not that he ever was; not only did the others make sure it didn't happen, but even to come last in the Tour is no mean achievement. You have to be pretty good to start, let alone finish.

But sometimes even the last can be first.

In 1969 Pierre Matignon was employed as all unknowns of the Tour have been employed: to sell their bodies and ride in the wind for their leaders and chase breaks and bring bottles and, in those days, raid bars for free drinks. He was just a curly-haired domestique in the little-fancied Frimatic team. Just two days remained by July 18 and he was 86th and last. He was as happy as everyone else to be so close to Paris and a night of rest rather than another team conference and another worried night.

Matignon was pleased to have got that far. It had been a hard Tour ever since the start at Roubaix, on the Belgian border. More than a third of the 130 starters had dropped out, among them Roger De Vlaeminck, Rik van Looy and Luis Ocaña. Lucien Aimar, who had won the Tour three years earlier was more than an hour behind. Jan Janssen, the winner in 1968, was at 48 minutes.

When the riders climbed out of bed in Brive that morning, they ate breakfast with thoughts of a hard traipse across central eastern France to the coil of road to the top of the Puy-de-Dôme. Matignon was in a slow bicycle race with André Wilhelm, a rider all of nine days older who rode for Sonolor, a maker of radios and televisions. Wilhelm was last but one and he had to lose two more minutes to be sure of his odd place in history and his string of contracts. But that didn't look like happening, so he decided to attack instead. Right from the start. Anything to get his name in the papers and on to start sheets.

Matignon happily, as he saw it, managed to puncture at the same time and, unworthy of support from his team, plodded on alone off the back.

Wilhelm was never going to stay out front all day, of course, least of all on a stage finishing on the Puy. But neither was the bunch going to make its legs ache too early by bothering to chase. The ride up the old volcano was the important part. Behind everyone else, Matignon pushed on and on and, with some relief, came back to the bunch. Everyone was looking forward to the hill at Chavanon, where crowds were gathering to see the Tour string out and grab food bags. And just as the riders did that, Radio Tour broke its silence.

"*On annonce le démarrage d'un coureur de la Frimatic Viva-De Gribaldy,*" the voice, dwelling on the syllables of De-gri-bal-dy, the name of a cuddly gray-haired millionaire known as The Count who'd been in bike racing for ages and would confirm his aristocratic lineage at the least prompting.

A few eyebrows rose. Ethics demanded a truce at feed stations and leaping away was badly thought of. The stars looked around and saw nobody of importance lacking and carried on riding. In time Radio Tour gave the rider's name, as unknown to the announcer as everyone else.

Matignon had decided that if Wilhelm could attack, then so could he. They were battling for press cuttings as well as the upside-down dignity of last place. And he wasn't going to stay away, that was for sure, so there was much to gain and little to lose. And maybe next day he'd be so tired that he'd flake off the back again. Being *lanterne rouge* has its own tactics. And so Matignon went off down the road and romantics smiled and cynics sneered.

There's a pride among the top names. None of them was going to chase a no-hoper. Lesser lights could do that if they chose, but not the stars. And so Matignon pushed on. After twenty kilometers he had three minutes. That grew to five minutes with 30 kilometers to go. Four riders did then set off after him, but two of them were Matignon's own team-mates, Jean-Claude Lebaube and Joaquin Agostinho. The little Portuguese climber would profit both ways: he could slow down the hunt for Matignon, and if that didn't work, well, he'd maybe get to the foot of the Puy before the other climbers.

Twenty kilometers from the line, Matignon had a startling seven and a half minutes. He could see the volcano, which sticks improbably out of the landscape like a cropped cone. But nothing was certain. He was flagging, repeatedly in and out of the saddle, a man out of his class. It would only take the chase to start seriously and he'd be swept up, passed, and left to a small paragraph in the thousands of words of reporting.

It was the largely French Peugeot team who got the chase going. Its leader was the hypochondriac, beak-nosed Roger Pingeon, who slept each night with paper stuffed in the bedroom key hole for fear it would let light flood in and disturb his sleep. He had won the Tour the previous year, when it was contested by national teams, and this time he was in second place to Eddy Merckx.

Pingeon and Merckx had been joined at the hip for days and so Merckx looked round, noticed Pingeon had shown no reaction, and joined in the chase. He could push Pingeon into obscurity and save his shame by winning on the Puy rather than be belittled by a man to whom he'd probably never spoken. He wound his body into an arch and rode so hard that only Poulidor and Paul Gutty, Matignon's teammate climber from Lyons, could go with him.

The result was Matignon was down to two minutes with ten kilometers to go. He had the class of neither Merckx nor Poulidor and he'd been riding on his own for hours.

The chase and then the bunch, itself chasing, turned through the gate to the narrow road of the Puy. The race twirled round and round its flanks, as it had with Anquetil and Poulidor five years earlier. For a while Merckx couldn't see Matignon, who was always too far round the circle. He spotted him as Matignon rode across the shadow of the final banner and the red triangle that announced the last thousand meters.

Once more Merckx curved his shoulders. He threw his bike from side to side. He dropped back into the saddle, elbows bent outwards, hands on the drops, back arched. Gutty broke, then Poulidor.

The gap was 500 meters and the great Merckx was about to be beaten by a man who'd never previously ridden the Tour. He must that moment have wondered if it would have been better to stay anonymously with the other stars rather than be pictured struggling behind a man whom nobody recognized.

Matignon began to zigzag. The crowds, the mayhem, surrounded him. He didn't have to look round to confirm it was Merckx, although he risked a nervous glance anyway. His woolen vest was soaked with sweat, his dark curly hair shone, his white handlebar tape was soiled by ungloved hands. He reached the short flat stretch at the summit, lifted one arm, loosened his pedal straps and freewheeled exhausted across the line.

Les Woodland

Matignon never did finish *lanterne rouge*. His lone break made him too fast and Wilhelm finished six and a half minutes slower. Matignon probably made more in fees from his triumph, but he never became a star. He rode one more Tour, in 1972, when he finished 75th. And he died in November 1987, just 44 years old.

Arsène Millocheau died in May 1948, when he was 81.

37

Revenge, Sweet Revenge

We don't see many breaks like today's, they said at the end of the day. But maybe what happened behind was even more remarkable. The story of an extraordinary day...

Orcières-Merlette, France, July 8, 1971: You see the *Closed* sign before you get there. It's hanging on a single strand of chain that hangs between two short posts. Few people wander that far up the path because they pass the main attraction before they get there and turn off to see the chapel of Labastide d'Armagnac. And it's not surprising because the church, like the one of Madonna del Ghisallo near Como, Italy, is dedicated to cyclists and full of jerseys and bikes and magazines.

The place that's closed is more of a junk heap. And it was dedicated not to cyclists generally but to one in particular: Luis Ocaña. Because the one man ever to humiliate Merckx lived in the area. And he carried the bruises of their encounter until the day he reached for his gun and shot himself.

In June 1990, Ocaña said: "*Bon sang*, I'd give hectares of my land to see Merckx come back to the bunch for just two weeks. Just two weeks. To show all those *mignons* what it was like to race against Merckx! That guy was unbelievable, for God's sake. They wouldn't have time to go curling their hair or putting rings in their ear. They only thing they'd want is to get to bed even faster and recover."

Whatever and whoever was at the Luis Ocaña museum have now gone. There's a padlocked wooden gate and a glimpse of a Tour de France judging stand, the sort they put on a flatbed truck in those days to give a better view. A sign in the church asks you don't send donations to the museum by mistake. The remains are sadly reminiscent of a troubled man who put an end to his life for reasons that even now aren't clear.

Ocaña was Spanish but he'd lived in France since his father emigrated to the Aran valley in 1957. He was loyal to Spain but he considered himself French. He bought his first bike from saved pocket money when he was twelve, and four years later began racing with a club at Aire-sur-l'Adour. From there he moved to the club in Mont-de-Marsan. And in 1971, as a professional in the orange jersey of the Bic ballpoint and razor company, he set out from Grenoble to Orcières, a ski station which wanted the publicity in an era when the Tour went almost anywhere that paid well.

Merckx, at his height, had planned to hold the yellow jersey from start to finish. And probably he would have done it had Ocaña not "at last paid up on his promising talent", as Geoffrey Nicholson put it, and "outdistanced him in the Chartreuse, along with Thévenet, the Swede Gosta Petersson and Zoetemelk, who took the yellow jersey."

According to Michel Crepel: "Ocaña had a single obsession. It was spelled in six letters: M.E.R.C.K.X. He even called his dog Merckx, for the simple pleasure of seeing it lie at his feet when he told it to." And that day, he saw the first signs of weakness in his devil.

Deposing Merckx, even for a day, seemed unbelievable. "We were resigned to it," van Impe confessed. "We thought Merckx was unbeatable, and I still think so today. He was very strong, too strong. And he had the best team." And yet, and yet...

On the night the riders slept at Grenoble, they went to bed with rumors of insurrection in their ears. Something was going to happen, they were sure, but what and who would do it, well, that was less clear. Zoetemelk had been dismissed, victim of his reputation for following Merckx rather than attacking him. He was naturally pale and didn't tan easily, so the joke was that the sun never shone on him because he was always in Merckx's shadow. Thévenet could be the man, but he was even more unpredictable than his team, Peugeot. So, who? Ocaña? He'd insisted in *L'Équipe* only the previous day that to attack was the only way to put Merckx in trouble. He hoped his own win on the Puy-de-Dôme "would give ideas to others."

Les Woodland

But would he put his money where his mouth was, this irritatingly arrogant man so often dogged by ill luck?

In the event, it was Joaquim Agostinho, whom his manager, Raphaël Géminiani, had told to attack in revenge for comments a couple of days earlier. He was cross with Lomme Driessens, Merckx's manager at Molteni. "He said unpleasant things about Merckx's opposition. He particularly singled out my little Portuguese, saying he didn't have the class and that he was too docile, the sort of thing not pleasant to hear. I repeated them to Joaquim and he reacted. We had made him his own bike, made to measure, very light, for the côte de Laffrey. He wanted to stuff the lot, and I encouraged him."

So Agostinho attacked, just after Vizille. The climb suited him. It's called a *côte*, a hill, but it's ten kilometers long. It was so steep that there were pull-outs for drivers whose engines had overheated. Ocaña saw the danger and chased him, and so did another climber, van Impe. On the flat stretch on the Pierre-Châtel, Ocaña waited for his chasers. There was a link of circumstance between him and Agostinho. Ocaña had joined Bic in the belief that Géminiani would be the manager there. But Géminiani had been fired and gone instead to Hoover, Agostinho's sponsor. The two stayed friends but Géminiani insisted there was no plot, that Agostinho and Ocaña joining on the road "was racing, that's all."

Back in the bunch, Ocaña's teammates surrounded Merckx, trying to fence him in. And the Spanish Kas team were no more helpful because their leader, José Manuel Fuente, was up the road trying to catch the break. And Merckx was uncomfortable. The fortress resistance no longer showed and his head had begun rolling. Small signs but unmissable.

Celestino Vercelli, a minor Italian but a keen observer, remembered: "Merckx never let anybody break away. But that day…we don't know.… The start was on an upgrade and he wasn't that brilliant in the beginning. Maybe he was still warming up and Ocaña, Agostinho, Zoetemelk, noticed that and decided to break away immediately. Maybe he didn't expect such an early breakaway from the others, or maybe he wasn't just prompt enough for that uphill start. Anyway the leading group never slowed down."

At St-Disdier, 70 kilometers from Grenoble, those leaders had a little more than three minutes. It was the start of the col du Noyer.

Few spectators saw it because the road is narrow and the climb less important than the others. But it was there that Ocaña attacked. Just as he passed 74 kilometers of racing, he leaned forward on his bike and the others never saw him again. Van Impe began chasing too late, despairing of the riders he was with ever working together because they had conflicting interests.

Back in the main group, more and more riders began relishing Merckx's discontent and resolved to make it no better. He had won everything, left them nothing, demanded so much in appearance fees that little was left for the rest. Fine, let him suffer now. And so he rode alone at the front for twenty kilometers, catching Agostinho and Zoetemelk and keeping the others in a wriggling string behind him. Yet still Ocaña gained. As the Spaniard reached the foot of Merlette, the last climb, he had 5 minutes 45 seconds on van Impe and more than seven minutes on Merckx.

The blackboard man shuttled back and forth, bringing good news to one, bad news to the other: *"Le 40 [Van Impe] à 5'15", Pel. à 6'30"."*

"Slow down a bit!" his manager, Maurice De Muer, shouted. "You've got six minutes."

"Bordel," Ocaña shouted back. "I'll make it seven."

He reached the final meters, straightened his jersey, then slowly lifted his arms, smiling. Nearly six minutes passed before van Impe followed him. And then another three minutes before Merckx, sprinting to save his third place from the group that had stayed with him. He was 8 minutes 42 seconds behind.

Of the 113 who left Grenoble that morning, only 40 finished the day within the time limit. The judges, realizing a Tour with little more than three dozen survivors would lack spectacle, extended the limit. But it still put out Walter Godefroot, who'd been in the running for the green jersey, and a whole peninsula of Italians. It might have put out Roger De Vlaeminck had he not given up anyway.

Van Impe said: "Ocaña had won the Tour. He was the only one who believed it was possible, the only one to think he could beat Merckx, and he did it. Just for that, I'll always admire him."

Merckx offered: "What Luis did was the great moment of our rivalry. He was courageous, free-spirited. He went to the limits of what he could do. He made me, too, go to the limit of my abilities and yet he made me concede nine minutes. I had never felt so bad."

Géminiani took a more balanced view: "Breaks like the one today, those we don't see often in the Tour. But I wonder if what Merckx did behind him, with all those guys on his wheel, whether what wasn't even more extraordinary."

38

Revenge, Sweet Revenge II

To bring a god to earth will earn your place in history.
But the vengeance will be dreadful.

Marseilles, France, July 10, 1971: Being knocked back by almost nine minutes was, as Geoffrey Nicholson put it in *Le Tour,* "the greatest affront the Belgian had received." And "affront" summed it up well. It was all very well being beaten in body but Merckx had been beaten in soul. And that he would not tolerate. The vengeance was terrible and its shock-wave had the Tour banned from Marseille.

There was a rest day when the race reached Orcières. There was just one topic of conversation, of course, and when that started wearing thin, it was helped along by rumors from the Molteni hotel. While Ocaña was in his room with the yellow jersey he had paraded at press conferences, Merckx had been down to the hotel garage. The team mechanics were working there and they were used to, although they never quite forgave, the extra work that his arrival always gave them. Merckx was notoriously difficult about his bike and could never settle on a riding position.

When the great man had left, reporters took over. What had he asked for? What did that mean for the following day? Not much emerged.

But while Ocaña had talked much of the day to the press, watched as ever by Plaud, Merckx and the Molteni team were crowded into a bedroom with their own manager, Lomme Driessens.

"We all looked as though we were at a funeral, but we had to come up with something fast," Jos Bruyère remembered. He was so close to Merckx and such a faithful supporter that more than once Merckx had to tell him not to try so hard, to take his own chances when they came.

"And Driessens explained his plan and twice, in the greatest secrecy, we rehearsed our plan for the next day."

It depended on the Dutchman, Rini Wagtmans, known as Kuifje, or Tufty, for the streak of white hair above his forehead in line with his nose. It's vanished now because his hair has turned uniformly gray but back then it was the first thing you noticed. Wagtmans was the race's fastest descender and he was to set the race alight from the start.

Celestino Vercelli remembered: "We had another incredible stage, from Orcières-Merlette to Marseilles. It was 300 kilometers long, with 20 kilometers of downhill and then 280 kilometers in the Reno valley."

It was those first 20 kilometers that Wagtmans was to exploit. He attacked the moment Félix Lévitan dropped the flag. Bruyère said: "Eddy, Rini and Roger Swerts plunged into the first descent. The peloton exploded immediately. I've never descended so fast. Everyone thought I'd punctured but in fact I was braking so hard that the glue holding my tire had melted."

He wasn't alone. Vercelli said: "This happened to two or three of Merckx's teammates and so they could not help him any more in the valley. And it also happened to me. This happened much more often to the heavy riders, like me, because we had to use the brakes more heavily. Because of this, Merckx lost some riders along the way who would have been a fundamental help to the plan."

Everyone was waiting for Merckx to try something, "but we never thought of that," van Impe said. We were all wearing leg-warmers and plastic covers on our shoes. We had to get rid of them in a hurry and ride flat out. Merckx had really duped us."

The peloton, unobliging when Merckx had wanted help to Orcières, now joined forces to beat him. Bic and Kas, which still had an interest in the race with Fuente, were the driving force. But everyone else joined in, except of course Merckx's Molteni team. The stage was run off at 45.4 kilometers per hour, and yet never did Merckx get more than two and a half minutes on his chasers. The race reached Marseille in such record time that nobody but the judges were ready.

"We went so fast that when we arrived in Marseille there were no television cameras there to broadcast our arrival," Vercelli laughed. "We were two and a half hours early! So the arrival was never filmed. At that time they usually showed only the last part of each stage on TV and we arrived before they could start doing that. In the ten years I have been a professional, this never happened again."

The whole Kas team, which had waited for Fuente when he had problems, arrived after the time limit. To the dismay especially of Molteni's riders, who had arrived on time but far more tired, they were all allowed to stay in the race.

A knot of spectators, alerted by radio accounts, had got to the track in time. But not the mayor. Gaston Defferre had run Marseille as a fiefdom since 1953. His 33 years as mayor, unbeaten in elections, is a record in France. It ended only with his death. Defferre was a genial-looking man whose appearance deceived. He was frighteningly direct and to the point. Defferre was Marseille and Marseille was Defferre. And he didn't take kindly to the Tour getting to his city before it was supposed to and before he was ready. He hurried to the track when he heard the news but he got there to find the riders had all gone, the officials packing up, and the heavy brigade taking down the podium and judging stand. He banned the Tour from returning to his city, a ban that stood until his death fifteen years later.

For all his effort, Merckx took back only two minutes from Ocaña, less than a quarter of what the Spaniard had taken out of him. So there had to be another attempt. And so Merckx waited for the Pyrenees where, in apocalyptic weather fitting the drama, he attacked in rain, wind and hail beneath a Wagnerian black sky.

The col de Menté stands on the D44, a secondary road that runs parallel to the Spanish border eight kilometers to the south, climbing to 1,349 meters. The Tour first climbed it in 1966 and now, in the worst of weather, it was to do it again. Merckx attacked, Ocaña countered. The following cars' headlights half-lit the road, reflecting on the rivers of rain.

Merckx attacked again and again and every time Ocaña stayed with him and sometimes he countered. And then four kilometers down the descent, Merckx missed a left-hand bend on the ice rink of a road and skidded in a puddle and fell. Ocaña slipped behind him and fell against a low wall that protected the road from the ravine. Both men got to their feet, Merckx to put his chain back in place, Ocaña to inspect his Motobecane for damage. De Muer was there and handed over a wheel.

The rest of the race was approaching in the half-light. Zoetemelk, descending on a deflating tire that handicapped his steering, pulled out to avoid De Muer's parked car and ran into Ocaña. Agostinho piled into the two of them, hitting Ocaña in the kidneys, followed by Vicente Lopez-Carril. Ocaña doubled over, screaming in pain, and fell back to the ground.

Jacques Goddet, ghostly in a gray waterproof jacket, arrived in his scarlet car, waving the followers to slow down. The race doctor arrived. But there was nothing to do. Merckx pressed on and won; Ocaña went by helicopter to the hospital at St-Gaudens. Jacques Anquetil, who had taken a mischievous pleasure in advising Ocaña publicly through his radio commentaries, went to see him that evening. Merckx, now the race leader again, declined to wear the yellow jersey next morning.

The yellow jersey that Ocaña wore that day still exists. It's slit from neck to waist, through the sticker that names Bic as his sponsor. The surgeon cut it to get at Ocaña's chest after he arrived on a stretcher. Someone thought to save his cotton cap, too; it's still gray and grubby from the rain and grit that dreadful day.

He did recover, Ocaña, and in 1973 he won the Tour and six of its stages, pushing Bernard Thévenet to fifteen minutes. But that was a year that Merckx didn't ride. It's a barroom debating point among those old enough to care whether the Spaniard or the Belgian would have won that year.

Ocaña retired in 1977 and spent his time growing vines around his house at Caupenne d'Armagnac and occasionally commentating on Spanish radio and television. On May 19, 1994, he walked from the house to the wine store that stood beside it. He was alone. It was a journey he had made a thousand times. But this time was different because he either took a gun from his house or he picked one up in the wine store. There was a shot and Ocaña was found dead beside his gun, which had fallen from his hands. There was blood everywhere.

His family called a doctor and the doctor called an ambulance, which carried him to hospital at Mont-de-Marsan, where he'd been a member of the town cycling club and where he's still remembered with affection. He was declared dead at 5:10 that afternoon, at the age of 48.

The records are at the local *préfecture*, home of the regional administration. They give the cause of death as a gunshot wound and the conclusion was that it was suicide. But why? Perhaps because little had gone right for him from the moment he stopped racing. He had two car crashes, one of them in 1979 during a car gymkhana and another on the road in 1983, for which he'd needed blood transfusions.

The vineyard was erratically profitable at best. He became steadily more morose. His wife left him. He developed hepatitis C and that provoked liver cancer in 1994. He told the few people to whom he spoke that he'd been given only months to live. And so he lifted a gun to his head and cut it short.

Merckx, obviously saddened, said: "He had told me about his financial difficulties, and his family problems, but I didn't think it was as severe as that. He was a fighter, an honest and courageous man. Nobody did me as much damage as him on the road to Orcières. We became close friends because we were both winners."

39

Go Home in Shame,
Young Man, Go Home

There are scandals and then there are scandals behind scandals. Little is as obvious as it first seems.

Alpe d'Huez, July 16, 1978: Michel Pollentier knew he'd be tested, that he could be caught. He told his roommate, Freddy Maertens, that he was going to take a charge, a dose of drugs, to make his mark on the day to Alpe d'Huez in the Tour de France of 1978. Both knew the risk but both knew, too, that controls were easily tricked. Both had done it in the past. Maertens looked quizzical and told Pollentier to be careful. Maertens took drugs in criteriums, "along with everyone else", but he is insistent that he never did in the Tour because the risks were too great. Now Pollentier was about to take those risks.

What neither knew that morning was that Pollentier would be betrayed not by medicine or even by rivals but from within his own camp. Because, as the writer Roger-Pierre Turine said: "That day, believe me, Pollentier was sold in the way that slaves used to be sold."

Michel Pollentier—it's pronounced POLLEN-teer—is a gentle, almost humble man hard to dislike. He learned English at school and then polished it as Sean Kelly's roommate. He enjoys saying "Why not?" with an Irish inflection.

In July 1978, he beat Bernard Hinault in a 52-kilometer time-trial that ended on top of the Puy-de-Dôme. And Hinault and Zoetemelk didn't challenge him when he sprinted for points on the col de Luitel on the fourteenth stage. That hesitation cost Hinault and Zoetemelk dearly; Pollentier sensed his moment and, blown down the mountain and then along the valley by a tailwind, he got three minutes ahead.

The effort to chase him on the Alpe d'Huez split the chasers into ones and twos. Ahead, Pollentier continued his twisted, crab-like ride to the summit. It took two decades before Chris Froome arrived to challenge his ungainliness. Pollentier reached the top of the mountain at 4:10, his knees and arms everywhere. His hat fell off and he caught it, collected his yellow jersey, his polkadot jersey and then his prize as winner of the stage, and rode away after 25 minutes.

There was a small caravan parked near the finish, where the drug checks were to be made. The rules said the five riders named for checks had to be there within an hour of finishing. Two were picked at random, the others because they'd finished in the leading places. Pollentier presented himself in a fresh black, yellow and red jersey of national champion, having ridden to the Castillan et des Cîmes hotel, which his team shared with Bernard Hinault's team, and then driven back with his team manager, Fred De Bruyne.

In the time he spent at the hotel, Maertens said: "Michel lifted up the first-aid box. It wasn't what you think. Inside were condoms, rubber tubes, a couple of thick veterinary syringes, sticky tape and plasters. That was how we got round the dope controls."

The trick was to fill a condom with urine, tape it beneath one arm to keep it at body heat, then run a pipe down beneath the clothes and into the shorts. Pollentier's plumbing was fitted by Jef D'Hont, the soigneur, and the condom filled by someone working with the team.

The condom is often politely described in reports as a pear, because *peertje* is its name in Dutch slang. A rule insisted riders raise their jerseys to their chests and lower their shorts. Many doctors thought that below their dignity and the rule hadn't been applied in the Tour until that afternoon. Then a new doctor had taken over, an Italian named Renaldo Sacconi, and he was about to insist.

Pollentier—Tjelle (*Chella*) to friends—entered the caravan with the two riders picked at random: José Nazábal and Antoine Guttierez. Nazabal, who'd won a stage of the Tour of Spain the previous year, gave his urine sample normally but left the race that night. Guttierez, a Frenchman born in Morocco, was next. He appeared to be having trouble. The doctor pulled up his jersey and found the plastic tubing. He then turned to Pollentier and tugged at his shorts and found him similarly entwined.

Pollentier didn't return to his hotel for an hour and a half. Reporters wanted to know why he had taken so long. He said: "Going up Alpe d'Huez was so hard that I pissed in my shorts." There wasn't enough liquid left to fill the two glass test bottles easily, he said. "The doctor told me I may have not urinated enough, but as far as I know, it's going to be OK."

The reporters went back to their press tables in the church of Notre Dame des Neiges. They were writing their *papiers* when in walked Félix Lévitan and Jacques Goddet. The room fell silent. Lévitan lifted a script and read a prepared statement. Pollentier had been caught and the judges had fined him 5,000 Swiss francs and suspended him for two months. The fine was in Swiss francs because the UCI headquarters is in Switzerland.

The UCI's strictness was new. Until that year, the penalty had been a ten-minute penalty, a fine of 1,000 francs and two months' probation. Such was the sympathy for Pollentier, and so different were the era's attitudes, that a rider from each of seven teams appealed to Lévitan to apply the old and not the new penalty.

John Wilcockson remembers going to Pollentier's hotel next day, when there was no racing. Maertens and Pollentier were in their shared room, number 32. "We all gathered on the balcony to his hotel room, in the sunshine, and listened to this mild-mannered young man say how he felt that he and his team were being victimized. His roommate, Maertens, said: 'They've all been after us for some time because we're a bunch of small-time Belgians who get in the way.' To which, Pollentier, whose yellow jersey was in the corner of the room, added: 'You see that *maillot jaune* there? Why don't you just deliver it to Hinault? It's his, and that must be what some of them have been wanting all along.' "

Later, talking to a French television interviewer, he supported Maertens' explanation.

"I think we were winning too much," he said. "We had the yellow jersey, the green jersey and the polkadot." The interviewer asked why a true champion like Pollentier would need to take drugs. Pollentier, in his red Flandria jacket and looking tired and distraught, snapped: "You think I'm the first rider in the Tour de France to...?"

The interviewer, fearing his time may have elapsed there and then, quickly said "*Non.*" Pollentier made a sulking, almost truculent, toss of the head to suggest "Well, there you are, then."

"Is it the first time you ever did that [tricking the controls]?"

"Yes. Yes."

Another interviewer asked: "Do you have the feeling that today's control was stricter than usual?"

"Well, what I can tell you is that the previous night, at St-Étienne, a rider from another team went to the control and pissed without the doctor even being there. That's not normal either, is it? I'm never going to ride the Tour de France again."

The Flandria team wanted to pull out of the Tour. But the race left next morning with Zoetemelk rather than Hinault in yellow and with all the Flandria team there apart from Pollentier. It wasn't until the time-trial on the twentieth stage, from Metz to Nancy, that Hinault took the lead and kept it to Paris.

It would be here that the story would end, just another tale of a doping infraction albeit by the race leader, were it not for assertions by Freddy Maertens. The background is that Flandria had got rid of Driessens as manager, largely at Pollentier's insistence. Maertens liked Driessens and did well under his guidance, seeing him as a replacement for his dominant father. Because of that, it's not surprising that he didn't like Driessens' replacement: Fred De Bruyne. Maertens says he was never asked about the decision.

"He was not a director. In the morning he was not at the table with us. In the evening he was in the bar with the girls. At Paris–Nice we already had a problem with Fred De Bruyne. For ten days we didn't have the Flandria team bus. It was good when we had the bus. We could finish the race and just get in. There was one door that wouldn't close. They called to have it repaired. The repair crew came to the hotel and the bus was driven there. The workmen asked if they could start work on the bus immediately because they had to go to the Côte d'Azur.

"Fred de Bruyne said: 'No, first you eat something. You eat with us and then you can repair the bus.'

"'No,' said the two men. 'We must go, we have many kilometers to travel to do all of our service work.'

"'No,' said de Bruyne, 'No.'

"While we were eating, I asked Fred De Bruyne three more times to get the bus fixed. Marc Demeyer didn't ask. He grabbed Fred De Bruyne, *boom*, he lifted him by the lapels and he went into his pocket. 'I have the keys, sirs', he said, and he gave the keys to the mechanics."

According to Willy Voet, the soigneur who moved in a world where colleagues exchanged notes and stories, Pollentier's *peertje* had been sabotaged. But, according to Maertens, it didn't need to be because the doctor had already been tipped off, either direct or through a third party.

"It was Fred De Bruyne's fault. He denounced Pollentier to the judges. He was paid, but not in money. He got the house where he lived in the south of France. Pollentier was sold."

Maertens wanted revenge. But "it was not easy. I was at the Tour de France, I had to defend my green jersey. I had to win one or two more stages. You have to race. I had to do a lot of things."

Pollentier wrote to the Tour's organizers to apologize. "The hardest thing to bear is the charge of sullying the Tour's standing," he wrote. "You know how I have committed myself to how I raced. That should have been the finest day of my career. Unhappily, it will be the saddest. Please accept my sincere regret."

Pollentier received "thousands of letters, all very sympathetic, wishing me well and telling me to fight it and get back again." The suspension cost him not only his fine but the rich criterium contracts he would have received. Many race organizers paid him as much to fire the starting gun as they'd have paid him to take part. He was an attraction, just being there.

It was the end of Pollentier's world, though. He raced again but his heart and his legs were never in it. He fell into a mental gloom, not helped by losing all his money in unsound investments. He spent a year under a doctor in Ostend before pinning on his last race number on October 8, 1984.

He lived in a pleasant but unremarkable house in Dead Horses Street—he assumed it had something to do with the first world war—and ran a small business selling car tires. In his spare time, he worked with youngsters in his local club.

"I was almost 34," he said of his retirement from racing. "You don't get to carry on much longer."

He has never been outspoken about that afternoon on Alpe d'Huez. Yes, he said, he took drugs when he was racing, but less than many. And yes, he took something that day: Alupin. He knew it didn't foul dope tests in Belgium but he tricked the control because he wasn't sure what would happen in France. In those days tests and analyses weren't standardized.

That trickery led to a change. The condom-and-tube method was no secret but, cycling being too scared to look for fear of what they'd find, as Tom Simpson's manager said, many a blind eye had been turned. Now it was public and a new, more convincing version had to be found. And it was. You may want to skip the next bit…

Maertens explained: "The condom had to be heavy-duty quality, like the ones they used back then in the army. The rubber pipe went into that, but not too deep so that the condom wasn't damaged and so the urine could flow freely. And you sealed off the end with a flexible metal ring.

"With Vaseline to help, you slipped the condom and the tube into your anus. Then one end of the tube was stuck beneath the anus with tape and taken along the underside of the penis and trimmed off. You then poured urine into the tube with a syringe. Clean urine, of course, from a teammate, a team official or from a Thermos that the rider himself had filled before taking any drugs. You kept it in a Thermos so that it stayed at body temperature. It'd be hard to give the doctor a bottle of ice-cold urine."

Maertens smiles: some riders with a bloated condom in their backsides walked to the test with such difficulty that it looked as though they'd laid an egg.

Fred De Bruyne died at 63 on February 4, 1994. Michel Pollentier and his son, Dimitri, still run their tire business on Albert I Laan in Nieuwpoort. Freddy Maertens is the curator and guide at the Tour of Flanders museum at Oudenaarde. And Jacques Goddet and Félix Lévitan are both dead.

40

Tomorrow You Will Win The Tour

Hell breaks out when gods bicker. Heaven arrives when they cooperate, as two days in the mountains can prove.

Izoard, France, July 18, 1949: It doesn't happen these days, that one great star will beat another by nearly 24 minutes in one of the big tours. And yet 23 minutes 47 seconds was the extent to which Fausto Coppi led in Gino Bartali in the Tour of Italy in 1949. The faster was rising to his peak, the slower sliding reluctantly from his. But, like Anquetil and Poulidor later, they were more than rivals. They symbolized different sides of Italy, still a provincial outpost of Europe. Bartali, the moaner, the man for whom things wouldn't go right but who succeeded nevertheless, was old Italy. He was the symbol of the religious, the landworker, the ugly man with the unprepossessing wife and too many children. Coppi was slim, elegant, handsome, the modern man, an atheist and an adulterer; he stood for Italy's industrial future and for men in suits and women who wanted more from life than perpetual motherhood.

The French star, André Leducq, bursting into purple prose, said of Coppi: "He seemed to caress rather than grip the handlebars. His long legs extend to the pedals with the joints of a gazelle. At the end of each pedal stroke his ankles flex gracefully, a movement which would be wonderful to analyze in slow motion on a cinema screen—all the moving parts turn in oil."

Bartali was clumsy, the toiler of fields; Coppi was the elegant heron, long-legged, perpetually sad-looking, stroking the pedals. "Bartali prayed as he pedaled," wrote Curzio Malaparte. "Coppi was the rationalist, the Cartesian [follower of the reductive logic of René Descartes], skeptical and riddled with doubts, believing only in his motor: his body."

Coppi followed the advice of Gayelord Hauser, a nutritionist whose views about food were just becoming fashionable; Bartali preferred to drink cider and, on the advice of his doctor, smoke cigarettes three times a day to regulate his heart. As Philippe Brunel observed, it was the perfect modern version of *The Little World of Don Camillo*.

The problem with the Tour de France was that the two would have to be in the same team. Anquetil had refused to ride for France if Bobet were there and now this time neither Coppi nor Bartali would ride in the presence of the other. Leaving out Bobet wasn't difficult. Not only did he take the hint and not seek a place but he was getting past his best anyway. He'd also won the Tour three times, which does a lot for a man's sense of self-achievement. But that did nothing for the Coppi-Bartali problem. All Italy wanted them to ride because all Italy wanted one or the other to win.

Both men remembered that Coppi had turned professional, or more precisely semi-professional, to be Bartali's domestique. That was in 1940 and even then Bartali didn't want him. It was his team manager, Eberardo Pavesi, who recruited him and Bartali was cross. Coppi, he said, was too fragile for races of more than two or three days. His concern turned to fury in that year's Giro when Coppi dutifully stayed with him after a crash on the first stage, and when he was still there after the rest of the team had been dropped by a series of attacks.

Bartali realized he had underestimated Coppi but Coppi realized he in turn had overestimated Bartali. The old man wasn't as good as he thought. In the guise of being a good team man, he chased after a breakaway. But instead of staying with it, to slow it down, he carried on over the Abetone pass and won by four minutes.

Bartali was so furious at what he interpreted as treachery that he organized the rival Legnano team into chasing him. And the wound didn't heal until both men stopped racing, by which time they'd turned into a stage show of personal appearances together.

It was in that turmoil of bitterness that Alfredo Binda had to bring them together. Binda was of an earlier generation, the first world professional road champion, a winner of 5 Tours of Italy and 41 of its stages. He would have won a sixth Giro had the organizers not paid him the equivalent of first prize to stay away. Coppi and Bartali saw him as an equal.

Binda remembered: "It was like being asked to put a cat and a dog in the same sack. No good pretending they were friends. Their rivalry wasn't an attitude they adopted out of vanity. It was real and never-ending. I had to show them I was boss and win them over to my ways. I had to turn two men accustomed to giving orders into obedient boys."

He did it at the Hotel Andreola at Chiavari, taking with him two witnesses from the Italian federation.

"I asked them to listen to me and not ask questions until I'd finished. Then I talked…one hour, two hours, three. Finally, I could say: 'Gentlemen, I've finished. Now I hope that you understand how and why an Italian team can't be and mustn't be beaten in the Tour de France.' I'd been talking for five and a quarter hours.

"Later I got, without having asked for it, a signed promise by Coppi and Bartali that they would obey me blindly, whatever happened, follow my orders, never dispute them either in public or in private."

Binda recognized that he had two winners, that he couldn't sacrifice one for the other. So he told half the team to support one and the rest to support the other. French reporters took that as a split, which angered everyone after the trouble they'd taken. In fact, the division had been needed not only to satisfy both men's ambitions but because they rode different derailleurs—in those days each company's gears worked differently—and needed their own supporting riders for a change of wheels. But quickly Binda realized that rumors of a split in his team could only help because rivals would never know where to look next. He didn't deny them.

Coppi's radio interviews added to the intrigue. He had a tic of saying "Bay…bay…bay…" before each answer. It was his way of gathering his thoughts but the hesitation added to suspicion that he was being guarded in what he said. And, again, journalists had reason to doubt when they saw what happened on the stage from Rouen to St-Malo.

Coppi was in a break that he had started and in which he'd been joined among others by the *maillot jaune*, Jacques Marinelli. The little Parisian hadn't made selection for the main teams and was riding instead for the Ile-de-France, nominally representing Paris. He was the surprise of the race, attacking repeatedly for five days until he changed his green jersey for the yellow of leader. It led Jacques Goddet to write that "our budgerigar has been transformed into a canary." For the rest of his career, Marinelli was known not as Canary, which would have reminded the world of his glory, but Budgie.

Marinelli took a bottle of beer that a woman was holding out by the roadside. He fell off and brought Coppi down with him. Coppi's bike was damaged and he looked for Binda in the team's Renault. But Binda was back with Bartali, who'd been delayed at a feeding point. Binda's assistant gave him a bike but Coppi refused it, angry that it wasn't the right size. He waited for his own bike and rode in such slow-pedaling sulk that he got to St-Malo more than 18 minutes after the winner, Ferdi Kübler, and nearly 37 minutes overall behind Marinelli.

He sulked so much that he wouldn't talk until he got to his hotel. There he told Luciano Pezzi, the closest of his domestiques: "It's not the bike. What you have to realize is that my morale took a dive when I saw that Binda wasn't there. Binda didn't want to help me: he's here to help Bartali. He doesn't want me to win the Tour."

That in turn produced a sulk among his domestiques. They stood to share Coppi's prizes if he finished the Tour. If he didn't, they'd go home penniless, because only the top riders were paid. And Coppi, a loyal man who at least once had demanded that other riders in show races were paid more than they'd been offered, changed his mind and said he'd carry on.

Chunk by chunk, Coppi made his way back up the rankings. The race left the Pyrenees with his gap down to 14 minutes 46 seconds. The sixteenth stage, from Cannes to Briançon, took in the Allos, Vars and Izoard. Bartali had ridiculed the Tour there in 1938 and 1948 and he planned to do the same in 1949. But he had barely broken away when Coppi rode up beside him. In support, said the optimists, to be sure Bartali couldn't win according to the doom-sayers. It was a bit of both.

Bartali, a year older that very day, acknowledged his time had passed. "Let's ride together," he shouted. "Today's my birthday and to-morrow you'll win the Tour." Or, in other words: "Don't make a fool of me on my birthday and I'll not bother you for the rest of the race."

The deal was done. They rode away from the rest. Coppi punctured on the Izoard and Bartali waited. Then Bartali flatted and Coppi waited. They came into Briançon together having taken twenty minutes out of the yellow jersey, Fiorenzo Magni, the leader of Italy's B-team. Bartali won for his birthday and Coppi took second place overall.

"Tomorrow you'll win the Tour," Bartali had said. And he was right. The two dreamed of again finishing together but this time in Italy. The stage finished across the border in Aosta. Again they broke away and again Coppi waited when Bartali punctured. He waited again when Bartali crashed on a descent and picked himself up groggily. There were only 40 kilometers to go. Bartali was stunned and limping. Coppi was unsure.

He turned to two men riding a motorbike for Italian radio.

"What should I do?"

The broadcaster, a man called Reschini, said he couldn't say. He was a commentator, not a strategist. "Ask Binda," he suggested.

Reschini found a way to ask, delighted to have only his hands on the story. "Tell him to ride for himself," Binda commanded. And Coppi promptly took nearly five minutes on Bartali and more than ten on the field, which Binda feared would catch him if Bartali didn't get going again. That afternoon Coppi pulled on the yellow jersey in the first summer it had the initials of Henri Desgrange on the chest. Jean-Paul Ollivier calculated that Coppi had taken 55 minutes from Marinelli in the mountains.

Coppi won the Tour, a year earlier than he'd planned to ride it, by 10 minutes 55 seconds. For the first time, a rider had won the Giro and the Tour in the same year. It's a small club. In the more than 60 years since, the only other members have been Anquetil, Merckx, Hinault, Stephen Roche, Indurain and Pantani.

Fausto Coppi, whose first name meant "happy", died of malaria in 1960. He was 40. Bartali died in 2000 when he was 85. Jacques Marinelli, still alive, was mayor of Melun, near Paris, from 1989 to 2002. He still rides a bike and still watches the Tour on television. "Wearing that yellow jersey gave me everything I have in life," he says.

Fausto Coppi on the Pordoi

41

The Day of the Franky Boys

He was 'le goldenboy' of Belgian cycling, finally a prince for Eddy Merckx. But no sooner was he at his peak than the slide began.

Ans, Belgium, April 18, 1999: They called themselves the Franky Boys, or sometimes Frankboys. It depended on who got the T-shirts printed. Their main qualifications were a paunch, a lot to drink and unbridled enthusiasm for their hero: Frank Vandenbroucke. "*Fay-day-bay, Fay-day-bay*," they used to shout, the Dutch pronunciation of his initials.

It used to be that you could ride through Ploegsteert, an ugly name for an unremarkable village, and see Franky's face and golden hair on a board above a bar. It was there that he grew up. Later the Frankyboys—"VDB forever"—put up their own board outside a bar at Oudenaarde. There were 400 of them in 1999.

They had every reason to be proud of their hero. His talent brought him a professional contract at nineteen, not in Italy as he wanted but, through family pressure, with his uncle, Jean-Luc Vandenbroucke. The two never got on.

The younger Vandenbroucke's golden day was in his native Wallonia, the southern half of Belgium that speaks French. Vandenbroucke's name, though, is Dutch. Turn the pedals half a dozen times, it seems in so small a land, and you ride into Dutch-speaking Flanders. Vandenbroucke was at home in both languages, and in English.

In April 1999 he went to the start of Liège–Bastogne–Liège with newly bleached hair, ribs that stuck through his chest, and what he believed was the lightest and most modern bike in the race. MBK had had problems with the bikes they gave the team. Vandenbroucke was among those who complained. And now he had his reward, "a gem of 6.9 kilograms with two bottle cages, a special American titanium frame, wheels of 1.2 kilograms with Kevlar spokes and high-sided rims of carbon from Cees Beers, two Vittoria tires of 180 grams and a special seat pin in carbon. All the screws of the frame were made in titanium by Campagnolo, the stem was carbon and the pedals titanium. It was a €7,000 bike designed to last 1,000 kilometers—a one-day Ferrari that cut through hills like a knife through butter."

There was an early break, of course. Laurent Jalabert was there, and Stefano Garzelli. But no Michele Bartoli. He was the only rider that Vandenbroucke cared about and so he didn't chase anyone else. He had team-mates to do that. He would wait until Bartoli attacked or he would himself attack. There was bad blood between them. Vandenbroucke had said he'd beat him.

"He was the king of La Doyenne," Vandenbroucke said, "while I was a peasant from Ploegsteert who should keep his mouth shut. He'd read all the articles, of course, and had all the headlines translated. How would I beat him? By riding him off my wheel. *Come batto Bartoli? Seminandolo. Ecco come!* It didn't strike him as funny. Italians don't have the same sense of humor."

And so Bartoli attacked on the Redoute, a climb of 2.2 kilometers with a short stretch at nineteen per cent. The toothy Dutchman, Michael Boogerd, struggled up to him and then Vandenbroucke. "When he saw *me* alongside him, it became a duel of prestige and we were sprinting for half the race for our honor."

Nico Mattan said that whereas he would use 39 x 21 or even 39 x 23 on La Redoute. Vandenbroucke had taken it on 53 x 21. "It showed he had good strength in his legs," he added with a half smile of understatement.

They turned into a group of fourteen, including the world champion, Oscar Camenzind, the Dutchmen Boogerd and Maarten Den Bakker, and a Frenchman, Laurent Roux. They rode more hills together, Vandenbroucke looking in Bartoli's eyes for clues, wondering if the double winner was worrying, suspecting he wasn't because he had the formidable Paolo Bettini to help.

Boogerd had three team-mates. Vandenbroucke had only one, Peter Farazijn. It was Vandenbroucke who should be worrying, even though he'd told insiders at the start that he had "legs of fire" and would have trouble restraining himself until his planned attack on the Côte de St-Nicolas.

"That was where the victory was to be had," he said afterwards. "Not at the start, not in the middle, but on the hard bit at the end. The bunch was at four minutes and the winner was in the lead group. I called to Peter to go to the front and give it all he had. The speed went up and some of them were struggling. And that's when I took off the covers. We approached the climb. Farazijn kept going and the others wasted their energy staying with him. We started the climb and the knight stepped aside [Farazijn: *knecht* is Dutch for a domestique]. Now it was up to the leader. Boogerd tried to attack but I could bring him back easily. We had a little battle and Bartoli looked spent.

"And I went for it. I rode so hard that I was on my big ring. It was less efficient for me but it drained the energy out the legs of the opposition. I was away and I never saw them again."

A commentator on RTBF, the Belgian French-language TV station, said: "We thought then that it would be the first of a long series of classics."

The Frankyboys were well into drinking at the Hostellerie de la Place in Ploegsteert, "just a sprint's distance inside Belgium from the French border", as Vandenbroucke described it. The customers had spilled into the square and much of the rest of the village had joined them. The Cofidis team drove there after the race, to celebrate Vandenbroucke's victory, among his own people. They dressed in the colors of the rainbow to climb on the podium they'd put up. Vandenbroucke paid the eight members of the team a million Belgian francs from his own pocket to share between, later adding the personal bonus that Cofidis gave him.

That café on the Place de la Rabecque was where Vandenbroucke grew up. "My whole life took place in that café," he said. "My diapers were changed on the tables. I made my first drawings on a beer mat and that's where I drank my first fruit juice. I've seen Bernard Hinault and Sean Kelly drinking a glass of Duivel beer there. I knew everybody and everybody knew me. Our café was the center of Ploegsteert and I was the center of the café.

"More than that, I had been the little prince, the emblem of Ploeg-steert, and for some people I got better the more they drank. Around eight o'clock I was another Rik van Looy. The beer flowed and I was Claude Criquielion or Eric Vanderaerden. By the time my mother filled the last glasses, I was the new Eddy Merckx."

And that was where his journey into the ashes began. Vanden-broucke and his team prepared to go north into Holland, for the Am-stel Gold Race. He spent the night with his friend, Philippe Gaumont, just across the border in France. The two "did almost everything to-gether in those days: races, drugs, fishing." They were preparing their bags and bikes in the garage at dawn when they had visitors.

"It's never good news when the door bell goes at 5:30 in the morn-ing," Vandenbroucke said, "and this was no exception. We stood there looking at five gendarmes."

"*Brigade des Stupéfiants. Venez avec nous.*" Drugs squad. Come with us.

Vandenbroucke panicked. Not Gaumont; he already had a color-ful history with the *flics*. For Vandenbroucke, "the only police I'd seen were standing at the side of the road to control the traffic."

The drugs police drove them to the headquarters of the criminal police at 36 quai des Orfévres, an address in Paris known to older French-speakers through Georges Simenon's *Maigret* paperbacks. And there both men began a complicated and ultimately disastrous flir-tation with drugs investigators. At first they were more interested in Bernard Sainz, a quack doctor more commonly known as Dr Mabuse, after a film character who also mumbled as he made countless unin-telligible notes. But then their interest widened and Vandenbroucke's life worsened. Drugs investigations and suspensions followed. His marriage floundered. He missed races, made comebacks, failed again. Teams gave him another chance and then wish they hadn't.

Sainz never claimed to be a doctor, although many, including Van-denbroucke, referred to him that way. He called himself a homeo-path, although that didn't stop his being appointed to the Munich Olympics. He worked with teams that included Zoetemelk, Poulidor, Knetemann and Guimard. In 1977 an amateur under his wing was found to have taken amphetamine as part of the treatment that he had prescribed. By 1985 he was banned from the Paris six-day and the following year he was investigated but cleared in an investigation into drug trafficking, although he was fined for working as a doctor without qualifications.

He moved to horse-racing, with more scandals, then returned to cycling and was again penalized for working as an unqualified doctor. Vandenbroucke said he once paid him 7,600 French francs for nose drops and, in six months of 1999, 50,000 francs for advice and treatment. Sainz was seen frequently with his rider and went on vacation with him. The two were stopped for speeding on the E17 highway in Belgium and police found what Sainz said were homeopathic products but which turned out to be clenbuterol, morphine and EPO. Vandenbroucke insisted that drugs found at his house were for his dog.

Sarah Vandenbroucke, the Italian model he married in 2000, a year after his childhood sweetheart Clothilde Menu had their baby daughter, described Vandenbroucke as a cocaine addict. She left him in 2006 after he fired a gun during an argument at their home in Nieuwkerke. That year, Vandenbroucke was discovered trying to start a race in Italy as "Francesco del Ponte", using a race license carrying the picture of world champion Tom Boonen.

He died, aged 34, in a hotel on the coast of Senegal.

Philippe Gaumont, died at 40 in May 2013. He was caught in dope tests in 1996, 1998 and 1999 and in 2004 was given a six-month suspended jail sentence for further offenses. He had taken drugs since the start of his professional career, he said in his autobiography, *Prisonnier du Dopage*.

Of the Frankyboys, membership fell from 300 in 2005 to half that after his disappearance in 2006. They still sold 600 Frankyboys T-shirts in 2006, most of them on the internet. There were just 70 members when he died.

"My world stopped turning," said their chairman, Adelin De Meulemeester. Look for them on the web now and all you'll find is a link to a German soccer club.

A Frankyboys banner

42

Moore The Merrier

Sports evolve. Nobody knows who played the first soccer match, or where someone first whacked a puck across ice. But we know just when and where cycle-racing began.

Rouen, France, November 7, 1869: It's written St-Cloud but it's pronounced *San-Cloo*. These days it's a western suburb of Paris, a multicultural area with one of the city's few surviving communist councils. If you leave the Métro at Pont de Sèvres rather than St-Cloud itself, you can cross the busy road and walk through a pedestrian tunnel marked "Parc-de-St-Cloud." At the other end a gravel path runs to the park's fountains 600 meters away. And it was from the fountains to the tunnel and back that an 18-year-old Englishman called Jimmy Moore lined up with the rest of the field to ride the world's first bike race. It was Friday May 31, 1868.

Now, there need to be several qualifications. The first is that Moore had lived in Paris since he was four and he was a lot more French than English. The second is that there must have been informal races for years. And the third is that historians dispute whether the race that Moore won that day was the first of the meeting or simply the most important.

All that said, it was Moore's race that the crowd turned out to see. They'd been promised speed and spectacle and they turned up in crinolines and top hats and frock coats to see it. It had rained that morning and many carried umbrellas because the Paris sky was still cloudy.

Jimmy Moore—his friends pronounced it *Jeemie*—was born on January 14, 1849, in Bury St Edmunds, in eastern England, in part of a street called Long Brackland that has since been been replaced by a supermarket. His father, also called James, was a blacksmith and far-rier and an amateur animal doctor. His mother, Elizabeth, was illiter-ate and signed Jimmy's birth certificate with an X. Why they moved from a quiet country town with little contact with the rest of England to what was then the unofficial capital of the world, nobody knows. All we know is that they moved to an alleyway between the Champs-Ely-sées and the avenue Montaigne, now the heart of the Parisian fashion industry. Their little road is no longer there and it's hard to imagine the area back in 1854 when the streets were full of horses and men worked in cluttered yards to keep them shod and to repair their carts.

Jimmy made friends with the Michaux family, who built carriages in a nearby street. It was to the family that a man named Brunel pushed his broken, iron-and-wood velocipede to have it repaired. Such things were new then and the Michaux family had never touched one. Leg-end says they reckoned it needed foot rests to roll down hill and only accidentally hit on fitting them to the wheel and then finding that a machine that once had to be scooted could now, with difficulty, be balanced and pedaled. The Michaux sons tried it along the Champs-Elysées towards the Arc de Triomphe and Jimmy joined them.

Michaux's accidental invention of the bicycle made them their for-tune. Napoléon III bought one and the Prince Impérial, Louis-Na-poléon, gave a dozen to his friends. The social status of the bicycle was born, which is why the royal family, which owned the park, allowed the race there and why the crowd was so well-heeled. René and Aimé Olivier whose Compagnie Parisienne financed Michaux's expansion, put on the race for the advertising and so the Michaux could repay their loan.

Moore, the youngest competitor, accelerated "as fast as lightning" according to *Cycling Record* and won in 3 minutes 50 seconds to "fre-netic hurrahs", receiving a gold medal engraved with the image of Na-poléon III.

A race that lasts less than four minutes wasn't going to make any-body's fortune, though. The future depended on showing that bicycles weren't toys, but the future. And that demanded something grander. The Olivier brothers therefore put on a race from Paris to Rouen. The organizer was Richard Lesclide, personal secretary to Victor Hugo, who wrote *The Hunchback of Notre Dame*. And on September 30, 1869, *Le Vélocipède Illustré* announced: "To further the good cause of the bicycle, it must be determined that the bicycle can be raced over considerable distances with incomparably less fatigue than running. Therefore we announce to our readers that a first long-distance race will take place in late October. The distance to race will be that separating Paris from Rouen, being a distance of 130 kilometers approximately."

No mention, you notice, that the brothers wanted to sell more bikes.

The paper had said late October but the date was Sunday, November 7, a morning which began with a rainstorm. Moore, like everyone else, had agreed not "to be trailed by a dog or use sails." People remembered the excitement of St-Cloud and those who weren't there and didn't want to miss out a second time were already on the street before dawn when the 325 competitors—the number has been disputed, which shows how chaotic arrangements had become—collected numbers and road maps at the Compagnie Parisienne's offices in the avenue Bugeaud. From there they were expected to ride gently to the Arc de Triomphe for the start at 8am.

The crowd, though, couldn't resist riding with them and, this being a first long-distance race, cycling clothes hadn't been invented and riders were indistinguishable from everyone else. The bigger the bunch that rode along the avenue Victor Hugo, the more excited everyone grew and the faster they went. Before long they were riding as fast as they could and the thundering iron wheels increased the excitement even more.

Nobody could be sure if the race had started. They weren't going to take a chance and so they swept past the start and down what is now the avenue Charles de Gaulle and off towards Rouen. One of the Olivier brothers expressed "strong astonishment" and stewards promised riders who *were* waiting at the Arc de Triomphe that they'd have half an hour deducted from their time. Some say the 30-minute delay had been planned all along, to split the field and avoid bottlenecks. In the end it didn't matter because the race was a great deal longer and harder than anyone imagined and riders split up and often just dropped out.

One, a Londoner called J.T. Johnson, had dressed in jockey's silks and carried a whip "to fend off dogs." By Vaudreuil at 60 kilometers he fell off exhausted on a railway crossing and couldn't pick himself up. Race officials had to carry him to a railwayman's cottage to recover and then to the home of a Monsieur Duval. There, Johnson ate and slept for an hour and set off once more and passed competitor after competitor to finish seventh.

Moore, on an Olivier bike with seven 9-millimeter ball bearings in the hubs, a rare and expensive refinement, won in darkness at 6:10pm after 134 kilometers. He was cheered in by a huge crowd after a little less than ten and a half hours. Not bad for 134 kilometers on unmade roads on a bike with no tires. It was fast enough, anyway, for the mayor of Rouen to be summoned earlier than he'd expected and was climbing out of his carriage as Moore arrived.

The runners-up at fifteen minutes were the curly-haired and self-styled Count André Castéra, who had come second to Moore at St-Cloud, and Jean Bobillier on a farmer's bike that weighed 35 kilograms. They asked to be placed joint second. Miss America, a well-built British woman who'd been chased by spectators throughout the day, finished at dawn next day, 22nd and the only woman inside 24 hours. A Miss Olga of Russia didn't finish in time.

Moore won a bike and a medal but not his train fare back to Paris. For that he had to pay 8 francs and 40 centimes. And he'd have been pleased to win a bike because he left the other one outside the café at the finish and it was never seen again.

Johnson, the silk-clad jockey, went on to set the first world hour record—13 miles 600 yards on the Aston Cross track at Birmingham—part of the series that stood until conditions were standardized and a new measure was set by Henri Desgrange. Moore won the MacGregor Cup, then with the status of a world championship, five times before following his father and working at Maisons Lafitte, the capital of French horse-racing. He may well have grown rich enough to have his own horses. At some time he moved to 56 Wildwood Road in Hampstead, in north London, and there he died on July 17, 1935, after a prostate operation that went wrong.

And the Michaux family? They expanded faster than they could afford and lost control to the Olivier brothers. They then went into opposition, which led to their being sued by the Oliviers and a demand for 100,000 francs in damages. That ruined the father and he died in a pauper's hospital in Paris in 1883. The factory was little luckier. By 1870 it had 500 workers and 57 forges but soon there were rival companies all over Paris and it started to founder. Then the city was besieged in the Franco-Prussian war of 1870–71 and German shells landed on the factory and destroyed it.

Something has survived, though: the bike on which Moore won at St-Cloud and the medals he won that day. The Science Museum in London wouldn't agree to a family condition that they go on permanent display there. So they're now in the little municipal museum in Ely, near Cambridge, the nearest city to the home of Jimmy Moore's son.

Les Woodland

43

The Track that Died of Shame

It had a magic whether there was racing or not. It stood a handful of streets from the Eiffel Tower in a city of Gaulloises and trams and Édith Piaf and Joséphine Baker. But many were glad to see it go.

Paris, France, April 17, 1959: Everyone knew it as the Vel' d'Hiv, the *Vell Deev*. All it means, were it to be spelled in full, is winter track. A track, in other words, that's not outside in the cold. There were plenty of them round the world even then, but the vel' d'hiv in Paris was special: it was the Vel' d'Hiv.

Ernest Hemingway loved it, "the smoky light of the afternoon and the high-banked wooden track and the whirring sound the tires made on the wood as the riders passed." But for thousands it was the last place they were seen alive, kicking, screaming and treading in excrement. It stood in the rue Nélaton a few streets south-west of the Eiffel Tower, a solid, uncompromising building, square with a huge glass roof, the insides dark and tobacco-stained and dimly lit by spotlights hanging individually in metal lampshades.

The pale wooden track was 250 meters round and it was close to perfect if you rode high. Keep to the bottom and you rode a gradient at the start of the banking. Pursuiters and six-day chasers learned to ride further out, the long way round but less tiring. It was fast but not the fastest. Roger Rivière rode 47.346 kilometers in an hour on the Vigorelli but managed two kilometers less on the closing night in Paris even though the track was indoors with no wind.

The seats rose in three tiers with netting above each to protect the crowd from discontented onlookers higher up. They reveled in hurling food and even beer on those below them, or across the track at the officials. In 1932 the crowd threw flaming newspapers when it objected to a judging decision. The police had to be called. When they'd restored order, officials tried to restart the race, only to find that one of the riders, Henri Lemoine, had despaired and gone back to his hotel for a sleep.

In 1935 the crowd threw bottles when the judges mistakenly put Charles Pélissier and Antonin Magne a lap behind two Italians. The crowd disliked Italians because they'd invaded backward Ethiopia and Pélissier disliked the judges and walked off.

"Why should I care if they're smashing the place up?" he sulked. He walked away and sat in the dressing room for an hour. When he came back, the others lined up to thank him for sticking up for himself and the other riders but also because he'd given them an hour's rest.

The Paris six-day had fifteen or sixteen teams. The five best pairs were members of the Blue Train, a mafia named after a luxury express that had society's big-rollers among its passengers. Blue Train riders demanded and got two thirds of the prizes. If they didn't, they wouldn't ride. And the also-rans, kept in their place for much of the week, used their bitterness at being paid less in fees and prizes to upset their masters when they could.

Sometimes huge jams—chases—could start in the night when a minnow pairing sought revenge. It happened once at 6am with no-one paying to watch. Riders were weaving and sprinting as if it were the final hour.

"Make them stop, make them stop!" the director, Louis Delblat, yelled, beside himself with rage. "They'll be too exhausted when the public comes in." But still laps were lost and taken. It was more than Delblat could bear and he began lifting the seating and throwing it on the track. Only then would the riders stop.

The track announcer, Georges Berretrot, could work the crowd. One week he had to overcome its disappointment with Jean Brunier, a road rider who never got the grasp of the track and kept crashing. He went down to Brunier's cabin during a pause and told him his plan.

"Next time you come off, stick on a huge plaster whether you need it or not. I'll whip up sympathy and we'll both profit. You'll get the cash and I'll take a percentage." The tradition of primes had been started. Brunier, it was said perhaps with exaggeration, fell off another fifteen times, often voluntarily.

"Look at that poor courageous Brunier!", Berretrot appealed in his distinctive southern accent, warm and friendly to Parisian ears. "A little prime will help his suffering." The money poured in. From around 1924 he was also taking his percentage from the companies he persuaded to put up larger sums in return for announcements of their virtues. In 1926, the London department store, Selfridges, put up 10,000 francs, or half the annual average wage. Lucien Faucheux won it "thanks to the rare power of his thighs," as one newspaper put it.

The last meeting at the smoky old track was in April 1959. The track was to come down two weeks later. It meant as much to the riders as to spectators. There were so many stars that it was a job to fit them on the posters. Jacques Anquetil was there, and Fausto Coppi, Louison Bobet, Rik van Steenbergen, Charly Gaul, André Darrigade, Jan Derksen, Peter Post and Miguel Poblet. Roger Rivière would try for the hour record. Plus there were all those all those who couldn't fit on the bills. The lines of customers stretched down the road.

It was a final happy moment to hide the shame and guilt that the track walls and Paris itself felt in its soul. Because the Vel d'Hiv wasn't just cycling and boxing matches and the other sports events held there. It was for general hire and no stranger to fascism. Jacques Doriot, who led the most popular far-right party, the PPF, used the track to rouse the masses. He was, he believed, Führer of France and under him France would be second only to Germany in the new Europe. The party's "Heil Hitler!" salute was matched by a hymn which urged "Listen to Doriot who summons you, child of France, to the noblest goal."

It was no surprise, then, that Doriot supplied 400 thugs in dark blue shirts and PPF armbands and a further 3,400 young sympathizers to help the Nazis round up Paris's foreign or stateless Jews. His help was part of the plan that the Gestapo worked out at their headquarters in the avenue Foch. They made only one change: reluctant to include France's national holiday, July 14, in the three days of *rafale*, they delayed their work until July 16.

It was swift and efficient, all over by 11am on the first day. French police pulled out 27,388 record cards from the census of September 1940 and gave copies to the Germans. Operation Spring Wind, a bitterly pretty name, included 9,000 French policemen, from cadets to senior officers. The French suggested their definition of a Jew because it was wider-ranging and likely to cause fewer problems.

German soldiers walked into Jacques Goddet's office and demanded the keys to the Vel' d'Hiv. He handed them over, for which he has been criticized but which he never mentioned in his autobiography. But, as Pierre Chany put it: "What did you expect him to do?"

Unmarried men were sent straight to a concentration camp. Women and children were housed first in schools and other buildings and then taken to the track by bus. Curiously for so large an event, only one picture survives, a single bus at the track door, taken from an upstairs window across the street.

The track still had its glass roof, although it had been painted blue to make it harder for bomber navigators. The heat of the sun through the glass—outside, happier Parisians were swimming in the Seine—added to the infamy. Thousands were pushed inside along with their bags and such belongings as they could carry. They were fewer than the Germans had hoped but nevertheless they kicked up clouds of unbreathable dust. Of ten lavatories, five were sealed because their windows offered an escape. The others were blocked, and people already shoulder to shoulder were forced to relieve themselves where they stood. Some threw themselves from the top seats to kill themselves. Ten succeeded.

Those rounded up were told to bring food for two days. Some did. Many didn't have food for even one day. They were held for a week. What they ate, and medical care, came only from Quakers, the Red Cross and a handful of nurses and doctors allowed to enter. The 3,031 men, 5,802 women and 4,115 children held there or dispatched directly were taken 1,000 at a time to Drancy, a concentration camp built in an incomplete apartment block on the city's edge. They replaced those already on their way to Auschwitz. Fewer than 400 returned. None of the children survived.

Fire broke out at the track not long after that final race day. Some say it was started deliberately. Demolishers flattened it and a housing block was built where it stood. Most were glad to see it go. René de Latour of *Sporting Cyclist* lamented its closure after his 38 years of hanging about there, as he put it, but not once did he mention its shabby history.

It took decades for France to admit its complicity. It hid behind the legal nicety that Philippe Pétain, the wartime leader, had scrapped the Republic and that therefore it wasn't France that existed under his control but some other country. The Republic, once reestablished, had nothing for which to apologize. Finally, in July 1995, president Jacques Chirac stood where the track had been and admitted: "These black hours will stain our history for ever.... France committed that day the irreparable."

Where the track once stood there's now a small garden, backed by a dull, gray wall which shuts off an ugly flat-fronted apartment block. Half a dozen steps lead up to a plaque. Its gold lettering recites the baldest facts and ends: "Let those who tried to come to their aid be thanked. In passing by, remember."

A plaque memorializing the stain on France's history, at the site of the Vel' d'Hiv

Les Woodland

44

Oh Canada! Oh Dear, Oh Dear, Canada!

The sun never set on the British Empire. So you'd think, somehow, it could come up with a decent bike team when required. But it didn't work out that way.

Lille, France, June 30, 1937: There are daily newspapers more down-market than the *Daily Star* in Britain but they write about film stars abducted by spacemen and doctors who turn their wives into turtles. The *Star* has held itself back from that. Just. Although it did introduce newspaper bingo to the British.

The people who rewrite reporters' words and design pages and write headlines are known in Britain as sub-editors. One of them, on the *Star*, was a 41-year-old called Jeff Connor. And since nobody else knew anything about cycling, the *Star* decided that Connor should ride a stage of the Tour de France. No other newspaper had come up with the idea and that made it a good idea. Except that, as Connor pointed out with a grateful sigh, you can't just turn up and ride.

Instead, he followed the 1987 Tour de France and the ill fortunes of its one British team, sponsored by a delivery company run by Anthony N. Capper and bearing his initials. The team fell apart and the sponsor vanished and Connor's book, *Wide-Eyed and Legless*, recounts it all.

Well, back before world war two you really could enter the Tour just because you fancied it, and that's how the British Empire, the greatest political area the world has known, brought together a team of just three in 1937, half a century before Capper's ANC team. Of

570 million people, a quarter of the world's population, it had found just three men. And they had entered as individuals.

It got even better when the combined millions were reduced to a single man by the third day. One had lost contact and the other had fallen off. The survivor, a man with a long, slender face, large eyes and slicked-back hair parted above the left eye, was Charlie Holland. Until the Pyrenees, a puncture and a broken pump after 3,200 kilometers brought his dream to an end, he rode with the French but in the name of the Empire. Hence the honorary title of Sir Holland, the French never quite getting to grips with foreign nobility. And hence the fascination, even the love, that France showed him and his "raven hair as sleek as molten tar [with] a melting brown eye that brings every bird off the twig for miles around."

It worked wonders on the women of France. One, signing herself Huguette, wrote to him from Marseille (which she carefully wrote with a final "s", the English style at the time): "Bravo! Holland! We are some little french girls, friends and admirers of the England and also, we are very glad to see an englishman in the bicycle-course. What you are making (for a first time!) is a wonderful thing. Next year you should come with a whole company and you should be the most powerful men. Go on courageously and I shall go to cheer you at the 'arrival' in 'Marseilles'. Bravo! Bravo, indeed! Bravo! Boy! With a friendly sympathy. Huguette."

Another, from Lacelle-Corrèze, wrote: "My Dear Holland. I am a French girl who likes very much her bicycle, and who is very fond of 'Tour de France'. So, I read 'L'Auto' and I listen to 'Radio-Luxembourg'. I have been very pleased to learn we would have an English 'équipe' this year. First, I congratulate you for this: to run 'Tour de France' because I know it is not very important in England; your people prefers tennis, golf and so on…and however not one other competition promises as well as this, to measure courage. Don't be sorry if you are not the first, it is impossible when one is alone."

Holland, a Londoner called Bill Burl and a French-speaking Canadian, Pierre Gachon, had all entered the Tour separately. They didn't know each other and only Henri Desgrange, trying to assemble a field into an order that might enthuse the public, thought of their riding together for the Empire. Burl had some talent, although probably not enough, but what he had vanished when he crashed in Ostend as he prepared for the Tour and broke two ribs. That put him in so much pain that he was eliminated on the second day after finishing outside the time limit.

Nevertheless, he spent a lot longer in the race than the third member, Gachon.

Pierre Gachon, the first North American to ride the Tour, was better known in Montreal as a track rider. Apart from in his own area, Canadians knew nothing about him. They could hear he wasn't from Québec because his accent in French was different. He had been born not there but in Paris, on March 9, 1909. He was five when his father died in the war, after which his mother married Henri van der Auwera, a garage owner from northern Belgium. Things weren't going well when roads were wrecked by war and so they looked around and decided the car business was better in north America. Henri went for a look in 1922 and in 1923 sent for his wife and three sons and one daughter. They set up in the rue Dorchester Est in Montréal.

Pierre grew up into a handsome lad with wide-spaced eyes, thin lips around a wide, friendly mouth and full, dark hair. Now considering himself French, Canadian and Belgian, he met another Belgian emigrant, Jules Matton, who had ridden the Tour de France in 1924. Matton encouraged him to ride a bike. Gachon got on well and rode as an amateur from 1926 to 1929. He then turned professional and, contracted by another immigrant, Willie Spencer, he rode eighteen six-days on the track in Canada and the USA between 1930 and 1937.

The idea that he should ride the Tour came from the magazine, *Bicycles*. The problem was that he had rarely raced on the road, and then mostly behind a motorbike, and that he had never ridden with a derailleur and rarely with a freewheel. He left Quebec on June 12 aboard the *Emperor of Australia* and reached France eight days later, still not knowing what he was in for.

He soon found out. His first training on the cobbles of northern France shook him, physically and morally. He bounced everywhere, lacking the weight to hold him down. "There is no pavé in Canada," he explained. "It gave me quite a shock. And I need to get used to riding with a derailleur because at home we ride on a fixed wheel."

The Tour gathered outside *L'Auto*'s office in the faubourg Montmartre. Gachon was nervous, impressed that Holland and Burl had been relaxed enough to visit the World's Exhibition beside the Seine. At 9am the race began rolling along the Champs-Elysées to the Arc de Triomphe and then to Le Vésinet on the outskirts. The finish was at Lille, on a horse-racing track 263 kilometers away.

Gachon went straight out the back on the first hill, the côte du Pecq. The rest never saw him again. *Miroir des Sports* sighed: "Let us bury straight away this poor Gachon, unique victim of the first stage. Straight after the start, since he was already well dropped, we got up beside him to ask what was wrong. But instead of answering in the language of Shakespeare, the Canadian replied in Molière's. 'Everything's going fine, very well indeed. Except that I can't go any faster.'

"He was riding at 25 kilometers per hour and the others at 35. Gachon and the Canadian officials who surrounded him must surely have known that he couldn't ride faster than 25 while all the European riders exceeded 30."

L'Auto noted with heavy irony that a rescue team found a cyclist heading for Le Havre at "a record speed of 18 kilometers per hour, asking in every town if anyone knew the times of liners back across the Atlantic."

Gachon presumably kept quiet about how things turned out and wished that others would do the same. Holland, too, felt bitter, and not just because something as trivial as a broken pump denied him, in the days before service cars, his hopes of getting to Paris. He felt cheated by the Tour itself.

"I felt," he said bitterly, "that they wanted me out of their race. They got all the publicity out of me but they wanted me out because what would people think if an individual rider with no support finished the race?"

He went back to England and, unable to race conventionally as a professional, he set about beating place-to-place records. By the time the second world war ended he was too old to start again and he opened two shops in Birmingham, returning to cycling in 1974 and 1975 to win the year-long time-trial championship for veterans. He died in December 1989.

Gachon left the sport after the Tour and opened a sports shop in Rosemont. He also helped run Cycles Gachon, founded by his brother-in-law, until 1950. He died in Joliette, Québec, in May 2004.

Nobody seems to know what happened to Bill Burl.

Les Woodland

45

Death of a Champion

Now and then a champion emerges whose convictions outweigh his safety. But sometimes even the most courageous of men have a shady side.

Berlin, Germany, December 9, 1939: It was a wonderful performance. Yet again the home crowd roared and applauded the handsome blond sprinter in front of them. But Albert Richter didn't know then that it would be his last race. And the supporters didn't know it was the last time they'd ever see him.

They weren't a pleasant lot at the German cycling association in those days. In fact the man in charge was sentenced to death for sterilizing Jews, the disabled and even the healthy and working them to death in labor camps. To be Germany's greatest cyclist and refuse to give the Nazi salute, well, that was going to get you noticed. Especially when your picture appears in *Berliner Zeitung*, your arms firmly by your side when all around the crowd is saluting the Fuehrer.

And that meant that Richter's success at the Grand Prix of Berlin on December 9, 1939, would be the last he ever had. He'd soon be beaten senseless and then tortured to death.

But take a step back. In July 1934 Richter was in Hanover. He had just won the national sprint championship for the second time. You can see in the photos how spectators and officials crowded round him. They're ecstatic. It's hard now to remember how sprinters were the cream of cycling and that the best could fill huge old velodromes. Maybe the anthem is playing. They all have their arms sloped to the ceiling. All except Richter. His right hand is down on his thigh and his left is on the shoulder of his manager, Ernst Berliner.

The photo of an unsaluting Richter in *Berliner Zeitung* was one of many that Viktor Brack kept in a file at the German cycling federation. He was not only the new man in charge but a *standartenfuehrer* in the SS. Those who worked with him were also Nazi sympathisers, or didn't care to say that they weren't.

For the moment they did nothing. The world championship was to be in Leipzig a month later. If an Aryan triumph in the Fatherland would please the Fuehrer, now wasn't the time to prevent it. And there Richter lost to the little Belgian, Jef Scherens. He had won the silver medal but he had failed. Worse, he refused to lift his arm when Hitler entered the stadium and when he presented his medal. He refused, too, to wear a national jersey with a swastika, preferring an older one with the German eagle.

Now Brack had all he needed. Richter was followed wherever he went in Germany. There'd always be a black car or a man in a leather overcoat. The trap was closing.

Richter's manager was a furniture dealer and former rider called Ernst Berliner. Berliner was Jewish and uncomfortably aware of what was happening in Germany, not least because his shop had several times been broken into and plundered. His advice was that Richter should leave the country and live in Paris. He had enjoyed the Grand Prix de Paris, he said, and the French greeted him as a hero. It was all very well being the perfect Aryan but that wasn't going to go far if you didn't believe in a master race. So, without a word of French, Richter left for France. He was a hit there and legend says the crowd at the Vel' d'Hiv shouted: "*Hitler, non, Richter, oui.*"

In 1939 the world went to war and Richter went to Switzerland. That he'd banked his start fees and prizes there was an open secret within cycling. Riders traveled abroad far more than anyone else and they stashed their money out of sight. Swiss banks kept secrets, from the world in general and tax inspectors in particular. And Switzerland was neutral.

Some accounts insist that among the money that Richter took to Switzerland were rolls of banknotes belonging to Berliner.

Much of Switzerland spoke German and most of the rest spoke French, a language he had now mastered. He had a friend in Switzerland, a man named Süter, and the two had spoken of opening a hotel in Engelberg, a pretty ski resort almost cut off by mountains in the center of the country. But Richter was as naive as he was an idealist. Rather stupidly thinking there was nothing behind the invitation, he agreed to ride the Grand Prix of Berlin, at the Deutschlandhalle on December 9, 1939.

Berliner was no longer in Germany. He had abandoned his business and fled to Holland before the Gestapo could arrest him for smuggling money out of the country. Richter spoke to Berliner in Holland, told him about the invitation to the Deutschlandhalle and mentioned, too, that a friend in Cologne, a florist called Schweizer, had asked him to smuggle money out of Germany when he traveled back to Switzerland.

It's worth mentioning now that Schweizer is German for Swiss. The coincidence is strong. Did this florist exist and was he paying a generous commission or was "Schweizer" some sort of code name or disguise for the smuggling of money that Richter needed to pay for his share of the hotel? Whatever the truth, Berliner told Richter not to do it. And then, as an afterthought, he asked if he had mentioned it to anyone else.

"Only Peter Steffes," Berliner remembered his answering.

Berliner froze. Steffes, a plump and round-faced man, and a lesser professional, Werner Miethe, were Nazis who earned money on the side as informers. It was Steffes who had informed on Berliner. Again Berliner begged Richter to stay in Switzerland. To no avail. Richter caught the train to Berlin and reported to the Deutschlandhalle. It was a magnificent, flat-fronted, flat-roofed and gleaming white building put up in the Westend area for the 1936 Olympics. His arrival was noted.

There he won, reveled in the applause, collected his contract fee and prizes, and went back out on the streets of the capital. He had just had his last victory and ridden his last race. He spent the night and went to the station for a train to Cologne. There he would see his family and old friends and relax until new year's eve, when he'd take the Rheingold Express to Switzerland. He had no intention of staying in Germany and dying as a soldier, the fate of rivals and friends such as Toni Merkens. He'd even considered taking Swiss citizenship.

Cyclists traveled frequently by train those days. Two of them looked out of the window as the Rheingold Express reached Cologne and they saw Richter on the platform. Kees Pellenaars and Cor Wals were Dutch stars on their way to a meeting in Basel, on the Swiss border. They'd traveled from Amsterdam. Holland was still neutral. Wals had ridden the London six-day that summer, where he came second. He was paired in London with Arie van Vliet but his most frequent partner was Pellenaars.

They saw Richter with his bags, a pair of skis and his bike. What they didn't see but may well have guessed is that there was money hidden in the bike: 12,700 marks sewn into the tubular tires. They may have guessed because, according to Pierre Chany, few international cyclists weren't black marketeers at best and war-profiteers at worst.

Weil-am-Rhein is where the train crossed from Germany into Switzerland. The station was unusual in that it straddled the border, the tail of the train in Germany and the front, where the German steam engine would be replaced by a Swiss electric locomotive, in Switzerland. It was a good place to catch smugglers. Anyone who stayed on the train couldn't argue that his behavior, however eccentric, was legal. He obviously planned to leave the country.

Pellenaars and Wals much later told the Belgian paper, *Het Volk*, that well-informed German soldiers had walked through the snow of the platform straight to Richter's compartment. Shortly afterwards Richter fell unconscious from the train. The Germans had pulled his bike from the baggage van—not bothering with his suitcase or anything belonging to other travelers—and cut the tires with a knife. And there inside was the money.

The Germans pulled Richter's unconscious body along the platform, his legs trailing. Other witnesses say he was then thrown into a truck. From there he was taken to nearby Lörrach, close to the Black Forest, where the Nazis had their "correction" camp. The Germans called torture "accelerated interrogation". And Richter was accelerated to death.

The Germans insisted he had died in a skiing accident. But given that Richter was still in Germany and his skis were by then awaiting collection wherever the Rheingold Express ended up, they weren't convincing. On January 3, they said he had committed suicide. He had hanged himself, they said—something unlikely when his jacket was found full of bullet holes.

One version goes as far as saying he was given the choice between suicide and a firing squad, that he chose to shoot himself with a revolver. But who shoots himself several times? The Germans then changed their mind again and announced he had died fighting Russia. But he had been seen on the train. To this day his death has not been formally registered. However he died, the Germans said: "He is condemned to dishonor and to be forgotten."

The DRV, the cycling association, was quick to join in: "In trafficking currency for a Jew, Albert Richter committed a terrible crime and suicide was all he had left to him. His name has been eradicated from our records, from our memories, for ever."

Richter was buried, without announcement in the Melaten Friedhof cemetery outside Cologne, on the road to the Belgian border. His simple headstone shows him in his German jersey, the one without a swastika, describes him as a *Rennfahrer* (racing cyclist) and shows the date of his birth and when he is supposed to have died, which still isn't certain. The inscription is the German equivalent of "To know you was to love you."

Had East Germany not kept his story alive as an example of Nazi behavior, he might have been forgotten. Only in 1967 did the authorities discount his suicide. And they reinstated him by dedicating Cologne's new velodrome "to the memory of Albert Richter, victim of Nazi inhumanity."

Ernst Berliner emigrated to the United States and died there after several failed attempts to open an inquiry in Germany. Cor Wals became a member of the Dutch Waffen SS and died in 1994, when he was 83. Werner Wiethe died at 62 in 1968, Peter Steffes at 85 in 1992. Kees Pellenaars died in 1988 at the age of 74, having become Dutch national team manager. Victor Brack was sentenced to death at Nuremberg and hanged on June 2, 1948.

Viktor Brack at the Nuremburg trial

Les Woodland

46

Wait, Wait: We Can't Find the Anthem

Sometimes a rider or a ride are remarkable not for what they were but for when they happened and for what they brought about. And so it was on a wet day in eastern Europe.

Brno, Czechoslovakia, August 21, 1969: Czechoslovakia no longer exists. It was one of those countries thought up by well-meaning men in conferences after the first world war. The Habsburg kingdom had vanished, nations had been victorious or been defeated, and borders had to be drawn and Europe reestablished.

The problem was that nobody had learned lessons that should have been obvious from colonial Africa: that drawing lines on maps never recognizes the interests of the people. And so it was with Czechoslovakia. The very name showed how a country had been cobbled from two peoples: the Czechs and the Slovaks.

They never were at the same level, although their forced marriage did start closing the gap. And their joint resentment of the Russians who occupied their country brought them closer. It was the end of Russian dominance which split the country in two: the Czech Republic on one side and Slovakia down on the north bank of the Danube.

In 1969 a dark-haired, round-faced woman named Audrey McElmury arrived in Czechoslovakia no better known than she was at home in America. Which is to say: unknown. She'd finished fifth in the previous year's world road race championship, in Rome, but that wasn't remarkable enough to remember because the race had finished in a sprint.

The rain threatened as the 40 riders waited for the start signal of the world road race in Brno, then still behind the Iron Curtain. The atmosphere was difficult: it was the anniversary of the night 2,000 Warsaw Pact tanks entered Czechoslovakia to end the country's easing of communism. The championship circuit was rutted in parts from their tracks. A happier coincidence was that the championships were held 100 years after, to the week, Czechoslovakia's first bike race was held in the city.

The riders that day in Brno came from sixteen countries. When they finally set off for 62 kilometers, they cruised rather than raced. It was a dull race. And having paid her own way to get there, McElmury thought she'd better do something if only to have something for her money. America didn't have the cash to buy tickets for the three women it sent to Czechoslovakia and McElmury reckoned she and her two teammates had paid $10,000 in fares, hotels and meals. As a comparison, a Chevy Impala cost $2,200.

So she went off the front by 15 seconds, only to crash as she rode alone down a hill. She stood beside the road and watched her race and her hopes go by. Rain was now pouring and it exaggerated the blood from her elbow although the cold numbed the pain in her hip. An ambulance stopped and followed her, a vulture stalking its prey.

The others hadn't even bothered to chase. Why worry about an unknown from a country where nobody rode bikes? So they passed slowly enough that McElmury could chase back and latch on during the last lap. Still they went no faster, so she rode away again on the last hill, this time not using her brakes on the bend where she'd fallen. She finished 1 minute 10 seconds ahead of Bernadette Swinnerton, daughter of a cycle dealer in the British city of Stoke-on-Trent. She'd felt so unconfident of staying clear that she kept looking over her shoulder for a glimpse of Swinnerton and the Russian, Nina Trofimova, with whom she was chasing.

America had won world track championships but she was the first, male or female, to win on the road. In fact she was America's first world champion since Frank Kramer won the professional sprint in 1912.

That was how little she was expected to win. The medal ceremony was half an hour late because the organizers had to find a recording of the American anthem.

"Americans simply didn't win rainbow jerseys back then," historian Bill McGann noted with a wry smile.

Americans also hadn't always been keen on women racing at all. The *American Cycling Gazette* once pronounced that "Female racing is to be deplored for reasons which have on many occasions been tersely and forcibly stated." The greater public took little notice and turned up at tracks regardless, prompting the magazine to say: "While the public popularize these exhibitions, so will enterprising promoters shame the racing path by holding them."

That was in November 1898 and it would be foolish to suggest that American cycling still held the same views. But few women raced, the American federation saw no point in spending the money of a dominantly male membership on women who stood no chance abroad, there wasn't a women's world championship until 1958, and hardly anyone paid any notice when there was one. When McElmury got home to San Diego, where she was a technician in a genetics lab at the University of California, her local television station waiting for her at the airport was more interested in what she had seen of the anniversary of the Russian invasion than in her gold medal.

Athletically, her performance was unremarkable. Women's racing was still a backwater and few riders had the lean athleticism they have now. Races could be dominated by a handful of strongly built riders, such as Beryl Burton of Britain and Keetie van Oosten-Hage of Holland, winners the two previous years, capable of going to the front and pushing the pace until the rest dropped off. McElmury regularly lifted weights heavier than she was. There was little cut and thrust: there was attrition rather than attack.

Nevertheless, a race is a race regardless and those who take part all want to win. McElmury was one of the few to attack that day and she won. But it was what happened next that made her ride remarkable. Because she inspired the generation that followed, and for a decade it was American women—Sue Novara (twice world sprint champion), Connie Carpenter (Olympic road champion), Rebecca Twigg (six world pursuit championships and two medals from the Olympics),

Beth Heiden (world road champion), Sheila Young (twice world sprint champion)—who won the most medals.

Historian Peter Nye points out that American women won four medals, one of them gold, at the 1987 world championship in Vienna: the men won none.

McElmury, who was born in Northampton, Massachusetts, grew up in La Jolla, California. She tried horse jumping, surfing and only then cycling, to strengthen the ankle she broke on a skate board in 1960. Two years earlier she had met a cyclist, Scott McElmury, when she was fifteen. They went on a cycling tour in Europe and married and Audrey then started racing and training, obsessively. She raced on the track because there was no racing for women on the road. She trained twice a day, rising at 4:30am for her first session, which she said ended her marriage to her teenage sweetheart.

By 1966 there were road races for women and she won the first national championship. In 1969 she won the national omnium championship and then, in 1970, the pursuit and road titles. She set a national hour record in 1969—39.91 kilometers—at Encino in California. It stood until 1990. By then, though, her racing was over. She crashed while training in 1976 and got up with such concussion and loss of sense of smell that she wondered whether she'd ride again. In fact she called it a day two years later.

"I didn't have the nerve to race any more after so many accidents," she told Peter Nye in *Hearts of Lions*. "You have to be fearless." She did ride a few races later but she took up cross-country skiing and distance running instead, with moderate success.

She died of cancer in October 2008, aged 70. She's buried in North Dakota Veterans Cemetery in Mandan, North Dakota. Bernadette Swinnerton, who finished closest to her in Brno, became a school headmistress and retired in 2012. Nina Trofimova, who finished third, rode the world championship again for Russia in 1970 and 1972, coming fourth and tenth.

Les Woodland

47

Lifting a Leg for Glory

It's an inconvenience that, circus performers excepted, it's impossible to ride a bike with neither hands nor legs in their right place. But sometimes lifting both hands and one leg can plenty good enough.

Roubaix, France, April 9, 2000: Which, a French journalist wanted to know, was Johan Museeuw's most beautiful memory of Paris–Roubaix? He must already have known the answer but it was for the Belgian to confirm it.

"The one of my second victory," he said, "in 2000, when I showed my knee as I crossed the line. I did it in a moment, although I hadn't planned anything in advance. I thought of all those people close to me who helped me get back on my bike after my accident in the Tranchée d'Arenberg in 1998. My happiness at winning two years afterward was theirs as well, so I wanted to share that moment with them."

That day on the worst cobbles of the race, Museeuw fell on his left knee and smashed it. Splintered bone mixed with blood, torn flesh and mud. An ambulance took him, only just conscious, to a hospital in Lille and then to Ghent, across the border in Belgium. His masseur, Dirk Nachtergale, had first met him in similar circumstances, when Museeuw was in hospital in Benidorm after being knocked off while riding the world championship course in 1992. He entered the hospital room in Ghent, where Museeuw was sitting in a wheelchair.

"He was talking very quietly, making a sign with his finger raised. 'Can you massage me?' There was so much pain in his face. I thought he'd never race again. I acted as though nothing had happened but I was all torn up inside."

By then there were rumors of gangrene, of amputation, of blood so thick that an operation was impossible. There were rumors that dope would kill him; everyone knew EPO had so thickened the blood of Dutch amateurs that it had killed them, that professionals sometimes had to be woken in the night before their heart slowed down so much that it happened to them as well.

"At that moment, something changed in the media," Museeuw recalled. "Some of them went in for sensationalism. You can do whatever you like with a pen and a sheet of paper, and who can undo it afterward? I never said anything and people misunderstood. I would rather live with the rumor than reply to it, because you can't defend yourself against other people's lies."

That first Paris–Roubaix of the new millennium wasn't the most dramatic. It was warm and dry for one thing, where the opera of the race demands streaming mud beneath a frowning sky. There were the usual early scurries by riders who knew they had more chance of getting on television than getting to Roubaix—in fact only 66 of the 178 starters got that far and an unlucky 13 finished outside the time limit— but the important move came a little after 200 kilometers with another hour and a half to go.

Museeuw always made a point of riding Paris–Roubaix at the front first, as he said, because he didn't know the course as well as he did that of the Tour of Flanders, and second because Paris–Roubaix "smiled on the strong." By contrast, the repeated hills of the Tour of Flanders called on a rider to keep strength and ambition in reserve. And so Museeuw attacked and only the American, Frankie Andreu, could cling to him. They gained three minutes in as many kilometers, other teams not chasing, which one reporter described as "very noteworthy."

They passed Max van Heeswijk, the one man left out in front, who was Museeuw's teammate but considered not worthy. They reached the cobbles at Ennetières-en-Weppes with Museeuw tired but Andreu even more tired. Museeuw sensed the time had come to leave him to his misery and went off alone. He rode the final cobbles, the Crupelandt stretch laid as a tribute to Roubaix's only winner of the race, and entered the stadium.

Les Woodland

There he rode his lap of the track and, freewheeling to the line, lifted the left leg he had broken in the same race two years before. Frankie Andreu, once so close to coming at least second, finished twentieth at more than three minutes, van Heeswijk thirty-fifth at four and a half minutes.

There was jubilation, of course. "Only the hardest heart would have been unmoved by Museeuw's victorious return to Roubaix," said one observer. But that didn't mean there was no complaining in the background. Mapei, the team's sponsor, was Italian. Andrea Tafi, who had won the race for Mapei the previous year, was also Italian. But the team was registered in Belgium, its manager was Belgian and the race finished a bidon's throw from the Belgian border. And instead of supporting an Italian, the team threw itself behind a Belgian.

"To some eyes," a British magazine wrote, "Andrea Tafi, not for the first time, was the sacrificial lamb on a Belgian altar, as the likes of Wilfred Peeters, Tom Steels and Dutchman Max van Heeswijk ignored the 1999 champion's chances (not to mention his fluency over the cobbles) and committed themselves to Museeuw's cause.

"Given that Tafi had told the Italian press, with some prescience but little tact, on the eve of the race that his teammates were also his 'most dangerous rivals', it was perhaps not surprising that he received little real support."

Johan Museeuw was born into a cycling household in October 1965. His mother was just 16 and his father was 22 and still a racing cyclist. There were many sideways glances of disapproval as the couple walked the streets of observant Flanders with their new-born. Eddy Museeuw was the first boy in the family to ride as a professional. He won as many as 40 races a year as an amateur and so a pro contract was to be expected. He signed in 1968 for Okay-Diamant. And he left five months later because he wasn't getting paid and the family needed the money.

He became his son's supporter and adviser, urging caution with those who tried to be close to the famous and asking him not to commit the same errors as Freddy Maertens and be taken in by financial advisers with a soft sales patter. Johan followed his advice. He was never a flamboyant personality. He married his childhood sweetheart. And when his former team manager, José De Cauwer, suggested he buy a Ferrari, "to impress the crowd," Museeuw declined. He once bought a Harley-Davidson but that was as far as he'd go.

While riders such as Laurent Jalabert kept their phone number secret and even then changed it every few months, Museeuw was always listed in the public phone book just beneath the entry for his father's Peugeot garage. He rode for only three team managers throughout his pro career.

There was no hoop-la when he retired. It was in the Churchill-laan in Schoten, a suburb of Antwerp, at the Scheldeprijs, or what French speakers call the Grand Prix de l'Escaut. He stood on the decorated podium at the finish beside his wife Véronique, and his father Eddy, and with his team manager Patrick Lefèvre, looking absent-minded at a distance. A little further on, Dirk Nachtergale, his masseur for the past eleven years.

They held a party that night at the Riddershove restaurant in Antwerp. More than 200 people celebrated into the night. Two opera singers had flown from Italy, guests of an Italian friend who provided the wine. The prime minister, Guy Verhofstadt, sent a colleague to recount how his boss had several times canceled meetings to watch Museeuw on television.

Life began to fall apart for the golden boy late in 2003. It was then that police went into action after six months considering the activities of a vet in the suburbs of Kortrijk on the French border and a cycling soigneur named Jos Landuyt. Detectives were convinced that both had been providing growth hormones to animals, in the case of Herman Versele, and to cyclists in the case of Landuyt.

Among the 21 people whose homes were searched was Museeuw, at that moment in Canada to watch the world championships. The newspapers *Het Nieuwsblad* and *La Dernière Heure* printed what they said was a transcript of text exchanges between Museeuw and Landuyt. It introduced the wider world into alleged code names for Aronesp, an EPO-like drug then in favor. Riders shortened the name to Nesp, then changed it to *wesp*, which is Dutch for a wasp.

Museeuw: "A wasp's nest, can you work one out? I'm leaving on Wednesday for a training camp. I can't see the wasp. I have no test until 28 July."

Landuyt: "Now, I would take 80-100 wasps and at the start of the training camp a minimum of 40 and a maximum of 60 wasps. Then completely clean from July 19. It has to be in the inner tube [into the vein]. Test with [your] washing machine [centrifuge]."

Museeuw: "Subcutaneously or in the nose?"

Landuyt: "Always intravenously with wasp. Otherwise, bingo. So certainly intravenously."

The Belgian federation knew the two men met frequently at the Den Engel, a bar in Ichtergem where Museeuw went sometimes with his family and where he had held press meetings. It waited no longer and banned Museeuw for two years with a further two years as a suspended sentence. Plus a fine of €6,500. In 2012 he accepted that he, like "near enough everyone", had taken drugs throughout his career. It was a sad end for a man who'd never turn away a kid from his home without a bottle or cap, because he remembered how he too had idolized the greats and how once merely seeing Bernard Hinault's house had thrilled him for months.

48

Anything to Make Myself Popular

It must be so frustrating: the better you do, the more unpopular you become. It can drive a man to exceptional limits.

Paris, France, May 30, 1965: It didn't matter what Jacques Anquetil did, he could never make people like him. Respect him, yes, admire him, certainly. But warmth and accolade? No. That all went to Raymond Poulidor, a rider whom others in the bunch thought a moaner and not worth the adulation but for whom the crowds shouted in the way they rarely did for Anquetil.

And yet, and yet...Anquetil had won the Tour de France five times. Nobody else ever had. What more could a man do? Certainly not win for a sixth time, of which he was capable but for which, because Poulidor would once more get the credit, he had no ambition. What he needed was an achievement—a stunt, frankly—to seal the deal.

It was Raphaël Géminiani who came up with the idea and other riders, even those paid to ride against him, who made it possible.

The battle between Anquetil and Poulidor had been going on since the two first met. It divided France as the struggle between Coppi and Bartali had split Italy a decade earlier. The two could never meet on the road without the greatest concern being not who would win but which of the two would do better. It mattered to them and it mattered to their fans. And so it was when Paris–Nice set off for the sun in 1965.

Anquetil won after an attack on the last day in which it was clear to Poulidor's fans that the Italians in the race had sided with Anquetil and that fans beside the road had done their best to hamper Poulidor's team men.

The battle continued at the Dauphiné Libéré, first one beating the other, then the reverse. Both lost six minutes in an icy stage through Mont Revard and Chamrousse. But neither lost time on the other. Anquetil would doubtless have won overall anyway because of the time-trials. But he was guaranteed his win by the connivance of his supposed rivals, who were determined that Poulidor should lose and that Anquetil should succeed in the craziest gamble of a crazy, gambling life.

Because Anquetil planned to go straight from the finish of the Dauphiné at Avignon to the start that night of Bordeaux–Paris, the longest road race in the world. Bordeaux–Paris doesn't exist now, which is a shame. It was unique not only because of its distance, and because as a result it started during the night, but because it was the last of an otherwise dead tradition of allowing riders to have pacers. Once all races were that way, first behind other cyclists, then tandems, even for a while behind giant motorbikes and cars. Bordeaux–Paris had had all of those and had finally settled for a hybrid bicycle-motorcycle called a derny, after the Derny brothers of Paris who designed it.

The idea that Anquetil should go from a mountainous stage race to a 557-kilometer one-day race run at the speed of a motorbike—and without a night's sleep between the two—didn't evolve. Géminiani blurted it out in the spring when Anquetil was once more down in the dumps about Poulidor and the public. Géminiani called Anquetil the Emil Zátopek of cycling, after the Czech runner who won at almost every distance up to the marathon. Both he and Anquetil had been at the Helsinki Olympics.

"You're the Zátopek of the bicycle," Géminiani told him. "When it comes to it, Bordeaux–Paris is just another stage of the Dauphiné Libéré. I'd bet 500,000 francs on your chances."

A month passed while Anquetil considered the idea. He kept it a secret until June. "*C'est bon: je tente le coup!*" he said and then set off for the Dauphiné and a week through the Alps. The idea enchanted many of the riders he met there. They respected Anquetil and called him Maître Jacques. Most would never have dared talk to him but they all knew what he'd done and what he was capable of doing. More than that, Anquetil had frequently spoken up for them and for that they were grateful enough to help him and to do down Poulidor.

For everyone else, though, everyone but the star-struck, the idea was ridiculous. It was all very well Géminiani saying, truthfully, that "A rider coming out of a stage race has a far better form and his body can stand far tougher challenges", but that had its limits. And Bordeaux–Paris straight after the Dauphiné exceeded them.

At 4:58 on May 29, Anquetil finished the eighth and last stage of the Dauphiné, beating Poulidor by 1 minute 43 seconds. He went straight to the podium, both the organizers and the crowd recognizing the urgency, and ten minutes later he pushed through the crowd behind his mechanic, then ran to the Ford Taunus in which Géminiani drove him to the Crillon hotel, two streets back from the Rhône in the center of town.

Anquetil got into the bath in room 18, washed and dried himself off. Tarcisio Vergani gave him a massage just as he had massaged Coppi, Bobet and Simpson before him. That finished, Anquetil ate steak, cheese and strawberry tart and drank two beers before taking to a team car with the higher-geared Bordeaux–Paris bikes on its roof. He drove away at 5:55 with his manager, mechanic and masseur and Louis Rostollan, a tall dark-haired man who was among his favorite domestiques.

They drove at up to 140 kilometers per hour with a police motor-bike escort and by 6:30 they'd covered the 60 kilometers southwest to Nîmes-Garons airport. There's a major highway between the two now but, then, there were only ordinary, winding roads.

The group went into the airport building, where Anquetil lay on a bench seat, being massaged again by Vergani while answering questions from reporters. He said he was anxious to know what the weather would be.

A Mystère 20, a business jet with an engine mounted each side to the rear of the fuselage, waited. Anquetil shook hands with the pilot, René Brigand, then did it again because the photographers and television crews weren't ready. The doors closed at 6:50 and, as the little jet went down the runway, Rostollan took the unladen team car and drove it back to Avignon.

Another massage on the plane and a cold chicken and a glass of champagne, perhaps more. Legend says it was a whole bottle. The plane landed at Bordeaux around the time that Rostollan and the police escort, now traveling more slowly, were entering Avignon. Anquetil's party made for their hotel beside the Gironde where, at 10pm, he was massaged again and ate another meal. And at 2am he was on the line in the city's northern suburbs, ready to ride with the little bunch of twenty towards Paris way to the north. Among them: Simpson, François Mahé, Jean Stablinski and Bernard Gauthier, this last a four-time winner who delighted photographers with the agonized expressions he made at the least effort.

A crowd, mainly male and in raincoats, watched the city's mayor drop the flag. The raggle-taggle army set off north in heavy rain and into the darkness of the countryside, their way lit haphazardly by the headlamps of the cars that followed. They made the rain look even worse than it was.

Tradition had it that the field would stay together for 150 kilometers, by which time it would be dawn and they'd all stop to take off their heavy night clothes and put on fresh shorts and jerseys before finding the pacers on their dernies who were waiting up the road at Châtellerault. In that time they'd ride briskly but without racing. Yet even that was too much for Anquetil. He looked haggard, he complained of pain in his thighs, and he protested that he couldn't breathe. More than that, the wind had swung into the riders' face. And there was worse to come.

One of the riders employed to help Simpson against Anquetil was the Belgian, Claude Valdois. It was his last season and perhaps he wanted to make a mark. He'd had only seven wins as a professional and none since a criterium a year earlier. Because nobody cared, nobody noticed that he'd dropped off the back and put on new clothes before the agreed stop. When the others rolled to a halt to change in the half-privacy of opened car doors, he attacked.

Simpson, whom he was there to support, recalled: "Everybody saw him go and a cry of 'the bastard' went up and it was pandemonium. I took my shoes off to change my sodden socks and suddenly I saw a

Peugeot rider go away. I struggled to get into my shoes again [but] the back of one shoe folded down so I stood there at the roadside minus my shorts, trying to get my shoe on."

He became even angrier when he found their manager, Gaston Plaud, had told Valdois to do it but hadn't mentioned it to Simpson. Anquetil, not in the best mood anyway, called Simpson a duplicitous bastard out to disrupt the race and exploit his tiredness.

Anquetil was riding with his teammate Jean Stablinski, then still a friend and a prospective winner, and with a British domestique, Vin "Vic" Denson. The two got on particularly well. Anquetil ordered Denson to chase after Valdois.

"I jumped after him with my shorts half on, fastening my braces [suspenders], and Stablinski followed with one sock on and still trying to get his heels in his shoes."

All that meant that Denson hadn't had a pee since Bordeaux. It handicapped his riding but he still caught Valdois just before where the pacers were waiting and even won a prize for being first to reach them. Each rider had two pacers, one to lead and the other to take over when needed. The two racers and their four pacers buzzed away from Châtellerault, Denson soon building a four-minute lead. His pacer, a man named Pleasance, was already dreaming of winning in Paris.

But Denson was in agony. "I could no longer ignore the insistence of nature and I called to Pleasance to stop, and I lined up at a tree."

There was, of course, nothing else going on and reporters and photographers resigned to a long uneventful morning were grateful for the diversion. They crowded round Denson and the tree and watched, along with the unhappy Pleasance, a couple of spectators and a gravedigger called Bernard Stoops who worked each summer as a soigneur.

Anxiety swelled in the little crowd, which began urging Denson to get on with it. But Denson couldn't. He gave up, he reckoned, after five minutes, by which time he had been passed by Anquetil, the man he was supposed to protect and who was already into a 350 kilometer battle with Simpson.

Simpson, too, wasn't without troubles. He too had had to set off sooner than he wanted after Valdois, which he couldn't do until he'd put on new and freshly creamed shorts. In those days shorts had a soft leather lining that needed a copious coat of lanolin cream.

"As I was belting off up the road, I thought 'What on earth is this?' What had happened was that, as I had put on my shorts, gravel from my socks and shoes had stuck in the grease and was now hurting like the devil. So there I am, riding along digging my hands inside my shorts and pulling out lumps of gravel."

Simpson was riding now with Stablinski, Anquetil haggard and exhausted behind them. He dropped back to Géminiani in the Ford car and told him he wanted to quit. Géminiani, characteristically, exploded. He let out a stream of invective that ended in "*Tu n'est qu'une fiotte, toi!*" Now, *fiotte* isn't a word you find in most dictionaries. It's a pretty vulgar word for a homosexual or, in this context, a limp-wristed pansy. And Anquetil was offended enough to keep riding.

Denson, meanwhile, had stopped again, this time for three minutes—an agony that ended only when Stoops obliged with a sponge soaked in warm coffee.

Anquetil, riding better as the day warmed up, caught Simpson in the rolling Chartreuse valley and then, five kilometers before the end, he caught Stablinski. Simpson had tagged on and there were now three.

"I was snookered because they were teammates," Simpson remembered. "I was well and truly hammered. I took quite a hiding as first Stablinski and then Anquetil attacked. I had to go every time and gradually they wore me down."

In the end, Anquetil attacked definitively on the hill at Buc, just south of Versailles, and then on the long straight road that followed he rode away from both Simpson and Stablinski and swept through the concrete tunnel and on to the track of the Parc des Princes. After fifteen hours and with little rest and little sleep, he had won by three seconds short of a minute.

Stablinski came second and Simpson, two seconds behind him, had to be helped off his bike in third place. Denson finished sixth at 18 minutes 14 seconds. And Valdois, who'd caused so many problems in the first place, was the only non-finisher.

Did his win improve the warmth of the crowd? Well, certainly he was cheered as he rounded the Parc des Princes. But in the end it changed very little. Later that year he won Liège–Bastogne–Liège, a

Les Woodland

race he rode only because he could fit it between two criteriums for which he was booked in Holland. And because Poulidor was going to take part.

Anquetil won and won alone, after Géminiani had reminded him that the fans wanted dash and bravery and not just the cold calculation that won his five Tours. And then he refused a drugs test and ruined the lot.

Anquetil following the derny at Bordeaux–Paris

Les Woodland

49

Falling before the East Wind

The day that international cycling decided to make cycling truly international, nobody could have imagined the consequences...

Leicester, England, August 29, 1982: Sometimes a single newspaper story sums up a career, or at least a style. So here's the *Ottawa Citizen* on August 30, 1982: "Where there is money and a world title at stake, charity and sportsmanship do not seem too high on a competitor's list of priorities. On the final day of the world track cycling championships Sunday, blood flowed when Canada's Gordon Singleton clashed with reigning champion Koichi Nakano of Japan in the final of the premier event, the professional sprint.

"Any sprint on a tight, steeply banked 333.3-metre track is certain to be a cut and thrust affair, but Singleton's best-of-three-battle with the six-time champion from Fukuoka took the in-fighting beyond accepted limits. The first heat had to be re-run after both riders hit the track and crossed the line on their backs. Singleton won that one at the second time of asking, but the 25-year-old from Niagara Falls crashed onto the hardwood surface once again as he and Nakano raced shoulder-to-shoulder for the finish.

"In all, championship officials were called upon to sort out alleged misdemeanours on three occasions. As a result, Nakano took his sixth straight title by simply sitting on his bike at the start of the third, the blood trickling from a cut on his right elbow and oozing through his racing suit from a graze on his back.

"Survival of the fittest it certainly was. Singleton was in even worse shape, nursing a suspected broken collar bone and a cut elbow that prevented him from riding."

Koichi Nakano is, from his record, the world's best ever track sprinter. He won the world championship ten times, every year from 1977 to 1986. But he did ride with, let's say, a vigor not seen in track sprinting since the roughhouse days that ended in the 1950s. Then, nobody thought they'd had a good day without spokes breaking and wheels crumpling.

Koichi Nakano was the consequence of international cycling wanting to make itself properly international. It has happened now in road racing but it happened much earlier in track cycling. The reason is that the masters of the sport looked jealously at a huge racing circus in Japan and decided they wanted to be part of it. Or, more precisely, that they wanted to integrate Japan into what they saw as established world cycling.

The keirin was, said Pierre Chany in a good description, "a strange and distant cousin of western cycling [which] grew only on its archipelago and became a monster. A golden monster, a gigantic Buddha on wheels, which reeked of fortune and dispensed fabulous riches."

It had fabulous riches because Japan in 1948 had allowed gambling on bike races, the government's interest being the commission it could draw on each bet to help rebuild the country. And the population did its best to help, although it was thinking of the winnings rather than the slice that the government took. The race they really went for was unknown in the west and looked ridiculous when it was introduced. It was called the *keirin*, from *kei* (wheel) and *rin* (race).

A string of riders was paced up to speed by a motorbike and then left to race to the line. It was hard to see what the fuss was about, but western cycling wanted to draw in riders reputed for their toughness and so the UCI introduced it to its world championships. In the event, few Japanese riders saw the appeal in leaving Japan and those that did travel not infrequently found themselves beaten at their own specialty.

Nakano was the only keirin star who made it regularly to Europe and elsewhere abroad—but perhaps because, unlike the others, he wasn't that easy to beat.

Les Woodland

The only time from 1977 to 1986 that he really looked likely to fall—and not just literally—was that Sunday in 1982. He wasn't up against just anyone that day in Leicester, an uninspiring city in the English Midlands that made its fortune from shoes and railways junction and has been in decline ever since. Gordon Singleton, almost angelic with his striking blond hair, simultaneously held world records at 200, 500 and 1,000 meters. In that week in Leicester he had become the first Canadian to win a world championship, ironically in the keirin.

Singleton and Nakano were no strangers. It was to Nakano that the Canadian had come second in the previous summer's final, in Brno. Neither was the sort of rider to back down, Singleton being an angel only in appearance. There was going to be a collision of wills, if not bodies, and the crowd was expecting its money's worth. And so it was that two of the three rounds ended with flesh on the wooden boards.

The first would have been comical if it were only for the decision the judges had to make. The two men came to the finish straight side by side, Nakano on the outside and gaining slightly. Neither would give ground. The English-speaking commentators on the day held that Nakano had left his line and closed in on Singleton. The Canadian's head bobbed down and then both men came crashing to the ground. The judges, though, decided the opposite, that Singleton had ridden up from the bottom of the track and barged into Nakano's backside.

Both men crossed the line without their bikes. Nakano got the win first because Singleton hadn't ridden straight and second because he did actually cross the line first, albeit on his back. The crowd settled back into the seats and watched first-aid men and team helpers attend to the wreckage. They expected more drama in the next round, but they didn't get it. Instead, they saw Singleton dive to the bottom of the track from second position and get enough of a lead that Nakano was left four lengths back.

One round to each man.

The rules say that sprinters must alternate who goes first in each round. For the final sprint, that meant Nakano. Singleton, content with tricking Nakano last time, tried to do it again. But this time it didn't work as well. He got two lengths lead, but Nakano had the greater speed and came up beside Singleton, on the outside, in the last hundred meters.

Singleton, in his pale blue Canadian jersey, leaned slightly into Nakano and down he went. The judges couldn't decide where the fault lay, whether even there had been any fault. Their first decision was to run the heat again and Nakano went to the start. But Singleton had had enough. He signaled defeat from the track center and Nakano became champion of the world for the sixth time in a row.

Singleton did have the satisfaction of winning the keirin, in front of a tough Tasmanian called Danny Clark, a star of the six-day circuit, and Toru Kitamara, one of Nakano's teammates. And that, really, was the last Europe saw of him until he came back to racing to win the over-35s championship in Manchester in 1998, one of his seven world championship medals. He is still involved in cycling, although now he earns his living running the car-supplies business that his father started in Niagara Falls in 1957.

Nakano, whose earnings are reputed to have been $10 million, is a commentator on cycling for a Japanese television station. The sport still debates just how good he was. There is no contest that he was the best professional sprinter. He never won a medal of any color but gold. What makes the assessment more complicated is that cycling still had the amateur and professional races—but not all the amateurs were as amateur as all that. Few from western Europe held steady jobs and those from the east certainly didn't. The kind term for them was state-sponsored amateurs. So Nakano didn't ride against Daniel Morelon, the top western amateur from 1966 to 1975, nor against East Germans and Russians such as Lutz Hesslich, Michael Hübner and Sergei Kopylov.

He was, though, far ahead of any professional in history, his nearest challengers being Antonio Maspes, who won seven championships between 1955 and 1964, and Jef "Poeske" Scherens of Belgium, who also won seven championships, between 1932 and 1947.

Nakano's last world championship was won in Colorado Springs in 1986. He was 30. He retired five years later, re-emerging in the 2000 Olympics in Sydney when he rode the keirin pacing motorbike.

50

Can 40 Million Frenchmen Be Wrong?

And to end, the story of a good idea that went gloriously wrong...but gave a complete unknown a great day out.

Plymouth, England, June 29, 1974: You've maybe never heard of Henk Poppe. He was a professional for little more than a single season and he won only two races: a criterium in Belgium and...a stage of the Tour de France. Since complete unknowns, no-hopers, don't normally win sprint stages of the Tour, an explanation is needed.

In 1974, the Tour de France held a stage in south-west England, the first time it had left the continent. It was the era when Félix Lévitan would take the race down a dead-end road if there was enough money in it. He was all ears, therefore, when an artichoke farmer called Alexis Gourvennec started his own shipping company to take crops to England. Britain had joined what is now the European Union and Gourvennec and his colleagues were tired of driving their produce halfway round France to reach the Channel ports for this new market.

Quite a man, Gourvennec. In 1961, when he was 24, he forced the government to change its agricultural policy. Since nobody else would sail from anywhere more convenient, he would do it himself. He persuaded Paris to put the equivalent of a million euros into building a port at Roscoff and he began sailing to Plymouth, a conveniently inexpensive port also looking for trade. Artichokes alone wouldn't pay for the venture so the new line accepted passengers as well. You may recognize it as Brittany Ferries, as it's known today.

What Gourvennec needed now was publicity, in France for his ferries, in Britain for artichokes. That's why English fans who went to the Tour de France in Plymouth went home with mixed memories but clutching a plastic bag advertising Brittany artichokes and maybe even an artichoke which, in the uncertain manner of British cooking, they didn't know what to do with.

Alf Palmer, the city official and club cyclist told to make the Plymouth stage possible, says he suggested the Tour ride over the demanding and bleak hills of Dartmoor, a rugged national park not far from Plymouth. That would give the race drama in what otherwise would be a dull opening week. And at first, says the British journalist Geoffrey Nicholson, Lévitan and Jacques Goddet agreed. Only to change their mind, without ever really explaining why, and asking to use a recently finished stretch of bypass road around the outlying town of Plympton. And that made the stage everything you'd expect.

Each end of the bypass had a roundabout to connect it to the road it was relieving. And the riders set off from a cluster of marquees in the middle of the loop, rode five miles down to the roundabout at one end, back to the roundabout at the other end, and round and round for fourteen laps and four hours.

"I've ridden twelve Tours de France and that was the most boring stage I've ever, ever ridden," was how the British hope, Barry Hoban, described it. "All you had were people at either end, and no-one in between.

The organizers had laid on seating for 5,000 at £2 a go and arranged standing space for another 75,000. *Cycling* wrote with happy misery that only the first come would be served, that accommodation would be strained, the roads clogged. Local clubs put on races for the crowds expected to spend the week in England's south-western peninsula. In the end, probably no more than 2,000 turned up.

Plymouth itself had hardly been *en fête* even though it had spent £40,000 for the right to hold the stage. There were posters in some shop windows but not much more. A city official asked to explain to French television why there was so little excitement, answered in English: "They do not show it with flags because, not yet, they do not appreciate that this is the way it is done in France. If we were to bring an England-Australia cricket match to Paris, the French would not understand. We hope the English will soon understand the Tour de France."

Geoffrey Nicholson concluded: "Half an hour after the start, the best guess that the police could make of the crowd was 15,000. The idly curious were rare. Nearly all the Devon accents came from the mouths of constables or men in Plymouth Corporation jerkins. As ever, it was the faithful who made up the numbers."

The riders weren't any keener. They were sulking at the way they'd been treated by immigration officials at Exeter airport and they refused to leave their hotels a minute earlier than they needed to. "We were treated like illegal immigrants," Hoban said. They were herded into a locked room, he said. "It's not my fault!" he kept saying. "I was embarrassed to be British."

Alf Palmer had gone to Exeter to meet the charter plane the Tour had laid on for riders. The team cars and officials took the overnight crossing from Roscoff and the advertising caravan drivers had simply stayed in France, playing cards and drinking wine until the Tour returned to France and sanity returned. "I had come to an arrangement with the customs and immigration officials," he said. He told them the riders would be tired after racing 200 kilometers that day and they would want to get to their hotels quickly.

"Come the actual day they let me down stinking. When I went to see the customs people, and said 'Look, this isn't what was promised', they said 'You keep out of it. If you want to get yourself in trouble, carry on doing what you're doing.'" There was even a story that Jacques Goddet had been followed all day because he'd left his passport at home, never having needed it any other time the Tour had gone abroad.

The British fans who *did* make the journey to Plymouth, which doesn't seem far from the main population centers if you live on a continent, but which in domestic minds was a challenging journey, were delighted to see the stars of cycling where they'd never before seen them. They saw Eddy Merckx in yellow and those who knew how these things worked wondered whether the riders would treat the stage as a show, as they would in a criterium, and let the star man ride off the front for a lap or two.

But nobody rode off the front. The race stayed together from beginning to end and even the most starstruck realized something had gone horribly wrong. And it stayed wrong to the end. A dull day ended with a dull sprint, not won by Hoban, one of the best sprinters in the Tour and one of just two British riders and a man who might well have been allowed to win this first time the Tour had ever visited his homeland. It was won by Henk Poppe. Hoban was ninth.

Nobody has admitted that the Tour contrived to spoil the Tour's day by letting a no-hoper belittle a stage. But it wasn't the first time it had happened and the first to cross the line that day didn't even get to Paris. Maybe it wasn't a protest at all. Poppe said he got the impression Merckx was going to allow Patrick Sercu, a close friend in a rival team, to take the stage. "They were good friends, those two," he said. "They used to ride six-days together." Poppe stuck to Sercu's back wheel as the field swept down from the road bridge to the finish 400 meters later and came round him to beat him on the line.

Sercu said he had never heard of him. And Jean Nelissen, the veteran commentator for Dutch radio, even mistook him for Michael Wright, the second Briton in the race. Whether it was deliberate or not, that evening the riders were doubtless glad about what had happened—because they were held up again when they got back to Exeter for their plane back to St-Pol-de-Léon. Palmer was bitter. "We thought they'd be glad to just shove them on a plane to get rid of them, but they kept them hanging about for a couple of hours, getting all the riders to fill in forms."

Next day the *Daily Mirror*, then the country's best-selling newspaper, asked in giant black type: TOUR DE FRANCE: CAN 50 MILLION FRENCHMEN BE WRONG? It was a question even fans couldn't answer.

The only man who thought the day a success was Alexis Gourvennec. Britain joined the European Union and Brittany now sells 50,000 tons of potatoes and 20,000 tons of cauliflower there a year. And a few artichokes. And, with black satisfaction, he could conclude that the staff at Exeter airport had given him publicity he could never have hoped possible. They had shown how much more convenient it was to go by ferry.

Decades passed before the Tour went back to Britain. By that time Henk Poppe was 42. He didn't ride a bike for twenty years, exhausted by the program of races that his team, Frisol, demanded he ride. His first and only season included the Tours of France, Spain and Italy.

Alexis Gourvennec (above) and Henk Poppe (below)

Cycling's 50 Triumphs and Tragedies

Index

Géminiani, Rafaël 7, 8, 11, 68, 74, 89, 130, 134, 166, 167, 195, 196, 199, 249, 251, 311–313, 316, 317
Gimondi, Felice 27, 48, 123, 196
Girardengo, Costante 62
Giro d'Italia 7, 8, 10, 46, 60, 143–148, 151, 153, 155, 167, 168, 172, 181, 182, 190, 204, 209, 217–219, 229–233, 266, 267, 269
Goddet, Jacques 34, 68, 87, 88, 106, 107, 122, 126, 130, 166, 184, 186, 187, 198, 217, 256, 261, 264, 268, 286, 324, 325
Goddet, Victor 32, 35, 106
Guimard, Cyril 37–40, 48, 81, 82, 87, 171, 174, 274

H

Hamilton, Tyler 54, 57
Hampsten, Andy 152–155
Hautacam 235, 236, 238
Herrera, Luis "Lucho" 73–77
Hinault, Bernard 79–83, 86–89, 181, 200, 212, 259–262, 269, 273, 309
Holland, Charlie 290, 292

I

Indurain, Miguel 180–182, 215–219, 269

J

Jacquelin, Edmond 33, 34
Jalabert, Laurent 172, 179, 272, 308
Janssen, Jan 123, 138, 142, 242

K

Karstens, Gerben 25, 26, 88, 139, 140
Kelly, Sean 17–19, 26, 41, 42, 218, 259, 273
Koblet, Hubo 49, 73, 74, 165–170, 186
Koppenberg 115, 117, 118, 119
Kübler, Ferdy 166, 170, 268

L

Leblanc, Jean-Marie 13, 192
LeMond, Greg 39–44, 172–174, 215, 217, 218
Lévitan, Félix 39, 46, 73, 74, 86–89, 254, 261, 264, 323, 324

Liège–Bastogne–Liège 15, 79–81, 86, 101, 190, 204, 271, 316
Lloyd, Dave 59, 60

M

Maertens, Freddy 25, 28, 29, 88, 115–119, 189, 190, 230, 259–264, 307
Magne, Antonin 130, 131, 183–187, 195, 196, 197, 284
Magni, Fiorenzo 8, 9, 166, 167, 229–233, 269
Mallejac, Jean 122, 123
Mattan, Nico 236, 237, 272
McElmury, Audrey 40, 301–304
Merckx, Eddy 45–51, 72, 82, 116, 118, 123, 130, 138, 139, 181, 204–206, 209–213, 230, 244, 247–257, 269, 271, 274, 325, 326
Michaux family 278, 280
Milan–San Remo 15–20, 27, 46, 50, 59–65, 101, 109, 172, 204
Millocheau, Arsène 241, 245
Monseré, Jean-Pierre "Jempi" 24–29
Mont Ventoux 51, 121–123, 127
Monte Bondone 7, 10, 15
Moore, Jimmy 277–281
Moser, Francesco 51, 60, 204, 209–213, 219
Motta, Gianni 153, 154
Mottet, Charly 179
Museeuw, Johan 305–309

N

Nakano, Koichi 319–322

O

Ocaña, Luis 51, 60, 242, 247–250, 253, 255, 256
O'Leary, Daniel 157, 158
Olivier brothers 278–280
Opperman, Hubert 221–227
Ottenbros, Harm 137–141
Otxoa, Javier 236–240

P

Pantani, Marco 177–182, 190, 236–240, 269

Les Woodland

www.ingramcontent.com/pod-product-compliance
Lightning Source LLC
Chambersburg PA
CBHW032031090426
42733CB00029B/85